THE REBIRTH OF CONTRACT

The Rebirth of Contract is a critical investigation for judges, academics, and students into the contrived genesis and ill-advised nature of the purported contract law doctrine of "promissory estoppel." It argues that this doctrine was artificially invented and historically unprecedented, and offers economic and moral grounds for repudiating it. The book also presents an analytic framework for deciding "promissory estoppel cases" using traditional contract law tools. By tracing the historical development of Anglo-American contract law since the Norman conquest of England, the book provides a forensic investigation into and refutation of the claims of historical precedent upon which promissory estoppel was marketed to the American judiciary and academy. *The Rebirth of Contract* further includes a law and economics analysis of both traditional contract law and promissory estoppel, focusing on Pareto improving transactions. Finally, it offers a roadmap for returning to traditional contract law.

Eric Alden has taught law as a Professor at Northern Kentucky University, a Lecturer at University of California Berkeley, and an Adjunct Professor at University of California Hastings. Prior to academia, he was a full equity partner in two global law firms, and worked in a senior capacity with the Securities and Exchange Commission in Washington, DC.

The Rebirth of Contract

PUTTING PROMISSORY ESTOPPEL TO THE SWORD

ERIC ALDEN

Northern Kentucky University

CAMBRIDGE
UNIVERSITY PRESS

CAMBRIDGE
UNIVERSITY PRESS

Shaftesbury Road, Cambridge CB2 8EA, United Kingdom

One Liberty Plaza, 20th Floor, New York, NY 10006, USA

477 Williamstown Road, Port Melbourne, VIC 3207, Australia

314–321, 3rd Floor, Plot 3, Splendor Forum, Jasola District Centre, New Delhi – 110025, India

Cambridge University Press is part of Cambridge University Press & Assessment, a department of the University of Cambridge.

We share the University's mission to contribute to society through the pursuit of education, learning and research at the highest international levels of excellence.

www.cambridge.org
Information on this title: www.cambridge.org/9781009367615

DOI: 10.1017/9781009367622

When citing this work, please include a reference to the DOI 10.1017/9781009367622

First published 2026

Cover image: Richard I Equestrian Statue / RFStock / Getty Images

A catalogue record for this publication is available from the British Library

A Cataloging-in-Publication data record for this book is available from the Library of Congress

ISBN 978-1-009-36761-5 Hardback

Contents

Acknowledgments

The Author would like to thank many for their inspiration, generous assistance, or sheer depth of knowledge, including, alphabetically, John H. Baker, Randy Barnett, Judith Daar, David Epstein, Chris Gulinello, Jean Powers, and Jeffrey Standen. The Author alone is responsible for any errors or omissions, and for the entire substance of the statements and arguments advanced herein.

Introduction

> [M]odern Restatements … are of questionable value, and must be used with caution.… Over time, the Restatements' authors have abandoned the mission of describing the law, and have chosen instead to set forth their aspirations for what the law ought to be.… Restatement sections such as that should be given no weight whatever as to the current state of the law, and no more weight regarding what the law ought to be than the recommendations of any respected lawyer or scholar. And it cannot safely be assumed, without further inquiry, that a Restatement provision describes rather than revises current law.[1]
>
> —Antonin Scalia

This book concerns the attempted and partially successful hijacking of a major domain of American law, conducted by prominent members of academia. The domain in question is contract law, and the conceptual tool those academics have used to attempt its subversion is the novel, artificial doctrine of "promissory estoppel."[2]

[1] Kansas v. Nebraska, 574 U.S. 445, 475–76 (2015) (Scalia, J., concurring in part and dissenting in part) (citations omitted).

Though stated in a holding related to the Restatement (Third) of Restitution and Unjust Enrichment, Justice Scalia's point is of general character and applies with equal force to the first and second restatements of contract law under discussion in this book, *infra* note 2. Moreover, in the restatements at issue here, the manipulatory ambition to alter rather than to describe extant law with fidelity was present from its very inception.

[2] The Author has previously published three articles on core aspects of this subject. *See* Eric Alden, *Rethinking Promissory Estoppel*, 16 Nev. L.J. 659 (2016); Eric Alden, *Promissory Estoppel and the Origins of Contract Law*, 9 Ne. U. L. Rev. 1 (2017) [hereinafter Alden, *Origins of Contract Law*]; Eric Alden, *Reversing the Reliance Revolution in Contract*, 93 Wash. L. Rev. 1609 (2018) [hereinafter Alden, *Reversing the Reliance Revolution*].

The doctrine of promissory estoppel was conceived and drafted by the American Law Institute ("ALI"), a private legal organization consisting of prominent academics, judges, and practitioners, in the mid- to late 1920s and was first published in 1932 as Section 90 of the ALI's first "restatement" of American contract law. Restatement of the Law of Contracts § 90 (Am. Law Inst. 1932) [hereinafter First Restatement]. The First Restatement was then modified through discussions during the 1960s and 1970s, leading to publication of the revised

This might perhaps at first strike a casual observer as only a skirmish along the frontiers of American jurisprudence. Yet, contract is one of the oldest and most fundamental fields of human law, providing the legal framework for commercial transactions permitting the creation of advanced, prosperous, civilized society. It is for this very reason routinely taught, along with criminal law, torts, civil procedure, and property, as part of the required curriculum during the first year of American law school, as the springboard for all further legal study.

Contract law is intimately connected with private ownership and control over property, a foundational and necessary requisite of any free and individualistic society.[3] Promissory estoppel fundamentally alters the underpinnings – effects a tectonic shift in the bedrock – of contract law. Such a proposition is inherently nontrivial to our civilizational exercise.

In Anglo-American jurisprudence, the ethical basis for the enforceability of promise in contract has rested upon the payment one makes for that promise. If a person has paid for property to be conveyed or acts to be performed, that person has a legitimate moral right to assert that claim at law.

Promissory estoppel at its conceptual core both strives and purports to render promise enforceable upon a theory of victimhood. If you, the reader – and this statement is deliberately phrased in the second person to the reader in order to bring home the ethical impact at a personal level – make a future-oriented statement of anticipation or intent, then later change your mind, anyone who has chosen detrimentally to rely upon your statement – without having paid you a whit or made a countercommitment to you therefor – may now bring suit against you for the "harm" you have caused them.[4] Even though they made a conscious choice to rely upon what you said, without your request, without having been required to do so, and without having promised or paid you anything in return.[5] This is not a theory of mutual exchange, of a voluntary market transaction rendering both parties better off. It is at heart a theory of injury, a theory of tort. And you are the putative tortfeasor.

The story of this doctrinal hijacking will here be told, and result in a recommendation and plan for how to recover to its proper origins this vital legal pillar of American civil society – free and individualistic – for future generations.[6] Contract is but one stone in the broad legal mosaic both expressing and underpinning a free society. Yet, it is one of those mosaic stones, and an important one. Promissory

version in 1981. Restatement (Second) of Contracts § 90 (Am. Law Inst. 1981) [hereinafter Restatement (Second)].

3 Indeed, Blackstone, who wrote the definitive treatise on English law in 1765, which served as the defining text for American judges and advocates, treated contract law as in essence a portion of property law. 2 Sir William Blackstone, Commentaries on the Laws of England ch. 30, at 440–70 (London, W. Strahan, T. Cadell in the Strand, & D. Prince, Oxford, 9th rev. ed. 1783) (New York & London, Garland Pub. photo reprint 1978) (1765–69).

4 *See infra* Chapters 6 and 7.1.

5 *See infra* Chapters 5 and 6.

6 *See infra* Part IV.

estoppel represents a particular legal usurpation as part of a broad philosophical and political movement over the course of the past century to reorient American society away from individual to collective control of property – thus away from individual freedom – and toward collectivism.

Historically, the two absolute requisites for the formation of legally binding contract – aside from certain limited species of so-called formal contract, to be discussed later – have been (i) mutual agreement and (ii) mutual exchange, the latter typically being referred to in Anglo-American law as mutual "consideration."[7]

The term "promissory estoppel" was first coined by Professor Samuel Williston of Harvard Law School in his treatise on contract law in the early 1920s.[8] Indeed, he invented the doctrine nearly single-handedly.[9]

Williston's artificially invented doctrine of promissory estoppel purports to render "promises" – on which more to follow – legally binding even if they have not been bargained for, even if they have not been paid for. In short, if you the reader say you are going to do something, and someone else changes their position in reliance on your statement, and you later change your mind, they can sue you and take your property, if a judge sees fit. Even though that other person never paid you anything for your promise, never paid you anything for any commitment on your part. Thus, even if there was no bargained-for exchange. And even if you did not seek to induce their change in position in reliance on what you said. A court may decide, backed by police power, to confiscate part of your property as damages for the supposed "injury" you have occasioned upon the other.[10]

It may well do at this juncture to lean back and consider for a moment how frequently each of us, in normal back-and-forth communications with others in everyday life, makes future-oriented statements of anticipation or intent. It is constant and ubiquitous. Only a portion of what we communicate to each other on a routine basis constitutes a statement of past or present fact, or of opinion. Much of what we say concerns what we intend, what we plan, what we anticipate. The future. And this is as it should be.

And under the purported doctrine of "promissory estoppel," this makes you a potential tortfeasor, subject to potential asset confiscation.

---

7 *See* Alden, *Origins of Contract Law*, *supra* note 2, at 35–42, 46–53; Alden, *Reversing the Reliance Revolution*, *supra* note 2, at 1613, 1619–22.

8 Samuel Williston, The Law of Contracts § 139, at 308 (New York, Baker, Voorhis & Co. 1924) (both copyright claimed and preface dated 1920) [hereinafter Williston Treatise].

9 There has been some speculation as to the role that Professor Arthur Corbin of Yale, who served as Williston's deputy during the ALI's First Restatement drafting process, may have played in Williston's decision to propose the doctrine of promissory estoppel. For further discussion in this regard, see *infra* note 223.

10 As to all matters described in this paragraph, see *infra* Chapters 6 and 7.

Promissory estoppel purports to require neither mutual agreement nor mutual exchange.[11] It is thus a direct abnegation of the two fundamental requisites for the enforcement of promise in contract.[12] As so accurately and tellingly predicted in the early 1970s by Professor Grant Gilmore of Yale, a major proponent of promissory estoppel, classical contract law and promissory estoppel are "matter and anti-matter," "Restatement and anti-Restatement," "Contract and anti-Contract."[13] "The one thing that is clear is that these two contradictory propositions cannot live comfortably together: in the end one must swallow the other up."[14] Gilmore was, of course, absolutely correct in this judgment. He welcomed, indeed encouraged, the cannibalization of contract by promissory estoppel.[15] The Author opposes such endeavor.

How did we come to such a pass?

The political and institutional mechanism utilized by Williston to instigate change was the Restatement of the Law of Contracts (the "First Restatement") published in 1932 by the American Law Institute ("ALI").[16] Williston served as the Reporter for the First Restatement – in other words, the individual who personally drafted the First Restatement, subject to consultation with designated advisors, comments and revisions by the Council of the ALI, and ultimate approval by the ALI at an annual meeting.[17] A revised version of the restatement, the Restatement (Second), was published by the ALI in 1981.[18]

The ALI arose at the invitation of the Association of American Law Schools as a consortium of prominent law professors, judges, and practitioners established for the purpose of reducing into condensed form the major principles of various areas of Anglo-American caselaw.[19] By reducing the tangled welter of individual court opinions into acknowledged and agreed caselaw rules generally present among most

[11] Restatement (Second) § 90, *supra* note 2. This point was made even more explicitly in the First Restatement, in which Section 90, which sets forth promissory estoppel, appears under a subchapter labeled "Topic 4. Informal Contracts without Assent or Consideration." First Restatement ch. 3, topic 4, *supra* note 2.

[12] *See supra* text accompanying note 7; *infra* Chapter 5.

[13] Grant Gilmore, The Death of Contract 61 (Columbus, Ohio State Univ. Press 1974).

[14] *Id.* As Gilmore further observed: "A remarkable passage in the Restatement (Second) § 90 Commentary explains how most 'contract' cases, if not all of them, can be brought under § 90 so that resort to § 75 and consideration theory will rarely, if ever, be necessary. By passing through the magic gate of § 90, it seems, we can rid ourselves of all the technical limitations of contract theory." *Id.* at 90.

[15] *See* First Restatement, *supra* note 2; Alden, *Reversing the Reliance Revolution*, *supra* note 2, at 1613–14.

[16] *See supra* note 2.

[17] First Restatement, *supra* note 2, at ix–xi.

[18] *See* Restatement (Second), *supra* note 2.

[19] *Report of the Committee on the Establishment of a Permanent Organization for the Improvement of the Law Proposing the Establishment of an American Law Institute, Proceedings of the American Law Institute*, 1 A.L.I. Proc. pt. I, at 1–3 (Feb. 23, 1923) [hereinafter *Report of the ALI Establishing Committee*]; First Restatement, *supra* note 2, at viii–ix.

of them, it was hoped to foster greater regularity and predictability in application of the common law.[20]

Yet, though the ALI's restatement project was ostensibly conceived, and by Williston publicly heralded, as an effort "to restate the law as it is, not as a new law,"[21] the germ of manipulatory ambition lay already pregnant in the enterprise. The ALI itself baked within its organizational documents a subtle head nod that the members of each restatement team might suggest avenues of development in the law that they might view as desirable, even if those avenues did not reflect the law "as it is."[22]

Such an endeavor might have been undertaken honorably, setting forth in full candor the current state of law and clearly identifying those developments that the professoriate wished to suggest, even though they did not stand on any solid precedential basis. But such was not to be.

Rather, the First Restatement simply presented its abridged summary of the common law of contracts without distinguishing between those elements resting on solid historical foundation from those invented by the ALI itself.

The doctrine of promissory estoppel itself is set forth in Section 90 of the First Restatement and the Restatement (Second).[23] The First Restatement quite bluntly placed Section 90 within "Topic 4. Informal Contracts Without Assent or Consideration," neatly illustrating the doctrinal conflict with classical contract law.[24] The Restatement (Second) was somewhat more circumspect, omitting the foregoing "Topic 4" heading, but expanding the reach of Section 90 yet further to permit third party nonpromisees – that is, people to whom the promisor was not even speaking – to sue as well.[25] Section 90 accordingly now reads in most relevant part as follows:

> § 90. Promise Reasonably Inducing Action or Forbearance
>
> (1) A promise which the promisor should reasonably expect to induce action or forbearance on the part of the promisee or a third person and which does induce such action or forbearance is binding if injustice can be avoided only by enforcement of the promise. . . .[26]

[20] *Report of the ALI Establishing Committee*, *supra* note 19, at 1–2, 6, 13, 41; First Restatement, *supra* note 2, at viii–ix.

[21] *Minutes of the Third Annual Meeting*, 3 A.L.I. Proc. 159 (1925).

[22] *Report of the ALI Establishing Committee*, *supra* note 19, pt. I, at 15, 18 (authority and encouragement to "take account of situations not yet discussed by courts or dealt with by legislatures but which are likely to cause litigation in the future," where conflicting precedent exists to "make clear what is believed to be the proper rule of law," and to present changes to existing law "on clear proof of its advisability"); First Restatement, *supra* note 2, at viii ("to promote the clarification and simplification of the law and its better adaptation to social needs").

[23] First Restatement, *supra* note 2, § 90; Restatement (Second), *supra* note 2, § 90.

[24] First Restatement, *supra* note 2, ch. 3, topic 4.

[25] Restatement (Second), *supra* note 2, § 90.

[26] *Id.*

As one can see, there is no whisper in Section 90 of either mutual assent or mutual consideration, the two fundamental requisites for the enforceability of contract under precedent existing prior to that time. This was clearly not "the law as it is."[27] Yet, there was no concession of the radical abnegation of classical contract law at the heart of Section 90.

Worse, Williston did not characterize accurately the historical record with respect to the novel, artificial doctrine of promissory estoppel. This lent the doctrine an appearance of respectability and established precedential authority, involving two central assertions.[28] First, that the wellspring of Anglo-American contract law in medieval England rested upon the same foundation as, indeed constituted a form of, promissory estoppel.[29] And second, that certain idiosyncratic categories, along with individual American cases in the decades preceding the First Restatement, clearly supported or had been predicated upon promissory estoppel, though not using that specific terminology.[30]

Neither assertion is accurate.[31]

In overview, this book recounts the origins of Anglo-American contract law, commencing with the Romans, proceeding to the Norman conquest of England, thence to the development and evolution of English contract law over the course of the Middle Ages and Renaissance. Particular emphasis is placed on the historical continuity across these time periods of the requirement for contractual enforcement that a promise be either "formal" – manifesting a high degree of formality both from the perspective of intent and admonitory notice to be bound legally, and the creation of a clear evidentiary record thereof – or part of a mutually agreed mutual exchange transaction in which each party is providing or doing something at the other's request – in other words, where the promise is one half of a quid pro quo exchange between the parties.

Following the long record of Western civilization's laws of contract leading up to the early twentieth century, the book then examines the structure of the purported doctrine of promissory estoppel, its radical rejection of the requirements of mutual agreement and mutual exchange for the enforcement of promise, and how it has

[27] *See supra* text accompanying notes 11–13; *infra* Chapter 5.

[28] *See* Alden, *Origins of Contract Law*, *supra* note 2, at 10–12.

[29] *See* Samuel Williston, Commentaries on Contracts: Restatement No. 2, at 14 (Am. Law Inst. Mar. 9, 1926) [hereinafter Williston, *First Restatement Commentaries*].

[30] *See* Alden, *Rethinking*, *supra* note 2, at 683–704; Williston, *First Restatement Commentaries*, *supra* note 29, at 14–19; Discussion of the Tentative Draft, Contracts Restatement No. 2 (Apr. 29, 1926), Proceedings at the Fourth Annual Meeting of the American Law Institute, IV App. A.L.I. Proc. 90 (Apr. 29 to May 1, 1926) [hereinafter ALI Debate on Section 90].

[31] *See* Alden, *Rethinking*, *supra* note 2; Alden, *Origins of Contract Law*, *supra* note 2; Alden, *Reversing the Reliance Revolution*, *supra* note 2.

played out in American court decisions since the publication of the First Restatement.

This leads to a detailed forensic analysis of and rebuttal to the assertions of Williston and other promissory estoppel proponents both as to Anglo-Norman medieval and more recent American contract law.

The book then turns to a microeconomic analysis of classical contract law versus promissory estoppel, focused on Pareto improving transactions. And it addresses the moral foundation of contract law and the ethical implications of the attempt to alter its doctrinal underpinnings.

Based on the foregoing, two recommendations are presented.

First, it proposes a conceptual framework for analyzing so-called promissory estoppel cases through the lens of classical contract law. In certain cases, this will lead to a different result than the advocates of promissory estoppel might follow, but in not a few others the classical framework may lead to the same result as a simplistically expedient promissory estoppel decision, though without resort to use of a novel, dangerously overbroad and ill-defined doctrine to do so.

Second, it recommends the drafting and publication of a Third Restatement of Contracts to reverse the doctrinal heresy of promissory estoppel and to return American contract law to its classical contours. The book then concludes.

Part I

The History

Genesis and Development of Anglo-American Contract Law

1 ROMAN CONTRACT LAW

It might at first strike the reader as anomalous that one would begin a theoretical exegesis of Anglo-American contract law with ancient Rome. Yet, ancient Rome served as deeply influential intellectual soil from which European culture regerminated following the civilizational collapse of the Dark Ages.

As will be seen, Roman law, in particular Roman contract law, appears to have informed the development of Anglo-Norman contract law following the Norman conquest of England in 1066.

As stated in a highly abridged presentation for the sake of brevity, the Romans developed over time a formulary system of binding obligation.[32] That is, certain specific, named types of promise, transaction, or bargain were recognized and enforceable at law.

[32] A leading and detailed English-language treatise on the subject of Roman contract law is W. W. Buckland, A Text-Book of Roman Law from Augustus to Justinian (Cambridge Univ. Press 2d rev. ed. 1950) (1921).

Other corroborative English-language discussion can be found in H. F. Jolowicz, Historical Introduction to the Study of Roman Law (Cambridge Univ. Press 2d rev. ed. 1952) (1932); R. W. Lee, The Elements of Roman Law (London, Sweet & Maxwell 3d ed. 1952); W. A. Hunter, A Systematic and Historical Exposition of Roman Law in the Order of a Code (London, William Maxwell & Son 2d rev. ed. 1885); Lord MacKenzie, Studies in Roman Law with Comparative Views of the Laws of France, England, and Scotland (John Kirkpatrick ed., London, Blackwood & Sons 1886); James Muirhead, Historical Introduction to the Private Law of Rome (Henry Goudy ed., London, Adam & Charles Black 2d ed. 1899); A. M. Prichard, *Leage's Roman Private Law Founded on the Institutes of Gaius and Justinian* (London, Macmillan & Co. 3d ed. 1961) (1906); 2 Henry John Roby, Roman Private Law in the Times of Cicero and of the Antonines (Cambridge Univ. Press 1902); 2 Charles Phineas Sherman, Roman Law in the Modern World (New Haven Law Book Co. 2d ed. 1922); Rudolph Sohm, The Institutes: A Textbook of the History and System of Roman Private Law (James Crawford Ledlie trans., Oxford Univ. Press 3d ed. 1907).

Some of these were "formal" contracts.[33] The major category under this rubric was *stipulatio*, a formal promise made with both parties present, following a stylized question-and-answer format.[34] The recipient of the promise would ask *spondesne?* (do you formally promise?), whereupon the promisor would answer *spondeo* (I formally promise).[35] Although it was not required to be written, presumably due to the difficulty in otherwise proving that the stylized exchange had in fact taken place, and the precise nature of what had been promised, it was typical to reduce the *stipulatio* to writing.[36]

Due to the admonitory character of the stylized exchange, the promisor in *stipulatio* was upon conclusive notice that the promise would be legally enforceable. Presumably for this reason, it was thus not necessary for a recitation of what, if anything, the promisor might have received or been promised in return. On its face, *stipulatio* only bound one party, the formal promisor, though both promisor and promisee had to agree to the arrangement by virtue of the requisite stylized verbal back and forth between them.[37] However, due to the simple human observation that in many, if not nearly all, cases a person might only have an incentive to make a highly formal, legally binding promise if they were to receive something in return,[38] *stipulatio* was routinely used as part of composite transactions involving consideration on both sides. The mere fact that *stipulatio* was entered into does not in and of itself indicate whether the legal obligation thus embarked upon was gratuitous in nature or founded upon an unstated but entirely extant mutual exchange. For

[33] *See* BUCKLAND, *supra* note 32, at 412, 414, 434–61.

[34] *Id.* at 434. Other categories of formal contract included *adpromissio* (suretyship) (using the formal phrases "*idem dari spondes?*," "*idem fidepromittis?*," and "*id fide tua esse iubes?*"); *dictio dotis* (dowry) (using the formal phrase "*Stichus* (or *centum* or *fundus Cornelianus*) *tibi doti erit*"); *iusiurandum liberti* (oath before manumission to render continuing services) (using formal language based on "*dare oportere*"); and *nomina transcriptitia* (written recordation of liability for loan) (formality apparently achieved through transcription of liability into record books). *Id.* at 445–61.

[35] For the Latin, see D. P. SIMPSON, CASSELL'S LATIN DICTIONARY 567 (Houghton Mifflin Harcourt 1968) [hereinafter CASSELL'S] and FREDERIC M. WHEELOCK, WHEELOCK'S LATIN 3 (HarperCollins 7th rev. ed. 2011).

[36] *See* BUCKLAND, *supra* note 32, at 434–35.

[37] As to the point that *stipulatio* clearly involved mutual agreement, see DAVID IBBETSON, A HISTORICAL INTRODUCTION TO THE LAW OF OBLIGATIONS 7 (Oxford Univ. Press 1999, reprinted 2002). As discussed in the Introduction to this book, one of the features of the modern so-called doctrine of promissory estoppel is that it purports to bind not only in the absence of mutual consideration but also in the absence of mutual agreement, thus attenuating or eliminating altogether the admonitory character of the promissory act. *See, e.g., supra* text accompanying notes 10, 24, and 27. By contrast, in *stipulatio*, with its stylized exchange of words between promisor and promisee, there could be no misunderstanding or ambiguity as to whether a legally binding obligation would ensue. Not so with the potentially voracious maw of promissory estoppel in its ability to attach to any communication, however casually or insouciantly uttered.

[38] Moreover, the "something" received in return might be tangible and easily monetizable, or might be of other form not so readily measured in coin.

example, *stipulatio* could be used to transfer land, without recitation of the consideration for that promise to transfer.[39] Another use of *stipulatio* was to promise to repay a loan, and to promise to pay interest on a loan, where there is clearly consideration for the promise present.[40]

Others were informal contracts, again falling into specific, named categories. These included among others *mutuum* (loan), *depositum* (bailment), *commodatum* (loan for use), *pignus* (security), *hypotheca* (security), *emptio venditio* (sale and

[39] *See* Buckland, *supra* note 32, at 421.

[40] *Id.* at 442, 463–64.

It is worth noting that Buckland describes the Roman formal contracts as "unilateral," in the sense that they only refer explicitly to one party's obligation, even if when viewed as part of an overall composite transaction there may clearly be consideration rendered by the counterparty therefor. *Id.* at 406, 411, 413, 434. They were referred to as *stricti iuris*, giving "rise to a *strictum iudicium*" (strict judgment) in and of themselves. *Id.* For the Latin, see Cassell's, *supra* note 35, at 329, 572; Merriam-Webster Unabridged Dictionary online, https://www.merriam-webster.com/dictionary/actio%20stricti%20juris (last visited Dec. 6, 2024) (definition of *actio stricti iuris*: "an action in Roman law that the judge was to decide according to the strict legal rules without reference to equitable considerations – contrasted with *actio bonae fidei*").

Buckland's usage of the term "unilateral" is thus broader and somewhat different than in modern American law, where a unilateral contract is defined solely as one in which the offeror has made an offer that does not invite acceptance by counterpromise or partial counterperformance but rather solely by completed counterperformance on the part of the offeree. *See* First Restatement, *supra* note 2, § 45 cmt. b; Restatement (Second), *supra* note 2, § 45 cmt. a.

This also illustrates a consistent pattern in Buckland's descriptions of Roman law to discuss the various elements of a transaction as discrete, rather than as linked and related components of an overall composite transaction. On quite a few occasions, he characterizes an agreement as "unilateral," or even "gratuitous," when in fact the agreement constitutes but one inextricably interwoven piece of an overall composite transaction that indubitably involves mutual consideration. Examples include *stipulatio* characterized as unilateral, Buckland, *supra* note 32, at 434, 437, yet "[a] *stipulatio* for land . . . would not usually be by way of gift; other transactions would be connected with it. Thus other property might have been transferred in return for the promise," *id.* at 421; likewise, cases where a "*stipulator* [the recipient of the promise] sued on a promise to repay a loan of money," and where it was requisite, if existence of the loan was denied by the debtor, for the *stipulator*/creditor to demonstrate "that there was a real debt, even a pre-existing one," as the predicate for the promise, *id.* at 442–43. Similarly, Buckland writes that in *mutuum* (loan for consumption), "[t]he contract was unilateral, binding only the receiver. It was *stricti iuris*. . . .", and "*[m]utuum*, as a result, perhaps, of its origin, was gratuitous, but the Roman business man did not lend gratuitously. What the rule meant was that interest, if any, and there usually would be, must be agreed for by a separate contract. This would normally be a *stipulatio*. . . ." *Id.* at 462–64.

The genesis of this formalistic, discrete approach appears to lie in the premise that where one has formally acknowledged an obligation in a manner universally known to entail legal liability, the promisor has implicitly conceded the human reality that there was most likely an underlying quid pro quo bargain transaction, i.e., one involving mutual consideration, from which the promise arises. As Buckland writes, "where a man had given a written acknowledgment of a loan," "[t]he man was bound by the *mutuum* and had provided evidence which barred him from denying that there was a *mutuum*. On this view the document . . . was conclusive evidence." *Id.* at 461. This theme will be reprised in discussion by Professor John Baker of Cambridge University as to the later English formal contracts evidenced by "deeds," *infra*.

purchase), *locatio conductio* (hire or lease, of either services or objects), *societas* (partnership, whether or not for profit), and *mandatum* (agency).[41]

Mutual agreements, "informal bargains," not falling within any of the foregoing ordained enforceable categories, were referred to as *pacta* (pacts),[42] though in modern terminology we would of course refer to such agreements likewise as contracts.[43]

The significant point about *pacta* was that they were not enforceable without mutual consideration. It was a firmly established principle of Roman law that a "bare" or "naked" pact – that is, one where a party had promised but was not compensated by the counterparty for that promise in some form that would today be recognized as consideration – was simply not enforceable.[44]

This principle was articulated in various grammatical formulations, all of equivalent substantive content. As will be discussed *infra*, one of the most prevalent Latin forms of the legal rule commonly used in later English contract law as it developed during the Middle Ages and, thereafter, is *ex nudo pacto nulla oritur actio* (out of a naked pact no action arises).[45]

One of the clearest and most definitive statements of the rule centuries earlier in Roman times was set forth in the Digest of Justinian, promulgated circa AD 533.[46] During his reign, the Emperor Justinian had called for a vast compilation and systematic treatment of existing Roman law to be undertaken, led by scholars at

[41] *See* BUCKLAND, *supra* note 32, at 462–526.

[42] *Id.* at 527. For a more abbreviated discussion of *pacta*, see LEE, *supra* note 32, at 335–37; HUNTER, *supra* note 32, at 545–50; PRICHARD, *supra* note 32, at 379–81; ROBY, *supra* note 32, at 7–8; SHERMAN, *supra* note 32, at 316–18; SOHM, *supra* note 32, at 414–16. *Cf.* MACKENZIE, *supra* note 32, at 230; MUIRHEAD, *supra* note 32, at 143.

[43] This is, of course, subject to the requirement in Anglo-American law of mutual consideration, as discussed *infra*.

[44] *See* BUCKLAND, *supra* note 32, at 407, 428, 464, 465, 532, 553.

Buckland states the principle in one location which, although upon no more than a superficial read might initially give rise to doubt, upon closer examination merely confirms the principle all the more clearly. He writes, "*Nudum pactum*. It is usually held that a nude pact did not create a natural obligation, but there were a few exceptions." *Id.* at 553. The exceptions he articulates are, "Pacts for interest . . .; hypothec . . .; pact promising master money for liberty. . . ." *Id.* at 533 n.2. Without any question, each of these "exceptions" do indeed involve mutual consideration when viewed as a composite overall transaction: a loan is given, in exchange for a promise not only to repay the principal but also interest thereon; security is given for a loan; a promise is made to pay in future in order to be manumitted.

[45] *See, e.g.*, Question from the Master of the Rolls, Y.B. Trin. 17 Edw. IV, fo. 4, pl. 4 (1477), *translated in* JOHN H. BAKER & S. F. C. MILSOM, SOURCES OF ENGLISH LEGAL HISTORY: PRIVATE LAW TO 1750, at 242 (Butterworth 1986) [hereinafter ENGLISH SOURCES].

Other commonly occurring grammatical variants of the identical concept appearing in both Roman and later English law include "*nuda pacto obligationem non parit,*" "*ex nudo pacto non oritur actio,*" and "*nudum pactum non parit actionem,*" as well as the simple, abbreviated phrase "*nudum pactum.*"

[46] THE DIGEST OF JUSTINIAN [DIGESTA SEU PANDECTAE] (Theodor Mommsen, Paul Krueger & Alan Watson eds. and trans., Univ. of Penn. Press 1985) (533 A.D.).

the Eastern Roman Empire law schools at Constantinople and Beirut.[47] The result was the *Corpus Iuris Civilis*, comprising the Codex, the Digest, and the Institutes of Justinian.[48] Of these three components, the Digest constitutes "the richest and most massive part of the Justinianic codification" and "the principal source of our knowledge of the classical period of Roman law."[49]

In the Digest, the commentary by scholar Ulpian sets forth the general rule as to *pacta*:

> Ulpian, Edict, book 4: By universal law some agreements give rise to actions, some to defenses. 1. Those which give rise to actions do not have a name of their own but take the proper name of the contract [to which they refer], such as sale, hire, partnership, loan, deposit, and other similar contracts. 2. But even if the matter does not fall under the head of another contract and yet a ground [*causa*] exists, Aristo in apt reply to Celsus states that there is an obligation. *Where, for example, I gave a thing to you so that you may give another to me, or I gave so that you may do something, this is, Aristo says, a* synallagma *[Author's note: in the original Greek, a reciprocal exchange] and hence a civil obligation arises .... 4. But, when no ground* [causa] *exists, it is settled that no obligation arises from the agreement. Therefore, a naked agreement [a nude pact] does not give rise to an obligation ....*[50]

(emphasis added)

[47] Wolfgang Kunkel, An Introduction to Roman Legal and Constitutional History 163–64 (J. M. Kelly trans., Oxford Univ. Press 2d ed. 1973, reprinted 1975, from Wolfgang Kunkel, Römische Rechtsgeschichte (Köln and Graz, Böhlau-Verlag 6th ed. 1971)).

[48] *Id.* at 168.

[49] *Id.* at 169.

[50] In the original Latin:

> Ulpianus libro quarto ad edictum. Iuris gentium conuentiones quaedam actiones pariunt, quaedam exceptiones. Quae pariunt actiones, in suo nomine non stant, sed transeunt in proprium nomen contractus: ut emptio uenditio, locatio conductio, societas, commodatum, depositum et ceteri similes contractus. Sed et si in alium contractum res non transeat, subsit tamen causa, eleganter Aristo Celso respondit esse obligationem. ut puta dedi tibi rem ut mihi aliam dares, dedi ut aliquid facias: hoc συνάλλαγμα [synallagma] [Author's note: word appearing in original Greek letters embedded in the Latin text] esse et hinc nasci ciuilem obligationem.... Sed cum nulla subest causa, propter conuentionem hic constat non posse constitui obligationem: igitur *nuda pacto obligationem non parit*.... (emphasis added)

1 The Digest of Justinian, *supra* note 46, bk. 2, ch. 14, para. 7, at 63 (first alteration in Latin original) (emphasis added) (with minor revision to English translation of final sentence to reflect sequence of original Latin).

What can be quite confusing in reading sources with respect to pacts is that the law in this regard evolved over time. The best sequential, historical description of this evolution that the Author has yet identified is by Professor Buckland of Cambridge University. Initially, pacts constituted a form of liability release: "The XII Tables [Author: the foundation stone of republican Roman law] contained a rule that proceedings for personal injury were barred by pact, and pact continued to be a complete civil defense to an action on delict [tort], in later law." Buckland, *supra* note 32, at 527. "The next step was to allow pacts to vary obligations. The recognition of so-called *pacta adiecta*, pacts added to contracts, was a gradual process...." *Id.* at 528. "The next step was to give an action on pacts not connected with a contract (*pacta*

At risk of repetition but to focus in on the central concept of the quoted passage, the Digest thus states that if there is mutual exchange, *synallagma*,[51] then, because of, due to,[52] this fact, a pact becomes enforceable at law. But a naked pact, one where no mutual exchange is present, does not give rise to an obligation.[53] This is,

vestita)...." *Id.* at 529. The law of pacts thus expanded dramatically over time to embrace far wider types of agreement than at inception.

Confusion or conflation among the various states of development in the law of pacts is particularly noticeable in reading Ulpian's commentary in the Digest of Justinian, as well as in many other sources. But what stands clear from Ulpian is that a bare or naked pact, i.e., one without *causa*, was not enforceable, and that the sole and only example of *causa* given by Ulpian in this connection was *synallagma*, i.e., reciprocal exchange. Without *synallagma*, without reciprocal exchange, a pact was simply not enforceable at law. This represented the state of Roman law on point, and as will be discussed *infra*, was the principle adopted by the English as they developed the Anglo-American law of contract.

51 Συνάλλαγμα (from syn = with, + állagma = thing taken in exchange). The etymology of the word "synallagmatic" can be found in Ernest Klein, A Comprehensive Etymological Dictionary of the English Language 1558 (Elsevier 1966). The Digest of Justinian used the word in the original Greek, written in the Greek alphabet. For discussion of same, see, e.g., Gottfried Schiemann, *Synallagma*, Brill's New Pauly, http://referenceworks.brillonline.com/entries/brill-s-new-pauly/synallagma-e1127030 (last visited Feb. 1, 2016).

52 The word "hence" in the quoted passage is translated from the original Latin word *hinc*, denoting causation, "from this cause." *See* Cassell's, *supra* note 34, at 276.

53 Just after the end of the quoted text, in the original Latin appear the words *sed parit exceptionem*, "but [does give rise] to a defense," meaning that although a naked pact cannot be used offensively to assert the existence of an obligation on the part of the promisor, i.e., cannot be used to assert de novo the existence of a contract, a naked promise by a potential plaintiff not to sue can give rise to a litigational defense for the promisee against lawsuit. 1 The Digest of Justinian, *supra* note 46, bk. 2, ch. 14, para. 7, at 63. "[A] pact not to sue was a praetorian defence in any action, so that it could destroy an obligation, though it gave no action: *nuda pacto obligationem non parit, sed parit exceptionem.*" Buckland, *supra* note 32, at 527–28. This principle arises from the historical genesis of pacts as liability releases, prior to their radical expansion in scope to encompass effectively any substantive type of agreement. *See* discussion *supra* note 50.

Building out on this concept, Ulpian goes on to state in his commentary in the Digest that, provided no performance by either party has yet taken place, a sale or other good faith action can be rescinded or even modified by a pact. This principle would of course run contrary to the modern preexisting duty rule requirement that a rescission or modification of a contract be supported by mutual consideration. However, again, this principle emerges from the genesis of *pacta* as a form of liability release and cannot be used to create a contract de novo without mutual consideration. *See* 1 The Digest of Justinian, *supra* note 46, bk. 2, ch. 14, para. 7, at 63–64.

As a separate point, the Digest indicates that a pact made contemporaneously with a named contract for the purpose of spelling out additional terms of the agreement will be enforced as part of the overall transaction. This treatment does not apply if a contract is entered into and then, only later, a naked pact is made. In such case, the naked pact is viewed as standing separately, and is therefore not enforceable:

> ... [A]greements by way of pact are incorporated in good faith actions. But this is understood to mean that only if the pacts have followed immediately upon [the main contract] [Author's note: bracketed text appearing in published translation] are they incorporated in the plaintiff's action; if concluded after an interval, they are not incorporated, nor will they avail the plaintiff, should he sue, since an action cannot arise from a

in modern parlance, nothing other than the doctrinal requirement of mutual consideration in order for a contract to be enforceable.

So, to sum up Roman contract law in relevant respect, an agreement between counterparties would be enforceable if it either (i) fell within a preordained, specified, and named category of enforceable contract or if it (ii) constituted a pact predicated upon *synallagma*, upon mutual exchange.

Moreover, of the recognized, defined categories of enforceable contract, many, if not most, if not nearly all, were likewise predicated upon mutual exchange, even if the defined category only explicitly referred to the obligations of one of the counterparties to what might in economic substance have reflected a genuinely mutual exchange.[54]

Upon this ancient basis, Western legal civilization as to contract was reborn as it emerged from the Dark Ages.

2 THE RECEPTION AND THE NORMAN CONQUEST

The great moment in that rebirth of Roman law was the recovery and propagation of the Digest of Justinian throughout Italy and parts of France shortly after the turn of the first millennium AD, during the early eleventh century.[55] The text thereof was copied, interpreted, and expounded upon by so-called glossators and commentators, providing the foundation for the growth of legal studies in the fledgling universities at Bologna and elsewhere.[56] In due course, Roman civil law was formally adopted across the continental European landscape, from principalities and municipalities

> pact. . . . For the pacts incorporated are those which supply a contract with its terms, that is, those agreed when the contract was originally made.

Id. at 63.

[54] Though in the formal and other *stricti iuris* "unilateral" contracts, no specification of any applicable quid pro quo need have been made in order to seek enforcement, as discussed *supra*.

[55] "[T]hrough the Digest all the greatness and strength of Roman jurisprudence was again bestowed upon western Europe." KUNKEL, *supra* note 47, at 182.

> The manuscript (no longer surviving) on which the Italian manuscripts of the high and late Middle Ages are based, the so-called Codex S(ecundus) was probably written about the middle of the eleventh century in southern Italy. The celebrated Florentine manuscript must also have been in that area at the time, as the writer of S used it, along with another manuscript, as his original. One tradition (up to now fairly generally disbelieved) has it that the Florentine manuscript was stolen by the Pisans in Amalfi . . . and brought to Pisa in 1135, whence it came to Florence in 1406.

Id. at 182 n.1.

[56] *Id.* at 182–83.

"At the time of the glossators huge crowds of students from Germany, France, Spain, and other countries had come to the Italian universities, and now the commentators became to an ever greater extent the legal instructors of Europe," in whose work "may be found the roots of the modern legal life of the peoples of continental Europe. . . ." *Id.* at 185.

all the way up to the mighty Holy Roman Empire comprising effectively all of central Europe, a process known as the "Reception."[57]

During this same period, English history took its own decisive turn. In the year 1066, William the Conqueror led his Norman troops – originally Vikings who had settled in the north of France and adopted the French language – to the southern shore of England and triumphed over Anglo-Saxon King Harold II at the Battle of Hastings. Over the succeeding years, William solidified his control over the country and established a well-organized system of royal administration, including in particular legal administration. The Normans were the Prussians of their day.

As a result of the Norman Conquest, English society took on a distinctive character at this juncture. A Norman aristocratic and clerical overclass now ruled over an Anglo-Saxon farming and working class. One of the many effects of this initially bifurcated yet gradually fusing social structure is the evolution of the English language, largely Germanic in origin for everyday, simpler words from the existing Anglo-Saxon population, with an overlay of more sophisticated vocabulary of French-Latin origin in use among the clergy, the nobles, and later in the universities that were to develop.[58] Another effect, and one that would have great impact on the development of the Anglo-Norman legal system, as will be discussed in detail *infra*, was the fact that William and his successors created a distinctive procedural mechanism – so-called royal writs – for taking royal jurisdiction over legal disputes that would otherwise be handled through legacy Anglo-Saxon local and municipal judicial processes.[59]

2.1 *The Impact of Roman Contract Law*

Returning now to the brief exegesis of Roman contract law set forth earlier, its principal relevance for this account lies in the extent to which Roman law influenced the development of Anglo-Norman law in England from the Norman Conquest forward.[60] In this regard, various historians have reached somewhat

[57] THEODORE F. T. PLUCKNETT, A CONCISE HISTORY OF THE COMMON LAW 298 (Little, Brown 5th ed. 1956) (1929).

[58] An example of this stratified social and linguistic structure may be observed by considering basic, commonly used words such as light, water, land, etc., which obviously have the same original roots as the modern German *Licht*, *Wasser*, and *Land*. By contrast, more advanced, clerical and university level words, such as malleable, clearly come from the French *malléable*, in turn from the Latin *malleus* (hammer). *See, e.g.*, https://www.etymonline.com, enter "malleable" in search box (last visited Dec. 8, 2024).

[59] For a detailed description of the system of Anglo-Norman royal writs as applied to contract law, see Alden, *Origins of Contract Law*, *supra* note 2, at 1, 17–53.

[60] England did not follow the continental example of the formal Reception of Roman law. *See, e.g.*, PLUCKNETT, *supra* note 57, at 43–44. Nonetheless, "[o]ur English law shows itself strong enough to assimilate foreign ideas and convert them to its own use," and "the effect produced on English law by its contact with the romano-canonical learning seems immeasurable. . . ." 1 FREDERICK POLLOCK & FREDERIC WILLIAM MAITLAND, THE

different conclusions, or at least different emphases. Some have focused more heavily on the distinctives, particularly the evolution of the writ system and its wide-reaching effect on Anglo-Norman legal development.[61] Others have focused more heavily on aspects of continuity and cross-fertilization from continental European legal thinking, based as it was on Roman law.[62]

As to contract law specifically, there is reason in the Author's view to believe that a fair amount of cross-fertilization did in fact occur, some explicit, some implicit. As will be discussed, this is particularly to be seen in English jurists' firm and unyielding adoption over the centuries of the ancient Roman principle of contract law as applied to *pacta* – which the English jurists routinely cited in the original Latin – namely, that a naked promise, that is, one unsupported by consideration therefor rendered by the promisee, is simply not enforceable at law:[63]

> In the twelfth century the revived study of Justinian's books ... tended also to confirm the notion that something more than a formless expression of agreement must be required if an action is to be given. *Nudum pactum non parit actionem* – so much at least was clear beyond a doubt.[64]

This principle, *ex nudo pacto non oritur actio*, along with linguistically variant but substantively identical expressions thereof (such as *nudum pactum non parit actionem* in the preceding quoted text, or *nuda pacto obligationem non parit* in the Digest of Justinian[65]), and its repeated articulation during the evolution of English contract law, are analyzed in further detail later on as this account develops through the course of the Middle Ages.

History of English Law Before the Time of Edward I, at 134–35 (Cambridge Univ. Press 2d ed. 1968) (1895) [hereinafter Maitland].

61 An example in this regard is Professor Wolfgang Kunkel, though at the end of the following passage he makes a possibly quite telling concession:

> The Anglo-Saxon area remained excluded from this great legal family because England, which in the twelfth century ... had come under the first influences of Roman law, later consciously closed itself to these influences. Here by the end of the thirteenth century a native legal profession had grown up, organized as a guild which rejected foreign law and its methods. It was this English legal profession which from its own traditions lent Anglo-Saxon law those features which distinguish it today so sharply from the legal world of the Continent: features which nevertheless for all their individual nature still often remind one surprisingly of the structure of classical Roman law.

Kunkel, *supra* note 47, at 185.

It is worthy of note that in the late 1200s, precisely when Professor Kunkel believes English law was establishing itself independently of Roman precedent, the great Bracton published his seminal and deeply influential treatise on English substantive law, in Latin, using the original Roman legal terms, as discussed *infra*, text accompanying notes 75–77.

62 An intermediate position is reflected in, e.g., 1 Maitland, *supra* note 60, at 78.

63 *See* Alden, *Origins of Contract Law*, *supra* note 2, at 35–44.

64 2 Maitland, *supra* note 60, at 194.

65 *See supra* note 45.

To begin with, the substrate legal culture of Anglo-Saxon (thus Germanic) England prior to the Norman Conquest appears consistent with the Roman approach of denying enforcement to uncompensated promises:

> We may take it as a general principle of ancient German law that the courts will not undertake to uphold gratuitous gifts or to enforce gratuitous promises.[66]

The Roman conceptual approach to the enforceability of contract would thus fall upon fertile ground in the Germanically populated England newly conquered by the Normans.

Following the Norman Conquest, we then have the background of certain individuals who moved from the continent to England and informed the creation of the Norman legal system and its rules. Two in particular stand out. First, Lanfranc, "a lawyer of worldwide fame"[67] who had taught at the law school in Pavia, Italy,[68] was deeply conversant with both Roman and Canon (i.e., church) law.[69] He became William's leading advisor and was named by William as the Archbishop of Canterbury.[70] He was "the Conqueror's right-hand man"[71] as William built out the fledgling Norman administrative state and its legal system. Second, Vacarius, likewise from Italy, in his case the university at Bologna; in the 1100s, he published a massive work on the Digest and Code of Justinian and taught Roman law at Oxford.[72] Despite the geographic impediment of the English Channel, a genuinely pan-European culture populated by persons with significant international experience existed in the day, which brought many learned individuals from the continent to the British Isles. Roman law profoundly informed their own education and background as they helped to lay the foundation stones of Anglo-Norman law and legal thought in England. They did not operate in a vacuum.

The legacy of this influence may be observed less in the work of the prominent Ranulph de Glanville, who in the late 1100s published a legal treatise concerned in large part with the procedural mechanics of royal writs,[73] than it can in the first

66 2 MAITLAND, *supra* note 60, at 213.

67 1 MAITLAND, *supra* note 60, at 77.

68 PLUCKNETT, *supra* note 57, at 297.

69 1 MAITLAND, *supra* note 60, at 78. "He was remembered in Normandy as one of the discoverers of Roman law." *Id.*

70 PLUCKNETT, *supra* note 57, at 297.

71 1 MAITLAND, *supra* note 60, at 77.

72 *See, e.g.*, ENCYCLOPEDIA BRITANNICA, https://www.britannica.com/biography/Vacarius (last visited Dec. 21, 2024) (Vacarius "prepared a treatise (nine books) on the Digest, or Pandects, and Codex of the Byzantine Emperor Justinian I. Known as *Liber pauperum*, this work became one of the chief legal texts at Oxford. . . . Oxford students of law soon were called *pauperistae*, in reference to his book.").

73 RANULPH DE GLANVILLE, TRACTATUS DE LEGIBUS ET CONSUETUDINIBUS REGNI ANGLIAE [A TREATISE ON THE LAWS AND CUSTOMS OF THE KINGDOM OF ENGLAND] (John Beames trans., John Byrne & Co. 1900) (circa 1188) (English translation) [hereinafter GLANVILLE]. The original Latin text may be found in RANULPHO DE GLANVILLA, TRACTATUS DE LEGIBUS ET

comprehensive legal treatise on substantive Anglo-Norman law published in 1235 by Henry de Bracton.[74] Like Glanville, Bracton wrote in Latin, not English.[75] In setting forth the principles of contract law, he literally used the precise Roman terminology for various contractual categories.[76] Bracton's epochal work served as the touchstone for later English legal thought over the course of centuries.[77] Most significantly, his position as to the requirement of mutual consideration (or in the alternative, formal deed/*stipulatio*, to be discussed later) for the enforcement of contract was firmly grounded in Roman law: "About one point Bracton and his epitomators are clear – *Nudum pactum non parit actionem*. . . ."[78]

2.2 *The Canonists and Nude Pacts*

Before entering upon an examination of the development of English contracts caselaw over succeeding centuries, it is worthwhile interstitially to note an important conflict in the doctrines of contract law between the secular and religious authorities. Parallel to, and separate from, the secular law, during this period the declared religious authority of the church, known as "canon law," grew to comprise many matters, some of which were tangentially or even quite directly related to the secular sphere.[79] Notable for our account here is the assertion by canon law authorities that a naked promise, that is, one uncompensated by consideration coming from the

CONSUETUDINIBUS REGNI ANGLIAE (John Rayner ed., London, White & Brooke 1780) (circa 1188) [hereinafter GLANVILLE LATIN TEXT].

74 HENRICUS [HENRY] DE BRACTON, DE LEGIBUS ET CONSUETUDINIBUS ANGLIAE [ON THE LAWS AND CUSTOMS OF ENGLAND] (Sir Travers Twiss ed. & trans., London, Longman & Co. 1878–83) (circa 1235) (Latin original and English translation on facing pages) [hereinafter BRACTON]. For an alternative translation, see Samuel E. Thorne's work at the Harvard Law School Library, http://bracton.law.harvard.edu/ [hereinafter BRACTON ONLINE]. Because the translations in BRACTON and BRACTON ONLINE bear certain differences from each other, reference to the original Latin is advised.

75 A detailed and highly learned inquiry into the influence of Roman legal principles on Bracton's description of English substantive law is to be found in the work of the great scholar Professor Güterbock of Königsberg, East Prussia (present-day Kaliningrad, Russian Federation). *See* CARL GÜTERBOCK, BRACTON AND HIS RELATION TO THE ROMAN LAW (Brinton Coxe trans., Fred B. Rothman & Co. photo. reprint 1979) (1866).

Similarly, Professor William Holdsworth has examined the influence of Roman law on Bracton's work in granular detail. *See* WILLIAM HOLDSWORTH, 2 A HISTORY OF ENGLISH LAW 267–90 (Little, Brown 4th ed. 1936). Holdsworth specifies that one of the areas in Bracton's work "in which the influence of Roman law is marked" is that of contract. *See id.* at 271–77.

76 See the heading "Of Actions," 2 BRACTON, bk. 3, ch. 2, *supra* note 74, at 118–19; BRACTON ONLINE, *supra* note 74, at 287.

77 HOLDSWORTH, *supra* note 75, at 286–89.

78 2 MAITLAND, *supra* note 60, at 197.

79 *See* 1 MAITLAND, *supra* note 60, at 112–35. These included ecclesiastical matters, marriage, divorce, legitimacy, testamentary disposition, and others. *See id.* at 125–31. The great statement of canon law was the *Decretum* of Gratian, circa 1139 to 1142 A.D. *Id.* at 112–13.

promisee, if "made by oath, or by 'pledge of faith'," should be considered enforceable at law.[80]

> [T]he canonists declared, in spite of the Roman maxim *ex nudo pacto actio non oritur*, that a simple promise was enforceable. It must have needed a great deal of courage to reach this position when against it was all the authority of Roman law and the custom and practice of most of the other systems of secular law.[81]

On this point, King Henry II and the religious authorities contended with each other, with Henry opposed. Henry prevailed.[82] This resolution to the secular versus canon law doctrinal conflict would affect all of subsequent English contract law, as shall be seen.

3 ENGLISH CONTRACT LAW THROUGH THE MIDDLE AGES AND RENAISSANCE

3.1 *From 1066 to 1350: Contractual Claims and Procedural Defenses and Requirements*

3.1.1 Development of the Royal Courts and Freezing of the Writ System

To assume control over the legal administration of matters of significant import, William and his successors established and over time built out a system of centralized courts under royal, rather than local, authority.

This process was evolutionary in nature. Initially, there was no clear demarcation between administration and adjudication in the modern Western sense.[83] Authority proceeded from the King, around whom was gathered his royal court (alternatively referred to as the King's Court, the King's Council, or the *Curia Regis*).[84] The King sent forth roving commissions, so-called Justices in Eyre, around the kingdom to assert royal authority and render decisions on various matters.[85] In time, this function came to be centralized at Westminster in London, ultimately becoming the Court of Common Pleas.[86]

For appeals from the Court of Common Pleas, and for matters of major importance to the Crown, a second offshoot formed from the royal court, namely, the King's Bench.[87]

[80] *Id.* at 128.
[81] PLUCKNETT, *supra* note 57, at 304. *See also* 2 MAITLAND, *supra* note 60, at 195–96.
[82] 1 MAITLAND, *supra* note 60, at 128–29.
[83] *See, e.g.*, the combined judicial and administrative functions of the roving General Eyre. PLUCKNETT, *supra* note 57, at 103. *See also id.* at 146.
[84] *Id.* at 142, 151.
[85] *Id.* at 102–3, 144–46.
[86] *Id.* at 149.
[87] *Id.* at 149–51.

As the King's Bench itself became more heavily bound by procedure, as had already earlier occurred with the Court of Common Pleas,[88] a third principal instance arose from the office of the King's Chancellor, namely, the Chancery, which exercised broad equitable discretion and the power to impose extraordinary remedies not available to the other royal courts.[89]

Alongside these operated the Court of Exchequer, which oversaw matters affecting the royal finances.[90] And throughout, the royal court, and later the developing and evolving institution of Parliament, exercised not only legislative but also judicial power.[91]

All of this centralized judicial apparatus arose against the backdrop of preexisting, pre-Norman Anglo-Saxon political, administrative, and judicial systems at the local level. These were the vill (village), the hundred (100 freemen) in the countryside or borough in the towns, and the county.[92]

[88] *Id.* at 151–52.

[89] As to the historical development and powers of Chancery, see *id.* at 139–40, 163–64, 673–89.

[90] *Id.* at 146–47. In a later development, there arose certain grand conclaves of all the judges:

> At all times judges of the common law courts have discussed important and difficult cases in meetings consisting of all the judges of both Benches, and sometimes the Lord Chancellor and the barons of the Exchequer. Sometimes the Council is also mentioned, and the judgment proceeded from this impressive assembly as a whole.... At the beginning of the fifteenth century such meetings were often in the "Exchequer Chamber"....
>
> ... [U]nder this system the case went at once for discussion by all the judges of all the courts sitting together in order to reach a definitive ruling, which very naturally was accepted with the greatest respect as settling the point.

Id. at 162–63.

For examples of such coordinated judicial action in practice, see *Doige's Case* of 1442, *infra* note 143, and *Slade's Case* of 1602, *infra* note 181, and in each case the accompanying text. *See also* PLUCKNETT, *supra* note 57, at 645.

[91] PLUCKNETT, *supra* note 57, at 146.

[92] *Id.* at 83–93; JOHN H. BAKER, AN INTRODUCTION TO ENGLISH LEGAL HISTORY 6–7 (Oxford Univ. Press 4th ed. 2007, reprinted 2011). Per Professor Baker of Cambridge University:

> The borough performed similar functions for townspeople, both administratively and judicially, as the hundred performed for country folk; borough and hundred were therefore reckoned to be mutually exclusive. In London, however, the husting was really the equivalent of a shire [county].... The London equivalent of the hundred was the "ward"....

BAKER, *supra*, at 7.

As stated by the Magna Carta of 1215, a century and a half after the Conquest of 1066:

> Et civitas London. habeat omnes libertates et liberas consuetudines suas, tam per terras, quam per aquas. Preterea volumnus et concedimus quod omnes alia civitates, et burgi, et ville, et portus, habeant omnes libertates et liberas consuetudines suas.
>
> [And the city of London shall have all its ancient liberties and free customs, as well by land as by water; furthermore, we decree and grant that all other cities, boroughs, towns, and ports shall have all their liberties and free customs.]

To take royal jurisdiction over an otherwise local matter, the Chancery (the office of the Chancellor of England) would issue a "writ,"[93] a formal letter of command, typically instructing a county sheriff to compel a defendant to take action satisfying a given plaintiff's complaint, or to bring the defendant before the royal courts to explain which such action should not be compelled.[94] Later forms of writ simply commanded that a defendant appear before the royal courts immediately to defend such an individual's conduct.[95]

Because the Crown chose to bring only certain more significant matters to the royal courts, there were a limited number of writs created, addressing certain specific factual situations or allegations. This gave rise to a formulary system of centralized justice reminiscent of the Romans' formulary system.[96]

Over time, the number and variety of writs increased until, in 1258, the Provisions of Oxford effectively put an end to the further creation of new forms of writ, thus freezing the existing formulary system in place at that point.[97] As will be seen, this

MAGNA CARTA LIBERTATUM [MAGNA CARTA] para. 13 (1215), *original Latin text from* CHARLES B. MONT, CHARTES DES LIBERTÉS ANGLAISES (1100–1305) (Paris, Alphonse Picard 1892), *English translation from* SOURCE PROBLEMS IN ENGLISH HISTORY (Albert Beebe White & Wallace Notestein eds., New York, Harper & Bros. 1915), *reprinted at* https://www.orbilat.com/Languages/Latin/Texts/06_Medieval_period/Legal_Documents/Magna_Carta.html (last visited Dec. 6, 2024).

[93] 1 MAITLAND, *supra* note 60, at 194.

[94] PLUCKNETT, *supra* note 57, at 355–57.

[95] *Id.* at 366.

[96] 2 MAITLAND, *supra* note 60, at 558:

> [W]e have yet to speak of the most distinctively English trait of our medieval law, its "formulary system" of actions. We call it distinctively English; but it is also in a certain sense very Roman. While the other nations of Western Europe were beginning to adopt as their own the ultimate results of Roman legal history, England was unconsciously reproducing that history. . . .

See also PLUCKNETT, *supra* note 57, at 354 (citing Maitland).

[97] As explained by Professor Baker, an emerging position to this effect in the years leading up to 1258 that

> . . . seems, then, already to have become the orthodoxy, was voiced two years later in the Provisions of Oxford 1258, under which the chancellor was to be sworn to issue no unprecedented writs without the consent of the king's council. After this period, although occasional innovations were sanctioned by parliament, the categories [of writs] became more or less closed. The effect was momentous. Finding the right formula was no longer simply a matter of consistency and routine. If a would-be plaintiff could not find a writ in the register he was without remedy as far as the two benches [king's courts] were concerned.

BAKER, *supra* note 92, at 56.

The technical legal manner through which this was effectuated was the appointment by the Provisions of Oxford of 24 individuals, 12 from the side of the King, and 12 from the side of the Earls and Barons, to constitute a council. *See* Provisions of Oxford 1258, 1 ANNALES MONASTICI 448 (Rolls ser. 1864–69), https://historyofengland.typepad.com/files/the-provisions-of-oxford-1258.pdf. Further, the Chancellor of England, who had the power and responsibility to issue any and all royal writs, swore therein as follows:

formulary writ system and the halt to its further expansion was to have tremendous significance for the development of English contract law.[98]

> Thus swore the chancellor of England[:] That he will not seal any writ except a writ of course without the order of the king and of the councillors who are present. Nor will he seal a gift or of a great wardship or of a large sum of money or of escheats without the assent of the full council or of the greater part of it. And that he will not seal anything that is contrary to what has been and will be ordained by the twenty four or by the greater part of them.

Id. This constituted a nontrivial administrative impediment to the creation of new writs.

98 It would distract from the principal focus of this book on substantive contract law to delve too deeply into a later, highly creative procedural invention in this context, namely the so-called bill of Middlesex. An abridged precis of the subject may perhaps, however, be necessary to avoid inadvertent confusion on an important point in regard to the royal writs as the centuries unfold.

Briefly stated, pursuant to the Magna Carta of 1215, the King's Bench was not eligible to take jurisdiction over "common pleas," meaning any "suits in which the Kind had no interest." BAKER, *supra* note 92, at 38. This meant that private "actions to recover property or debts, the greater part of all civil cases," through the royal courts went to the Court of Common Pleas, not the King's Bench. *Id.* Actions for trespass, however, could be heard by both of those courts. *Id.*

Over time, in response to a relative dearth of cases coming before the King's Bench, that court took action to reassert its competitive position in the English legal construct. *Id.* at 40–41. Specifically, "King's Bench developed its own bill system, with swift process and procedure to vie with that of the Chancery, and acquired a jurisdiction over most common pleas by a combination of procedural devices." *Id.* at 40.

"A bill, in this sense, was a petition addressed directly to a court in order to commence an action. Procedure by bill was more convenient for litigants than writ procedure, since the latter required the first complaint to be made in Chancery so that an authorising writ could be addressed to the court where proceedings were to be taken." *Id.* at 41. "When the King's Bench settled at Westminster, the bill procedure remained available for Middlesex cases [Middlesex being the county in which Westminster was located], and was commonly so used by 1420; cases from other counties required writs." *Id.* "The Common Pleas litigant still needed an original writ from the Chancery. . . ." *Id.* at 43.

And from here the jurisdictional sleight of hand, indeed fraud, took full flower in due course. It came to be accepted and common practice for a plaintiff's attorney seeking King's Bench jurisdiction first to present an entirely fictive bill of trespass against the defendant (and recall, under Magna Carta the King's Bench had jurisdiction over claims of trespass), called a "bill of Middlesex," followed by a second bill (which could be "in respect of matters arising in any county in England" and not just Middlesex, *id.* at 42 n.28) setting forth the true cause of action against the defendant: "By the use of two bills, the first alleging an imaginary trespass to secure arrest, and second a genuine complaint against the person arrested, the King's Bench litigant could thus sue in debt without writ." *Id.* at 42.

Lest one accidentally misapprehend that this jurisdictional legerdemain altered the substantive law to be applied, consider, e.g., the crucial and decisive *Slade's Case* of 1602, discussed in detail *infra* note 181 and accompanying text. The record shows that in 1595 John Slade brought a bill against Humfrey Morley before the King's Court, alleging nonpayment for certain wheat and corn in Devon. *Slade's Case*, *infra* note 181, at 420. The entire case was then fought out over the substantive contractual law question of whether the complaint need be brought as an action of debt, permitting the defendant to "wage his law" as an affirmative defense, or whether it could be brought as an action on the case sounding in assumpsit, as to which no wager of law defense would be available. As unsuccessfully argued by utter barrister John Dodderidge, "here is a ready framed writ in the register: the action of debt, the natural remedy, the writ of form.

3.1.2 The Contractual Writs

In the field of contract, for our purposes, the following principal royal writs worthy of note were debt sur contract (debt upon contract), debt sur obligation (debt upon obligation), and covenant.[99]

3.1.2.1 INFORMAL CONTRACTS AND DEFENSE BY WAGER OF LAW. The first of these contractual writs, debt sur contract, can be characterized as "informal," as no written document was required to evidence the transaction.[100] It did, however, require the plaintiff to have performed the plaintiff's own contractual commitment, and thus delivered value to the counterparty, as a necessary precondition to enforcement.[101] The latter two writs, debt sur obligation and covenant, are characterized as

Therefore here is no place for the action upon the case, the writ without form, the usurped remedy." *Id.* at 421.

Though brought by Slade as a bill, the substantive law and rights to be decided were predicated entirely upon the existing forms of royal writ.

For our purposes, therefore, the focus shall remain on those writs and their respective characteristics, rather than on the procedural mechanics utilized to obtain jurisdiction before the King's Bench.

[99] *See generally* SAMUEL JACOB STOLJAR, A HISTORY OF CONTRACT AT COMMON LAW 3–15 (Australian Nat'l Univ. Press 1975); BAKER, *supra* note 92, at 318–25. We will not here delve into the writ of detinue, which could be used by a plaintiff buyer who had paid in whole or in part for goods but not yet received the same from the seller. As to detinue see, e.g., STOLJAR, *supra*, at 13–15, 17; BAKER, *supra* note 92, at 321.

[100] *See, e.g.*, BAKER, *supra* note 92, at 322.

[101] It was necessary for the enforcement of debt sur contract that the plaintiff have performed either in whole or in part the plaintiff's own obligation under the agreement before suit could be brought:

> But a purchase and sale are effectually perfected from the moment the price is settled between the contracting parties; provided possession of the thing purchased and sold be delivered, or that the price, either wholly, or in part, be paid, or, at least, that Earnest be given and received.

GLANVILLE, *supra* note 73, at 216 (citations omitted); GLANVILLE LATIN TEXT, *supra* note 73, at 172. *See also* 2 MAITLAND, *supra* note 60, at 207 (citation omitted) ("To make a binding sale there must be either delivery of the thing, payment of the whole or part of the price, or giving of earnest."); STOLJAR, *supra* note 99, at 11 ("The general principle then was that debt would lie for a fixed reward, provided the agreed benefit or *quid pro quo* was already conferred. . . ."; "A plaintiff was unable to recover unless the debt had fully arisen; that is, he had in fact completed the whole, not just part, of the agreed services.") (citation omitted).

As a consequence, for informal debt upon contract, "[w]hen there is neither writing, Earnest, nor delivery, the parties, says Bracton, may retract." GLANVILLE, *supra* note 73, at 216 n.5 (citation omitted). In the words of Professor Stoljar:

> So far only covenant furnished a "consensual" contract, in the sense of permitting an entirely future relationship. A buyer and seller, having covenanted under seal, could sue each other independently, without prior execution: one for the money, the other for services or merchandise. Outside covenant, on the other hand, the "real" constituents of debt and detinue excluded purely executory obligations. A seller could not claim the price unless he had fully performed, while the buyer had a corresponding duty to pay for

"formal," as enforcement depended on the existence of a sealed, formal document evidencing contractual liability.[102]

The broadest and most widely applicable of these contractual writs was debt sur contract.[103] It covered not just what we in modern terms would consider debt but any and all contractual obligations where one party had performed and the other had then failed to counterperform upon an agreement between the two parties.[104] This included, for example, failure to pay for goods, services, or upon a lease granted.[105] As such, debt sur contract claims manifestly required mutual exchange – mutual consideration in modern terminology.

The grand limitation upon debt sur contract in the King's central courts was the defendant's near-conclusive ability to defeat the plaintiff's claim by "wager of law."[106] This involved first the defendant denying the grounds for the alleged liability, for example, by asserting that the plaintiff had not in fact conveyed the specified goods, or performed the specified services, and so on, or by asserting that

> executed performance but not for anything less. It follows that there could not even be a contractual relationship until a debt arose upon a completed quid pro quo....

STOLJAR, *supra* note 99, at 16 (citation omitted).

The conceptual underpinnings of this framework were explained by Professor Maitland:

> In its earliest stage the action [of debt] is thought of as an action whereby a man "recovers" what belongs to him. It has its root in the money loan; for a very long time it is chiefly used for the recovery of money that has been lent. The case of the unpaid vendor is not – this is soon seen – essentially different from that of the lender: he has parted with property and demands a return. It enters no one's head that a promise is the ground of this action. No pleader propounding such an action will think of beginning his count with "Whereas the defendant promised to pay"; he will begin with "Whereas the plaintiff lent or (as the case may be) sold or leased to the defendant." In short, he will mention some *causa debendi* and that cause will not be a promise.

2 MAITLAND, *supra* note 60, at 207 (citation omitted). As to service contracts:

> Probably the king's court would have put services rendered on an equality with goods sold and delivered. The fact that we cannot give an instance of an action brought by a servant to recover his wages may well be due to the existence of local courts which were fully competent to deal with such matters. But we much doubt whether at the end of the thirteenth century the action extended beyond those cases in which the defendant had received some material thing or some service from the plaintiff.

Id. at 211 (citation omitted).

[102] *See infra* Chapter 3.1.2.2.

[103] Debt upon contract:

> was the great exemplar of debt, being the action applicable to the most usual and often entirely informal transactions which, executed on one side, therefore called for the recovery of either money lent, or the price of goods sold, or the rent for land, or the agreed reward for services rendered.

STOLJAR, *supra* note 99, at 10–11.

[104] *Id.*

[105] *See* BAKER, *supra* note 92, at 322; PLUCKNETT, *supra* note 57, at 633.

[106] *See* STOLJAR, *supra* note 99, at 8.

the defendant had in fact already paid for such. If the defendant could then find a group of "compurgators" willing to swear that they believed the defendant's denial of liability, this was regarded by the courts as an effectively irrebuttable defense to the plaintiff's claim.[107]

As one can imagine, this led to significant frustration among contractual plaintiffs in debt sur contract cases. Though during that era an oath upon one's faith was regarded in the most serious possible manner, human nature is of course sinful. A dishonest defendant, aided by loyal compatriots, could defeat a justified contractual claim by the plaintiff through the expedient of wager of law.[108]

3.1.2.2 FORMAL CONTRACTS AND THE REQUIREMENT OF A SEALED DEED. Turning now to the first of our two categories of formal contract, debt sur obligation constituted a solemn promise by one to pay a certain sum to another.[109] By contrast to debt sur contract, debt sur obligation avoided the potential pitfall of

[107] *See* BAKER, *supra* note 92, at 322–23; STOLJAR, *supra* note 99, at 8.

The precise number of compurgators required for wager of law is variously stated among differing sources as either twelve persons other than the defendant, or eleven persons with the defendant rounding out the group swearing under oath to twelve. For the former, see, e.g., STOLJAR, *supra* note 99, at 8. For the latter, see, e.g., A Lecture on Wager of Law, Reading on Magna Carta, c. 28: CUL MS. Ii. 5. 43, fol. 40v. (15th century), *translated in* ENGLISH SOURCES, *supra* note 45, at 214. There were certain circumstances in which wager of law was not available. *See id.*

[108] *See, e.g.*, CHRISTOPHER ST. GERMAN, DYALOGE IN ENGLYSSHE/ BYTWYXT A DOCTOURE OF DYUYNYTE/ AND A STUDENT IN THE LAWES OF ENGLANDE, *reprinted in* 91 SELDEN SOCIETY 232 (Theodore F. T. Plucknett & J. L. Barton eds., 1974) (1523, 1530) [hereinafter DOCTOR AND STUDENT].

[109] In a nod to Roman conceptual origins, "[t]he most carefully worded documents that will be sealed in the England of the thirteenth century, the bonds given to Lombard merchants, will speak of stipulation." 2 MAITLAND, *supra* note 60, at 193.

The implicit conceptual structure underlying debt sur obligation appears to have mutated somewhat over time.

"In its earliest stage, the action is thought of as an action whereby a man "recovers" what belongs to him. It has its roots in the money loan...." 2 MAITLAND, *supra* note 60, at 212. "It enters no one's head that a promise is the ground of this action." *Id.*

Later, the so-called conditioned (that is, defeasible) bond came into widespread use to provide a certain and easily defined remedy for breach of contractual promise:

> A bond (or "obligation") was a deed containing an acknowledgment that a sum of money was owed by the "obligor" to the "obligee." ... When it was desired to draw up an important written agreement, a common practice was for one or both of the parties to make a bond to pay a sum of money to the other unless a certain condition was performed.... The wording of a performance bond was usually in the form: "The condition of this obligation is that if *AB* shall build a house according to the following specifications ... then this obligation shall become void, or else it shall stand in full strength." ... So popular were conditioned bonds that by Tudor times actions of debt on an obligation were the commonest single class of actions in the Common Pleas rolls; and so they remained for three centuries.

BAKER, *supra* note 92, at 323–24.

wager of law by the defendant, but did so at the cost of requiring a formal written, signed, and sealed "deed" to evidence and establish conclusively the indebtedness.[110] From an evidential standpoint, the deed was entirely sufficient to establish the defendant's liability.[111] Under such circumstances, a denial of liability by the defendant was as a general matter to no avail; the defendant had, after all, confessed the indebtedness in a formally sealed writing. Wager of law was thus unavailable as a defense to this contractual writ.

Covenant operated similarly in terms of formal procedure. This writ covered the entire scope of conceivable contractual obligations, that is, it was not limited solely to a sum of money owed.[112] Just as with debt sur obligation, covenant avoided defense by wager of law[113] at the cost of requiring a sealed deed as the necessary prerequisite to enforcement.[114]

[110] A sealed deed was a signed written document to which the signatory had affixed a red wax seal, impressed by the signatory with their own personal identifying mark using a seal die or embossed ring. Ribbons were not infrequently attached to the document by means of the wax seal as well. *See generally* P. D. A. HARVEY & ANDREW MCGUINNESS, A GUIDE TO BRITISH MEDIEVAL SEALS (Univ. of Toronto Press 1996).

Deeds were also often referred to at the time as "specialty." *See, e.g.*, Anon., Y.B. Pas. 5 Edw. II, CUL MS. Hh. 2. 4, fo. 118v (C.P.) (1312), *translated in* ENGLISH SOURCES, *supra* note 45, at 285.

[111] "A deed was of such a 'high nature' for evidential purposes" that it constituted a near conclusive basis for enforcement by the courts. BAKER, *supra* note 92, at 324–25. *See also* STOLJAR, *supra* note 99, at 10.

In the words of Professor Maitland: "Perhaps we may doubt whether in the thirteenth century a purely gratuitous promise, though made in a sealed instrument, would have been enforced if its gratuitous character had stood openly revealed." 2 MAITLAND, *supra* note 60, at 213–14. Explaining further:

> The ordinary bond of this period generally states that there has been a loan of money, and, even when both parties are Englishmen, it often contains a renunciation of the *exceptio non numeratae pecuniae*.... This was probably an unnecessary precaution learnt from the Italian bankers.... But in any case the bond *is no mere promise; it is the confession of a legal debt.* It says, *Sciatis me teneri*. As Bracton puts it, the obligor *scripsit se debere* and is bound by his confession.

Id. at 214 n.1 (emphasis added as to English words).

[112] Initially, the principal application of covenant concerned land, and leases to land. *See* 2 MAITLAND, *supra* note 60, at 217 ("In all the oldest specimens we have seen ... the subject matter of the *conventio* is land...."; "[T]he action ... becomes popular as leases for terms of years become common.").

Over time, it became clear that covenant was by no means confined to land-related contracts. The Statute of Wales 1284 stated unambiguously that "because covenants bind in an infinite variety of ways, it is difficult to mention each one in particular...." Statute of Wales 1284, 1 STATUTES OF THE REALM ch. 10, at 65 (Eng.), *translated in* ENGLISH SOURCES, *supra* note 45, at 281. *See also* BAKER, *supra* note 92, at 318 (the writ of covenant "was applicable on the face of it to all consensual agreements....").

[113] *See, e.g.*, STOLJAR, *supra* note 99, at 6.

[114] 2 MAITLAND, *supra* note 60, at 219.

In the absence of a sealed deed, however, the great welter of less formal everyday commerce was left either to adjudication in the local courts or to the risk of defendant's wager of law in the King's courts.

3.1.3 The Forty Shilling Jurisdictional Division between Royal and Local Courts

Given the parallel existence of the legacy local and town courts capable of addressing contractual disputes,[115] the foregoing procedural regime applicable in the King's central courts – involving as it did the Scylla of wager of law on the one hand and the Charybdis of the requirement of formal deed on the other – might not have created tremendous tension but for a development of singular importance. Over time, contract disputes came to be strictly divided between the local and the King's courts by the amount in controversy, with smaller claims allocated exclusively to the former and larger claims exclusively to the latter.

The fulcrum of this development were the Statutes of Gloucester, enacted by Parliament in 1278.[116] "The thirteenth-century royal courts discouraged minor litigation, and came generally to exclude claims under forty shillings, a principle confirmed for trespass actions by a statute of 1278."[117] The critical further evolution of this division was "the fifteenth-century interpretation of the 1278 legislation which limited county jurisdiction generally to forty shillings. . . ."[118]

The result of the foregoing was a bifurcation of contractual dispute resolution in the kingdom. Claims at forty shillings or more necessarily went before the royal courts, where either a deed was required or wager of law loomed over the plaintiff's

[115] *See, e.g.*, BAKER, *supra* note 92, at 318, 320.

[116] Statuta Gloucestr' [The Statutes of Gloucester 1278], *translated in* 1 STATUTES OF THE REALM 45 of hard copy statutory section (internet page 225) (London, Dawsons 1963, *reprinted in* Hathi Trust Digital Library collection online https://www.hathitrust.org/, *available at* https://babel.hathitrust.org/cgi/pt?id=pst.000017915496&view=1up&seq=3&size=125&q1=statute%20of%20gloucester%201278) (last visited Dec. 10, 2024).

[117] BAKER, *supra* note 92, at 22. For the statutory text in its original medieval Anglo-Norman French:

> Purveu est ensement, qe Viscuntes pleident en Cuntez les plesz de trespas ausi com il soloient estre pleidez. E qe nul eit desoremes bref de trespas devaunt Justices [se il na fie] par fei, qe les biens enportez vaillent qaraunte souz al meins.
>
> [It is provided also that Sheriffs shall plead pleas of trespass in their Counties, as they have been accustomed to be pleaded. And that none from henceforth shall have writs of trespass before Justices, unless he swear by his faith, that the goods taken away were worth forty shillings at the least.]

Statutes of Gloucester 1278, *supra* note 116, at 48 of hard copy statutory section (internet page 228).

[118] BAKER, *supra* note 92, at 23. *See also* PLUCKNETT, *supra* note 57, at 93 n.5.

For a detailed investigation into the subject, see John S. Beckerman, *The Forty-Schilling Jurisdictional Limit in Medieval English Personal Actions*, *in* LEGAL HISTORY STUDIES 1972, at 110 (Dafydd Jenkins ed., 1975).

claim; while claims at less than forty shillings must perforce go before the local courts, free of such procedural limitations but limited in amount in controversy. As one might expect, tremendous numbers of plaintiffs brought claims at just under forty shillings in the local courts,[119] obviously to avoid the defenses and procedural requirements applicable in the royal courts. But what of significantly larger claims? Where was justice to be found for a contractual plaintiff, deserving in equity but failing or fearful of the royal defenses and procedural requirements?[120]

3.2 *From 1350 to 1600: Use of Tort to Circumvent Procedural Defenses and Requirements*

This tension led from roughly 1350 onward to creative jurisprudence on the part of plaintiffs' attorneys and judges on the bench.

3.2.1 Tort Not Subject to Wager of Law or Requirement of Deed

As noted earlier, the Provisions of Oxford 1258 had as a practical matter brought an end to the creation of new royal writs by the office of the Chancellor, thus barring one avenue to legal innovation in English contract law in the King's central courts.[121] Yet, as pent up water will flow around an obstruction to continue its course, litigants and judges began to search for ways for a plaintiff's meritorious contractual claim to succeed despite the otherwise applicable defense of wager of law in debt sur contract cases,[122] and the requirement of a formal deed in debt sur obligation and covenant cases. The inventive means used to achieve justice in such cases was an ever more malleable and expansive application of the tort writ of trespass to contractual claims in the royal courts.

119 *Id.* at 111 ("Helen Cam, reporting her researches on the rolls of hundred courts, wrote of debt claims of 39s. 11½d. recurring there 'with monotonous regularity'.").

120 Certain contract cases came to be handled by royal authority through a different venue separate from the Court of Common Pleas and the King's Bench, namely, Chancery. Chancery enjoyed certain distinct powers and remedies, and was free of certain rules adhered to by those other courts. This enabled Chancery to be flexible in its decisions in pursuit of what it considered an equitable result. "By 1500 the chancellor had assumed a general jurisdiction in contract, and it was said that 'a man shall have remedy in the Chancery for covenants made without specialty [i.e., without a deed] if the party have sufficient witnesses to prove the covenants.'" BAKER, *supra* note 92, at 327. Similarly, though the common law rules concerning the near-conclusive nature of an existing deed for purposes of enforcement were extraordinarily strict and unforgiving, in Chancery a "creditor who lost his deed might yet enforce his debt or covenant, while the debtor who had paid would be relieved from paying again." *Id.* Nonetheless, "the Chancery was not the ideal forum for commercial cases since it . . . lacked the common-law writs of execution for recovering money." *Id.*

121 *See supra* text accompanying notes 97–98.

122 *See, e.g.*, IBBETSON, *supra* note 37, at 132 ("Plaintiffs might wish to bring assumpsit in place of the older action in order to prevent defendants waging their law. . . .").

The significance of the use of a tort writ to address contractual claims is that this tort writ of trespass was not subject to defendant's wager of law,[123] nor of course for obvious reason was any kind of formal written document required between a tortfeasor and tort victim. If a plaintiff could somehow, by hook or by crook, shoehorn an essentially contractual claim into the category of tort – or more precisely, if the tort writ of trespass could be instrumentalized to address a contractual dispute – claims of forty shillings or more could then be brought in the King's central courts without fear of wager of law and without having to present a deed.

The expansion of trespass to embrace contractual matters ever more broadly occurred incrementally over centuries. And as it did so, as will be seen, the specific form of trespass used to address contractual disputes itself mutated in its preconditions, becoming subject to the core and foundational requirement of contractual liability that both parties have given or promised something to the other in exchange – in other words, mutual consideration.

Originally, trespass in the King's courts applied only to "wrongs committed 'with force and arms' (*vi et armis*) and 'against the king's peace' (*contra pacem regis*), or which infringed royal franchises."[124] Ignoring for the moment royal franchises, trespass thus constituted an apparently intentional tort involving violent harm to another person. Examples include where "[t]he plaintiff has been beaten, wounded, chained, imprisoned, starved, carried away to a foreign country, and has suffered many 'enormities'."[125]

3.2.2 Trespass Brought for Negligence in Contractual Transactions

The slow process by which litigants and judges came gradually, incrementally to cross-apply the tort of trespass in order to address contractual situations in which the strict requirements for use of the existing contractual writs in the King's courts were not satisfied is generally viewed as having commenced with the *Humber Ferry Case* of 1348.[126] The owner of a horse and a ferryman agreed that the ferryman would carry the animal in his boat across the River Humber in northeastern England, presumably in exchange for the owner paying for the transport.[127] Plaintiff owner alleged that the ferryman "overloaded his boat with other horses, as a result of which overloading his [plaintiff's] mare perished, wrongfully and to his damage."[128] The

[123] *See, e.g.*, BAKER, *supra* note 92, at 329, 331.
[124] *Id.* at 60 (footnote omitted).
[125] PLUCKNETT, *supra* note 57, at 465.
[126] Bukton v. Tounesende, *record at* KB 27/354, m. 85, *report at* 22 Lib. Ass., pl. 41 (corrected from LI MS. Hale 116) (1348), *translated in* ENGLISH SOURCES, *supra* note 45, at 358 [hereinafter Humber Ferry Case]; *alternative translation of record at* 82 SELDEN SOCIETY 66 (1965).
[127] *Id.*
[128] *Id.* at 359.

damage alleged was forty shillings,[129] precisely the sum necessary to access the royal courts (in this instance, King's Bench) rather than local jurisdiction.

Defendant's counsel countered that the plaintiff "should have had an action by way of covenant rather than by way of trespass."[130] A writ of covenant would of course have required a formal written deed in order to enforce in the royal courts – and who has the time, means at hand, or inclination, to go through the high formality of creating a sealed deed for every day-to-day contractual transaction with others?[131]

The court disagreed with defense counsel, declaring boldly that "[i]t seems you did him a trespass when you overloaded his boat so that his mare perished."[132] No longer was trespass confined to intentional conduct, but rather extended to what presumably constituted no more than negligence. Nor was direct physical harm to another's person required; here the physical harm occurred to another's property.

Thus, where negligent contractual performance caused injury to another's property (or *a fortiori* to another's person), this failure could be addressed through the now significantly liberalized tort of trespass, which came to be known as "trespass upon the special case" (i.e., a complaint alleging specialized tortious circumstances not covered by the general *vi et armis* and *contra pacem regis* recitations ordinarily applicable in writs of trespass), "trespass upon the case," "action on the case," or quite simply "case." The particular species of action on the case based on an undertaking by the defendant soon came to be referred to as "assumpsit."[133]

Subsequent judicial decisions confirmed the doctrinal development of the *Humber Ferry Case*.

For example, in *Waldon v. Mareschal* in 1369, the plaintiff alleged that the defendant "undertook to cure" plaintiff's "horse of an illness, and afterwards the aforesaid [defendant] John so negligently applied his treatment that the horse died."[134]

Predictably enough, defendant's counsel objected that the plaintiff "should ... have had an action of covenant."[135] Plaintiff's counsel immediately pointed out that plaintiff "cannot have that [i.e., a writ of covenant] without a deed."[136] Thus, we see

[129] *Id.* at 358.
[130] *Id.* at 359.
[131] In addition to the impracticality of creating formal deeds for everyday contractual relationships, Professor Baker has observed that "[c]ovenant did not then lie in the King's Bench...." BAKER, *supra* note 92, at 330.
[132] *Humber Ferry Case*, *supra* note 126, at 359.
[133] *See, e.g.*, BAKER, *supra* note 92, at 330.
[134] Waldon v. Mareschal, Y.B. Mich. 43 Edw. III, fo. 33, pl. 38 (collated with LI MS. Hale 187, fo. 104v) (1369), *translated in* ENGLISH SOURCES, *supra* note 45, at 359.
[135] *Id.*
[136] *Id.*

precisely the same dynamic play out yet again of a plaintiff before the King's courts who has entered into an everyday contractual arrangement without going through the formality of creating a sealed deed, and thus could not bring a writ of covenant.

For this reason, plaintiff's counsel argued, "[t]his action is brought because you performed the treatment so negligently that the horse died, and therefore it is right to maintain this special writ according to the case, . . . for we can have no other writ."[137] In other words, justice must be done, and the only path to that goal was to permit the recently broadened form of trespass – namely, "case" – to be applied.

Defendant's counsel objected to the broadened form of trespass urged by plaintiff: "You could have had a writ of trespass, alleging in general terms that he killed your horse."[138] In other words, defendant's counsel was arguing the traditionally correct point that the tort of trespass only applied where force had been used (*vi et armis*) and such recitation had explicitly been made in the writ.

Plaintiff's counsel urged the court, just as in the *Humber Ferry Case*, to permit trespass – in the broadened form of "case" – to be used to apply to a situation involving negligence rather than violent force: "We could not have had a general writ, because the horse was not slain by force but died for want of being cured."[139] The court agreed to the view of plaintiff's counsel, and "the writ was held good."[140]

It is thus not that the concept of contract developed out of tort, as more recently asserted by the latter-day American advocates of the artificial doctrine of promissory estoppel.[141] Clearly, the situation in *Waldon v. Mareschal* was contractual in origin, and the litigants so recognized. Tort was brought into the equation due to failure to satisfy the requirements necessary to pursue the claim through the contractual writ of covenant. Moreover, it was not tort in its historical form, but rather the newly mutated and minted trespass on the case.[142]

137 *Id.*

138 *Id.*

139 *Id.* at 360.

140 *Id.*

141 *See infra* Chapters 8.1 and 11.1.

142 Similar discussions took place in Stratton v. Swanlond, Y.B. Hil. 48 Edw. III, fo. 6, pl. 11 (corrected from LI MS. Hale 181, fo. 105v) (1374), *translated in* ENGLISH SOURCES, *supra* note 45, at 360. Stratton v. Swanlond involved an allegation that defendant surgeon "undertook to heal her [plaintiff's] injured hand; and by the negligence of this same John [defendant] and his cure her hand was made so much worse that she is now maimed. . . ." *Id.* at 361. In that case, the court observed that "this action of covenant [in fact brought by plaintiff as a writ of trespass, not covenant] is of necessity maintained because a man cannot always have a clerk to make a specialty [i.e., a sealed deed] in respect of such a small matter." *Id.* at 361–62. In other words, the court considered the matter at its heart to be one of covenant, thus contract, but had no objection to a tort writ of trespass being brought in order to permit justice to be done where plaintiff did not have the deed required for a writ of covenant. As it turned out, the writ was ultimately rejected on completely unrelated grounds, namely, "because the place where the cure was undertaken was missing from the writ. . . ." *Id.* at 362.

3.2.3 Trespass Brought for Simple Nonfeasance, without Negligence

The real crossing of the Rubicon, however, came in *Doige's Case* of 1442,[143] "debated by all the judges of England in the Exchequer Chamber"[144] and thus carrying enormous decisional and precedential weight.[145]

The trespass cases discussed heretofore involved misfeasance on the part of the defendant. The *Humber Ferry Case* and progeny had established that violence was no longer necessary for trespass, and that mere negligence causing injury to person or to property would do. But what if the contractual defendant, instead of performing imperfectly, had simply not performed whatsoever? How could that possibly be characterized as the tort of trespass?[146]

The manner in which litigants and judges circumvented this conceptual roadblock was to turn to and instrumentalize another branch of trespass on the special case, namely, an action on the case based not upon misfeasance leading to injury or damage, but rather upon tortious deceit by the defendant.[147]

In *Doige's Case*, William Shipton

> had bargained with the said Joan [Dogge] . . . to buy from her . . . [certain] land . . . for a certain sum of money paid in advance to the same Joan; and the same Joan

[143] (a) Shepton v. Dogge, Record: CP 40/725, m. 49d (Pas. 1442) (1442); (b) Shipton v. Dogge, Record: KB 27/717, m. 111 (1442) (*abstracted in* A. K. R. KIRALFY, A SOURCE BOOK OF ENGLISH LAW 192 (1957); (c) Shipton v. Dogge, Y.B. Trin. 20 Hen. VI, fo. 34, pl. 4 (Selden Soc. vol. 51, p. 97), *appearing in* ENGLISH SOURCES, *supra* note 45, at 390–95 [all three of the foregoing hereinafter collectively Doige's Case]. The first of these was filed as an initial action with the Court of Common Pleas. In the second "Shipton commenced another action in similar form, but in the King's Bench." *Id.* at 391. "[T]he matter was adjourned into the Exchequer Chamber for consultation with the other judges. . . ." *Id.* The debate in the Exchequer Chamber is set forth in the third item, the transcript. *Id.*

[144] BAKER, *supra* note 92, at 337.

[145] See Professor Plucknett's discussion of the significance of such grand conclaves in the Exchequer Chamber *supra* note 90.

[146] As put by Professor Baker of Cambridge University: "There is all the difference in legal theory between misfeasance and nonfeasance. Misfeasance is often legally wrong in the absence of contract, whereas nonfeasance is not." BAKER, *supra* note 92, at 334.

[147] As excellently summed up by Professor Stoljar:

> So far, the action of assumpsit extended to typical acts of negligence resulting in physical injury to the plaintiff or his goods. Assumpsit did not go further than this for . . . "if a covenant is made with me to keep my horse or to carry my goods and nothing more done, the action of covenant lies and no other action; for in these cases he only fails to execute his promise." This non-liability for non-feasance became an article of faith. Not because . . . medieval law found it difficult to move from mis-feasance to non-feasance, but rather because non-feasance did not normally give rise to an injury to person or property but rather to a special (economic or financial) injury, the loss of a promised advantage, for which the remedy still had to be covenant and could not be trespass or case or (more broadly) tort. . . .
>
> How, then, was this non-feasance rule overcome? The brief answer is: as yet only partly, and even then through an attack from another direction, that of deceit or (to speak more technically) the action on the case in the nature of deceit.

STOLJAR, *supra* note 99, at 30–31.

had there undertaken to make a feoffment thereof to the said William ... within a certain period now elapsed; the aforesaid Joan, craftily scheming to defraud him the said William in that behalf, sold the aforesaid ... land ... within the aforesaid period to John Melburne, and within the same period falsely and deceitfully made a feoffment thereof to the same John ... to the damage of the selfsame William. ...[148]

Shipton's action before the King's Bench was "entered as 'plea of falsity and deceit. ...'"[149] "Mrs. Dogge entered a special demurrer, on the express ground that the facts alleged amounted to a covenant, and so the plaintiff should have brought an action of covenant rather than deceit."[150]

In the discussion that followed among the judges, it is evident that had the writ been brought in covenant it would have failed for lack of a sealed deed.[151]

The critical point is this: The judges regarded this case as one of contract. Yet, if the plaintiff had sued pursuant to the contractual writ of covenant, there would have been no remedy. This, the judges concluded, was unacceptable. Several key statements illustrate their thinking with clarity.

First, Newton, Chief Justice of the Common Pleas, stated unambiguously that in a bargain transaction, that is, in contract, both parties must have a remedy against the other for breach. And if a remedy was barred by the evidentiary requirement of a deed, then a different solution must be found in order to do justice to the core principle in contract of mutual reciprocity, of mutual obligation:

> Now, when the plaintiff has made a firm bargain with the defendant, the defendant may at once demand her money by a writ of debt. ... It would be amazing law, then, if there should be a perfect bargain under which one party would be bound by an action of debt but would be without remedy against the other. *Therefore* the action of deceit clearly lies.[152]

Fortescue, Chief Justice of the King's Bench, echoed this line of thinking:

> If the case put by Newton be law, then there is no question concerning the law in our case: for if each party to a bargain should be bound by an action, *it must follow that* this action of deceit is maintainable.[153]

Likewise Paston, Justice of the Common Pleas:

> In your case the contract is good without any specialty [any deed]. And *a good contract must bind both parties*. What reason is there, then, why one should have an action of debt and the other should not have an action?[154]

[148] *Doige's Case*, *supra* note 143, at 390 (Common Pleas record).
[149] *Id.* at 391 (King's Bench record).
[150] *Id.* (King's Bench record).
[151] *Id.* at 395 (Exchequer Chamber record).
[152] *Id.* at 392–93 (emphasis added).
[153] *Id.* at 394 (emphasis added).
[154] *Id.* at 395 (emphasis added).

Judgment in the case was given for the plaintiff.[155]

We thus have the most prominent judges of the realm concurring that in a bargain, in a contract, both parties must have a remedy against the other for breach, meaning that both parties must have obligated themselves in some manner, both parties must be bound. This is the modern-day principle of mutual consideration as the foundational requirement for all contract, and the direct abnegation of the alleged doctrine of promissory estoppel that purports to bind one party but not the other.

Later assertions by the proponents of promissory estoppel to the effect that contract emerged in medieval England in essence from the tort of deceit,[156] that contract is a stepchild of tort, are thus entirely inaccurate in essential philosophy and programmatic intention. Those assertions precisely invert the truth. A detailed, meticulous reading of the arguments made and thinking articulated in *Doige's Case* reveals that the origin of the dispute was clearly considered contractual in nature, and that the procedural expedient of a tort writ was brought into play in order to vindicate the core principle of reciprocity at the beating heart of contract.

That the use of the tort writ of deceit as applied to contract served principally as an expedient, a pretext, for the purpose of circumventing the requirement of deed in covenant can be observed in the fact that

> [b]y the sixteenth century it was usual to insert a 'craftily scheming to defraud the plaintiff' clause in every assumpsit action, even when there was nothing in the facts to justify it; the allegation itself helped to dispose of the technical objection about nonfeasance, and the substance ceased to matter.[157]

As put by Professor Baker of Cambridge University, "the main reason for the delictual approach was to find a justification for using actions on the case [namely assumpsit] instead of 'general' writs of debt or covenant. . . ."[158]

[155] *Id.*

Citing additional cases in the years leading up to *Doige's Case* that illustrate a related line of thinking, Professor Ibbetson wrote:

> In cases in the fifteenth century in which attempts were made to use the action of trespass on the case as a remedy for non-performance of contracts it is stressed in argument that the plaintiff's claim would be well founded . . . only if the defendant had received *quid pro quo*.

IBBETSON, *supra* note 37, at 83. The citations are to: (i) Watkins' (or Wyke's) Case, Y.B. Hil. 3 Hen. VI, fo. 36, pl. 33; CUL MS. Gg. 8(10), fo. 34; Bod. Lib. MS. Rawl. D. 363, fo. 35; BL MS. Harley 452, fo. 57 (C.P.) (1425), *in* ENGLISH SOURCES, *supra* note 45, at 380; and (ii) Anon., Mich. 19 Hen. VI, HLS MS. 156, unfol. (C.P.) (1440), in *id.* at 389.

[156] *See infra* Chapters 8.1 and 11.1.

[157] BAKER, *supra* note 92, at 337.

[158] JOHN H. BAKER, *Origins of the "Doctrine" of Consideration, 1535–1585*, *in* ON THE LAWS AND CUSTOMS OF ENGLAND: ESSAYS IN HONOR OF SAMUEL E. THORNE 336, 356 (Morris S. Arnold et al. eds., Univ. of North Carolina Press 1981).

3.2.4 The Core Contractual Requirement of Mutual Reciprocity

3.2.4.1 QUID PRO QUO VERSUS "NAKED" PROMISES. Learned commentary of the time further illustrated that reciprocity, mutual obligation, was considered to constitute a core requirement for all enforceable informal contract.[159]

This can be seen, for instance, in remarks by John Rastell, a barrister of Lincoln's Inn and Member of Parliament, writing in 1525, with bracketed text added in 1579:

> "Contract" is a bargain or covenant between two parties where one thing is given for another, which is called *quid pro quo*; [as, if I sell my horse for money, or if I make you a lease of my manor of Dale in consideration of £20 that you shall give me, these are good contracts because there is one thing for another]; for if a man make a promise to me that I shall have 20s. and that he will be debtor to me thereof, and after I ask the 20s. and he will not deliver it, yet I shall never have no action for to recover this 20s., for that this promise was no contract, but a bare promise: *et ex nudo pacto non oritur actio*. But if anything was given for the 20s., though it were not but to the value of a penny, then it was a good contract.[160]

Very much the same point was made by Christopher St. German in his famous "Doctor and Student" exegetical dialogues in 1531:

> [A] nude contract is where a man maketh a bargain or a sale of his goods or lands without any recompense appointed for it. As, if I say to another, "I sell thee all my land (or all my goods)", and nothing is assigned that the other shall give or pay for it, that is a nude contract and (as I take it) it is void in the law and conscience. And a nude or naked promise is where a man promiseth another to give him certain money such a day or to build him a house, or to do him such certain service, and nothing is assigned for the money, for the building, nor for the service. These be called naked promises, because there is nothing assigned why they should be made. And I think no action lieth in those cases, though they be not performed.[161]

159 Again, for formal contracts, namely, those required to have been evidenced by a sealed deed (debt sur obligation, covenant), mutual reciprocity may very well have been present in many if not nearly all instances, though recitation of what the obligor had received in return for entering into the highly formal obligation need not have been recited. *See* discussion *supra* text accompanying notes 37–40.

In addressing "the requirement of reciprocity or quid pro quo in cases of informal contracts," expressed in English cases of the time by means of the Latin phrase *ex nudo pacto non oritur actio* (out of a naked promise there shall arise no action), Professor Ibbetson observes that this operated "to exclude informal gratuitous arrangements from the domain of the law of contract." IBBETSON, *supra* note 37, at 81–82. This reflected "the conception of … [informal] contract as a reciprocal relationship, as an exchange." *Id.* at 78. "[I]n informal contracts, the law was concerned only with relationships of reciprocity…. The basic framework … was the model of exchange." *Id.* at 71.

160 JOHN RASTELL, EXPOSITIONES TERMINORUM LEGUM ANGLIAE (circa 1525), *reprinted in* ENGLISH SOURCES, *supra* note 45, at 483.

161 DOCTOR AND STUDENT, *supra* note 108, at 228–29, *reprinted with modern spelling in* ENGLISH SOURCES, *supra* note 45, at 483–84. The original spelling by St. German himself reads as follows:

Continuing, St. German wrote:

> [W]here the party to whom the promise was made is bound to no new charge by reason of the promise made to him but as he was bound before, there they think that no action lieth against him though he perform not his promise; for it is no contract. . . .[162]

The foregoing statements are the direct antithesis of promissory estoppel.

3.2.4.2 EMERGENCE OF THE TERM "CONSIDERATION" AS SHORTHAND DESCRIPTOR. By the latter half of the 1500s, the word – and requirement of – "consideration" came into use to denote in shorthand manner this unambiguously enunciated principle that a naked promise is unenforceable, that there must exist a mutual bargain in order for a promise to be enforced.[163] In the words of Professor Baker, consideration given in exchange for a promise was "the key to liability in *assumpsit*."[164] Multiple cases during this period discussed the requirement of consideration and its doctrinal contours.[165]

This articulation of the fundamental requirement of reciprocity through use of the word "consideration" meant that:

> [A] nude contracte is where a man maketh a bargayne or a sale of his goodes or landes wythout any recompence appoynted for yt. As yf I saye to a nother I sell the all my lande or all my goodes & nothynge is assygned that the other shall gyue or paye for yt/ that ys a nude contracte/ and as I take yt: it ys voyde in the lawe and conscyence/ and a nude or a naked promyse ys where a man promyseth an other to gyue hym certayne money suche a daye or to buylde hym an house/ or to doo hym suche certeyne seruyce/ and nothynge is assygned for the money/ for the buyldyng/ nor for the seruyce/ these be called naked promyses bycause there ys nothynge assygned why they shold be made/ and I thynke no accyon lyeth in those cases thoughe they be not perfourmed.

162 DOCTOR AND STUDENT, *supra* note 108, at 231, *reprinted with modern spelling in* ENGLISH SOURCES, *supra* note 45, at 484. St. German's original spelling:

> . . . where the party to whome the promyse was made is bounde to no newe charge by reason of the promyse made to hym but as he was bounde to before/ there they thynke that no accyon lyeth agaynst hym thoughe he perfourme not hys promyse/ for yt is no contracte. . . .

163 *See* BAKER, *supra* note 92, at 339–41; IBBETSON, *supra* note 37, at 144 ("[T]he core of the doctrine of consideration was the same idea of reciprocity that had lain behind the *quid pro quo* of the action of debt. . . .").

164 BAKER, *supra* note 92, at 339.

165 See, e.g., the following cases:

(i) Lucy v. Walwyn, KB 27/1198, m. 183 (1561), *reprinted in* ENGLISH SOURCES, *supra* note 45, at 485–87;
(ii) Lord Grey's Case, HLS MS. 2071, fo. 18v; Bod. Lib. MS. Rawlinson C. 112, fo. 292; CUL MS. Li. 3. 8, fo. 51v (C.P.) (1567), *reprinted in id.* at 492–93;
(iii) Hunt v. Bate, Dyer 272 (C.P.) (1568), *reprinted in id.* at 494;
(iv) West v. Stowell, CP 40/1346, m. 719 (1577), *reprinted in id.* at 494–95;
(v) Stone v. Withipole, YLS MS. G. R29.6, fo. 81 (Q.B.); 1 Leon. 113, pl. 156 (untr.) (1589), *reprinted in id.* at 498–500.

By 1598 a binding contract could be defined in terms still acceptable today, as "a mutual agreement between the parties for something to be performed by the defendant in consideration of some benefit which must depart from the plaintiff, or of some labour or prejudice which must be sustained by the plaintiff."[166]

3.2.4.3 ASSUMPSIT ADAPTED TO THE RECIPROCITY REQUIREMENT. Much as the historical record has shown, the adaptation of assumpsit to the essential substantive rules of contract has been described by Professor Ibbetson of Cambridge University:

> *The medieval notion of contract had been built on two elements. First was ... bilateral agreement as its base, rather than a simple voluntary undertaking of responsibility by one person to another. Second was the restriction of the legal horizon to reciprocal agreements....* [B]y the beginning of the seventeenth century at the latest *assumpsit had to all intents and purposes adopted the structure of contractual liability found in the medieval law.*[167]

He continued:

> *In medieval law informal contracts were enforceable only if they were reciprocal: the debtor must have received something in exchange,* quid pro quo.[168]

One will recognize in these statements that medieval contract law was thus built on the very same two fundamental requirements stated at the outset of this book, and which have governed at all times since, until the invention of promissory estoppel, namely: (i) mutual assent; and (ii) mutual exchange, quid pro quo, reciprocity, aka mutual consideration.

[166] BAKER, *supra* note 92, at 340. Professor Baker's citation for this quote is to *Slade's Case* of 1602, *infra* note 181 (1598 hearing, per Tanfield, *in* ENGLISH SOURCES, *supra* note 45, at 429); and to "Coke's similar formulation in Stone v. Withipole (1589)," *in* ENGLISH SOURCES, *supra* note 45, at 499, 500.

This quote from *Slade's Case* is of such fundamental importance that it shall be repeated in the detailed discussion thereof, *infra*.

[167] IBBETSON, *supra* note 37, at 135 (emphasis added).

In the middle of the quoted passage, Professor Ibbetson also wrote: "This is not to say that the law would inevitably ignore arrangements that were unilateral or gratuitous, but it insisted that they should be made under seal and hence marginalized them." *Id.* However, it is important to recall in this context Professor Maitland's conclusion, discussed in note 111 *supra*, that "[p]-erhaps we may doubt whether in the thirteenth century a purely gratuitous promise, though made in a sealed instrument, would have been enforced if its gratuitous character had stood openly revealed." 2 MAITLAND, *supra* note 60, at 213–14.

Against the backdrop of American contract law and practice having over time relegated the use of a seal to create formal contract to the tenebrous shadows of relative desuetude, the possibility of using some species of legal formality to render gift promises binding in American doctrine will be explored *infra* in the final portion of this book.

[168] *Id.* at 141 (emphasis added).

And Professor Ibbetson in summation:

> *[T]he introduction of the action of assumpsit did not herald any wholesale shift from the exchange model of contract that had prevailed in the fourteenth and fifteenth centuries. . . .*[169]

As shall be seen *infra*, precisely these historical truths were to be denied by the latter-day proponents of promissory estoppel in their effort to conjure out of thin air precedential pedigree for promissory estoppel.

3.2.4.4 EXTENSION OF ENFORCEMENT TO BILATERALLY EXECUTORY AGREEMENTS. Contemporaneously, during the latter half of the 1500s the courts took a significant conceptual step forward by extending the enforcement of mutual exchange transactions – that is, those predicated upon quid pro quo and thus mutual consideration – to those that were still bilaterally executory. The judges resolved that where one party has made a promise to another, a counterpromise by the initial promisee will provide consideration for that initial promise. A promise-for-promise bargain between two parties was now clearly enforceable.[170] This permitted both parties to sue the other for breach even though neither party had yet performed, that is, the contract was still "bilaterally executory" – in contrast to the traditional requirement in debt sur contract that a party must have performed their own duty before being able to sue upon the counterparty's unfulfilled promise. The doctrinal significance of this step will be touched upon again *infra*.[171]

[169] *Id.* at 145 (emphasis added).

[170] *See, e.g.*:

(i) Lucy v. Walwyn, KB 27/1198, m. 183 (1561), *reprinted in* ENGLISH SOURCES, *supra* note 45, at 485–87, *discussed in* BAKER, *supra* note 92, at 341;
(ii) Strangborough v. Warner, 4 Leon. 3 (1589);
(iii) Wichals v. Johns, Croke. Eliz. 703 (1599), *discussed along with Strangborough v. Warner in* C. H. S. FIFOOT, HISTORY AND SOURCES OF THE COMMON LAW: TORT AND CONTRACT 399–400 (London, Stevens & Sons Ltd. 1949).

As explained by Professor Fifoot:

> The doctrine of consideration involved the assumption that his own outstanding undertaking, not yet discharged by performance or by subsequent agreement, was itself actionable and therefore a "charge" upon him. In the words of Chief Justice Popham in *Wichals v. Johns*, "there is a mutual promise, the one to the other, so that, if the plaintiff doth not [discharge his promise], the defendant may have his action against him; and a promise against a promise is a good consideration."

FIFOOT, *supra*, at 400.

[171] In the words of Professor Baker: "From this point the English law of contract might truly be said to be consensual; despite its trespassory guise, liability was based on reciprocal agreement." BAKER, *supra* note 92, at 341.

3.2.5 The Use of Assumpsit Despite Availability of Debt sur Contract

One final step remained in the ascendancy of assumpsit as an action for plaintiffs to use in contract cases.

The position of the Court of Common Pleas up till now had been that where debt sur contract was available to address a given contractual dispute, then the plaintiff could not choose to proceed under assumpsit as an alternative thereto. This stance preserved the defendant's right to wage their law as a near-conclusive affirmative defense, the principal thorn in the side of contractual plaintiffs.

In 1532, however, the King's Bench broke with Common Pleas on this point in *Pykeryng v. Thurgoode*.[172] The plaintiff had purchased malt for his brewery from the defendant, to be paid in cash part up front, part upon delivery.[173] "[T]he defendant had then and there promised and undertaken to deliver the malt accordingly," but "the defendant, scheming to cause the plaintiff loss in his trade as a brewer, did not deliver the malt on time or at all. . . ."[174] Plaintiff brought an action on the case, and defendant pled "non assumpsit" on the traditional theory that "this action [on the case] does not lie, since an action of debt lies: and where a general action lies, a special action on the case does not lie in the same case."[175]

In favor of the plaintiff's choice of action, Justice Spelman argued that "although Pykeryng could have an action of debt, that is immaterial; for the action of debt is founded on the *debet et detinet*, whereas this action is founded on another wrong, namely, the breach of the promise."[176] It was, of course, from a logical perspective paper thin to distinguish between a failure to deliver that which was owed and promised (and to which the plaintiff in legal theory now had a property right), and a failure to carry through on a promise to deliver that which was owed. The argument could strike one as nearly sophistical, particularly in light of the significant impact it had on defendant's substantive rights of defense.

Justice Port accordingly objected that "[t]his promise is part of the contract, and it is all one."[177] But Spelman's position carried the day and "judgment was given for the plaintiff."[178] Henceforth, before the King's Bench, any plaintiff bringing a suit for defendant's failure to perform a contractual promise could avoid the potential

[172] Pykeryng v. Thurgoode, Record: KB 27/1073, m. 70 (Selden Soc. vol. 94, p. 247) (1532), *reprinted in* English Sources, *supra* note 45, at 411–12.

[173] *Id.* at 411.

[174] *Id.* We note here again the pro forma "scheming" allegation commonly employed ever since *Doige's Case* of 1442 to bring the matter within trespass. *See supra* text accompanying notes 150–151. What defendant's true motive for nondelivery may have been – either a scheme "to cause the plaintiff loss in his trade as a brewer," as distinct from the many other day-to-day possible reasons for breach – is not known from the cited record but might well perhaps be doubted.

[175] *Id.*

[176] *Id.* at 411–12.

[177] *Id.* at 412.

[178] *Id.* at 413.

pitfall of defendant's wager of law by simply bringing the claim through an action on the case sounding in assumpsit, rather than through an action of debt sur contract. "The possibility of suing for debts without the risk of debtors waging their law attracted creditors to the [King's Bench] … in droves."[179]

It is worthy to note at this juncture that what was not suggested was a general new tort for any and all unfulfilled promises. That is, there was no articulated theory akin to "promissory estoppel" put forth. Rather, the failure to perform a contractual promise constituting part of a mutually reciprocal bargain transaction was treated – quite potentially pretextually[180] – as a species of tortious deceit such that the matter could now be brought under a writ immune to defense by wager of law. As we have seen, it was already accepted principle at this time that an uncompensated promise, one for which the plaintiff had given the defendant no consideration, was considered *nudum pactum* and thus entirely unenforceable. *Pyckeryng v. Thurgoode* involved alleged deceit for failure to fulfill a promise part and parcel of a mutual exchange, not alleged deceit to be applied in a free-floating manner to any unfulfilled promise unmoored from a specific mutual contractual bargain.

That this principle is true was openly conceded in the epochal *Slade's Case* of 1602,[181] in which the simmering jurisdictional conflict in the wake of *Pykeryng v. Thurgoode* between Common Pleas and King's Bench – as to whether plaintiffs could freely choose assumpsit even where debt sur contract was available – was decisively engaged and resolved.[182]

[179] BAKER, *supra* note 92, at 343.

[180] *See supra* text accompanying notes 157–158.

[181] Slade v. Morley, Record: KB 27/1336, m. 305 (4 Co. Rep. 91);

(a) Exchequer Chamber, Mich. 1597: Dodderidge's speech from LI MS. Maynard 55, fo. 246; and BL MS. Harley 6809, fo. 45 (untr.); Coke's reply from BL MS. Hargrave 5, fo. 67v;
(b) Serjeant's Inn, Mich. 1598: BL MS. Add. 25203, fo. 12;
(c) Serjeant's Inn, 13 May 1602: BL MS. Add. 25203, fo. 496;
(d) Queen's Bench, 9 November 1602: BL MS. Add. 25203, fo. 607;
(e) Coke's retrospective summary: 4 Co. Rep. 92; collated with Coke's autograph report, BL MS. Harley 6686, ff. 526–530v; *reprinted in* ENGLISH SOURCES, *supra* note 45, at 420 [all of the foregoing collectively hereinafter Slade's Case].

[182] Credit here is due to Professor Plucknett, who wrote of "a new variety of assumpsit appearing in the middle of the sixteenth century called *indebitatus assumpsit*, in which the plaintiff declares that the defendant, being already indebted (*indebitatus*), undertook (*assumpsit*) to pay a particular sum." PLUCKNETT, *supra* note 57, at 644. Continuing:

> At this point there enters a factor of much importance in the legal history of the sixteenth and seventeenth centuries – the competition between the courts for jurisdiction. *Assumpsit*, being a form of trespass, could be brought either in the King's Bench or Common Pleas: debt, on the other hand, could only be brought in the Common Pleas. The King's Bench therefore could not resist the temptation to use *indebitatus assumpsit* as an equivalent to debt. This was easily done by holding that where a debt existed, a subsequent *assumpsit* would be presumed in law, and need not be proved as a fact. This device captured much business [for the King's Bench]. …

In modern American terms, the mutually incompatible positions of Common Pleas and King's Bench on so consequential a matter represented the approximate equivalent of a major Circuit split, with multiple Circuits lining up on each side, finally going before the Supreme Court to cut through the Gordian knot. *Slade's Case* was heard "before all the justices of England and the barons of the Exchequer"[183] and lasted all the way from 1595 through 1602.[184] It set the definitive precedent and treatment for the foundation of English contract law going forward.

In *Slade's Case*, the plaintiff

> Slade brought a bill against ... Morley ... complaining that ... the defendant, in consideration that the plaintiff (at the defendant's request) had bargained and sold to him all the ears of wheat and corn then growing on [a certain tract of land] ... promised the plaintiff to pay him £16...: nevertheless the defendant, little regarding his undertaking and promise, but scheming and intending subtly and craftily to deceive and defraud the plaintiff of the £16, did not and still has not paid it, though often requested to do so.[185]

As previously and unsuccessfully argued by the defense in *Pyckeryng v. Thurgoode* in 1532,[186] defense counsel in *Slade's Case* more than half a century later likewise contended that the availability of an action in debt sur contract precluded the use of an action upon the case sounding in assumpsit.[187]

After years of deliberation and debate, in 1602 Chief Justice Popham announced the collective decision of the judicial body in favor of the plaintiff as follows:

> First, that every contract executory implies in itself a promise or *assumpsit*. Secondly, that although an action of debt lies upon such a contract to recover the duty, the plaintiff may nevertheless have an action on the case upon the *assumpsit*.[188]

The position of the King's (now Queen's) Bench ever since *Pyckeryng v. Thurgoode* had thus prevailed over the position of the Court of Common Pleas. Wager of law was therefore, as a practical matter, from this moment forward a dead letter. After all, what plaintiff in a contract dispute would voluntarily choose to proceed in debt sur contract rather assumpsit when the latter was not subject to defendant's potential wager of law?

Id. at 644–43.

This was a precursor to the formulation of the concept applied in the decision of *Slade's Case*, in which it was held inter alia that "every contract executory implies in itself a promise or *assumpsit*." *See infra* text accompanying note 188.

183 *Slade's Case*, *supra* note 181, at 437.

184 *Id.* at 420–37.

185 *Id.* at 420.

186 *See supra* text accompanying notes 175–179.

187 *Slade's Case*, *supra* note 181, at 421.

188 *Id.* at 437.

Of absolutely central importance in *Slade's Case* for our purposes was the statement by plaintiff's counsel that although assumpsit was not subject to defendant's wager of law, assumpsit could only be brought by a contractual plaintiff who had provided consideration to the defendant in exchange for defendant's promise:

> Before all the justices of England, assembled at Serjeant's Inn, *Tanfield* ... prayed judgment for the plaintiff.... [A]n assumption is nothing other than a mutual agreement between the parties for something to be performed by the defendant in consideration of some benefit which must depart from the plaintiff, or of some labour or prejudice which must be sustained by the plaintiff.[189]

The same principle was reiterated shortly thereafter in 1618 in the King's Bench case of *Hurford v. Pile*: "[E]very assumpsit is made by the mutual agreement of both parties and on reciprocal considerations, and through this creates a contract...."[190]

But for the attempted hijacking in American law by the proponents of promissory estoppel – which purports to render promise enforceable as "contract" without the presence of either mutual agreement or mutual consideration – these doctrinal statements at the start of the 1600s, fully consistent with the medieval philosophy and principles that preceded them and from which they flowed in natural historical progression,[191] did and do constitute the true and legitimate foundation of enforceable contract not under seal from that day to this, centuries later.

3.2.6 English Contract Law Following Slade's Case of 1602

To recapitulate, in English law, contract in the King's central courts did not descend from nonviolent tort; it preceded it. Nor did the essential requirements of enforceable contract – namely, mutual agreement and mutual consideration – descend from the tort of deceit. Rather, the tort of deceit was instrumentalized by litigants and judges in such a manner as to permit contractual plaintiffs to proceed without facing the risk of defendant's wager of law affirmative defense.[192] And as the tort of deceit came so to be instrumentalized, in tandem therewith it became subject to the fundamental requirements of enforceable contract.

The distinction between the doctrinal basis for contract (mutual consideration, i.e., mutually agreed exchange) and the doctrinal basis for tort (a unilateral wrong – in the commercial context generally harm arising from negligence or more culpable

[189] *Id.* at 428–29.

[190] Cro. Jac. 483; Ro. 21, 39 (*sub nom.* Winter v. Foweracres); HLS MS 105f f.291; LI MS Misc. 791d ff.80ᵛ, 85ᵛ; *cited and discussed by* IBBETSON, *supra* note 37, at 139–40 ("It would be difficult to find a better statement of the classical bargain theory of contractual liability.").

[191] *See supra* Chapter 3.2.4.2 and 3.2.4.3.

[192] Professor Maitland summed up the historical consequence of the wager of law defense: "The ease with which the defendant could escape [through wager of law] was in the end the ruin of this old action [of debt sur contract]." 2 MAITLAND, *supra* note 60, at 215.

conduct) was fully clear to English lawyers at the time and since.[193] That assumpsit had been instrumentalized – and in that process altered to take on the requirements of contract – is clearly seen in the fact that following *Slade's Case* two forms of assumpsit existed. The first was true tortious assumpsit, which did not require mutual consideration but of course did therefore require negligence or more culpable conduct to impose liability. The second was contractual assumpsit, which did not require negligence but, instead, required mutual consideration as the prerequisite to enforcement.[194]

4 THE CONTINUATION OF ENGLISH CONTRACT LAW IN AMERICA

4.1 *Civilizational Significance*

There may be temptation at this juncture for students of the younger generation to inquire what all this Roman and English legal history, what the animating principles of the legal structures they erected, have to do with America at present. Are we not our own country, operating on our own principles, incorporating immigrants from

[193] See, e.g., the remarks of Vampage in Somer v. Sapurton: "[I]t would be unfitting to have trespass and debt for one same thing, because they are contrary: for one begins by contract and consent of the parties, . . . and the basis of the action is an indebtedness; and the other begins by a wrong, and without the consent of the parties. . . ." Somer v. Sapurton, Y.B. Mich. 7 Hen. VI, fo. 5, pl. 9 (Selden Soc. vol. 51, p. 38, pl. 13) (1428), *translated in* ENGLISH SOURCES, *supra* note 45, at 234, 235.

As stated by Professor Ibbetson, "by the end of the fifteenth century there was a clear polarization between liability in tort (typically in trespass), which was essentially fault-based, and liability in contract (typically in debt), which was essentially strict." IBBETSON, *supra* note 37, at 90.

As to the word "tort" itself, this is of course from the French, in which *un tort* translates as "a wrong" or "a fault." *See* COLLINS ROBERT FRENCH COLLEGE DICTIONARY 658 (HarperCollins Publishers 8th U.S. ed. 2012).

[194] *See* BAKER, *supra* note 92, at 347:

> It must not be thought, however, that all actions of *assumpsit* were the same in form. The historical differences lingered in the pleadings until the procedural reforms of the nineteenth century. *Assumpsit* for misfeasance continued to be brought as an action in tort, without the need for consideration in the contractual sense; and to this day a negligent carrier or private surgeon may be sued in tort or contract at the plaintiff's election. *Assumpsit* for breach of covenant, for not performing an act as promised, varied from case to case and was therefore labelled 'special *assumpsit*'. In such actions the details of the promise and the consideration had to be proved. . . .

Accord IBBETSON, *supra* note 37, at 133, 135. *See also* OLIVER WENDELL HOLMES, JR., THE COMMON LAW 284 (Boston, Little, Brown, & Co. 1881) ("It was long recognized . . . that, in cases where the gist of the action was negligent damage to property [i.e., tort, rather than simply contract], a consideration was not necessary.").

Not all tortious "wrongs," of course, necessarily entail economic harm. In the context of commercial relationships, however, harms – typically economic in nature – caused by negligent, grossly negligent or reckless conduct, or by outright fraud, are obviously the most relevant categories of tort analytically and descriptively for our purposes here.

many countries and cultures over time, which has broken free from the fetters of the past? Has England not lost its empire in the wake of World War II, has it not receded into normalcy as one of a handful of mid-size European powers, with Europe itself but one of several major centers of world civilization? Should we simply invent ourselves anew, simply construct new fundamental legal rules wholecloth as we imagine might be best?

In the commercial and economic domain, the answer to this immoderate and hubristic query is "no," at least not without grave risk of adverse consequence. The reason therefor is age-old and remains continuously vital in all human affairs over the millennia. We are part of the grand sweep and tradition of Western civilization. That civilization developed rules of law founded upon the realities of immutable human nature, grounded in the practicalities of daily life and human interaction – technological advancement notwithstanding – and constructed to address certain common recurring patterns in those interactions. Roman and English principles and rules of law developed out of and in response to those realities, crafted by some of the finest minds those societies produced, and were in nontrivial respect responsible for the commercial success, indeed stellar growth, of their economies and thus national power. Wise, balanced, and sensible laws governing commercial exchange are likewise vital to our continued success as an American nation.

Moreover, America was in its inception and to an overwhelming degree remains an integral part of the world-spanning civilization created by Great Britain, the Anglosphere. Following its victory against the Spanish Armada in 1588, and taking a decisive step forward with its overseas triumph over France in 1763 at conclusion of the Seven Years' War (known in the British colonies in America as the French and Indian War), Great Britain became far and away the leading colonial power in Europe's global imperial expansion.[195] The Anglosphere, comprising both the British Empire (later Commonwealth) and its powerful offspring the United States, has been, both in its geographic extent and its impact on human affairs, the greatest civilization since Rome.

And the United States – despite the Revolution, despite all the immigration – is, in both the genesis and continuation of its legal culture, no more separate from the rest of the Anglosphere than one child is from its siblings. We constitute a single cultural family.

4.2 *Colonial America, the Revolution, and Adoption*

Our history bears this out.

From Jamestown in 1607 and Plymouth Rock in 1620, for more than a century and a half until the American Revolution in the 1770s, the American colonies were

[195] As to these events and their broader historical significance in the rise of British global power, see WINSTON S. CHURCHILL, A HISTORY OF THE ENGLISH-SPEAKING PEOPLES, VOL. 2: THE NEW WORLD 124–33, AND VOL. 3: THE AGE OF REVOLUTION 148–61, 169 (New York, Dodd, Mean & Co. 1962); J. M. ROBERTS, HISTORY OF THE WORLD 531–32, 564–66, 579–80, 582–83 (New York, Alfred A. Knopf, Inc. 1976).

part of the British Empire. The common law of the British colonies in America was, quite simply, English common law.[196]

Nor did the American Revolution alter the foundation and traditions of the common law fields such as contracts. Following the Revolution, the English common law was ratified and adopted as the original foundation of American common law, uninterrupted in historical line.[197]

To study American contract law is, therefore, necessarily and ineluctably to study English contract law, back through its genesis and doctrinal articulations. American contract law was and is a temporal extension of, originally, English contract law.

Nor was this point ignored by Williston. In his justificatory arguments in favor of the adoption of promissory estoppel as a feature of American law, Williston's central assertion was the false claim that the English common law of contract in the Middle Ages was, essentially, premised upon the enforcement of promise irrespective of whether founded upon an actual exchange transaction. That is, he asserted precedential authority in American law for his novel doctrine of promissory estoppel by misrepresenting the law of England centuries ago.[198]

4.3 *Blackstone*

That Williston's concept of promissory estoppel was alien to English contract law prevailing in the British colonies, later American states, is demonstrated by reference to Blackstone.

Rarely has a single figure featured so prominently over the landscape of legal exposition as did Sir William Blackstone in his time. As an English jurist, Blackstone in his 1765–69 comprehensive *Commentaries on the Laws of England* set forth in abridged form the major legal principles, rules, and structures of the English-speaking world.[199] His Commentaries were treated in the American colonies and later states as the authoritative, definitive statement of existing English, and thus American, common law.[200]

Although Blackstone's exegesis has a brief stretch of choppy water to navigate, we do have his following strong, clear doctrinal statements that at the end firmly anchor the conceptual ship.[201] As stated by Blackstone, "[t]he civilians hold, that in all

[196] *See* Herbert Pope, *The English Common Law in the United States*, 24 HARV. L. REV. 6, 16 (1910).

[197] *See id.*; Alton B. Parker, *The Common Law Jurisdiction of the United States Courts*, 17 YALE L.J. 1 (1907). This extended not only to state courts but also to the federal courts. *Id.* at 6, 12–20.

[198] *See* Alden, *Origins of Contract Law*, and Alden, *Reversing the Reliance Revolution*, *supra* note 2.

[199] *See* BLACKSTONE, *supra* note 3.

[200] *See, e.g.*, PLUCKNETT, *supra* note 57, at 287; Pope, *supra* note 196, at 7; Parker, *supra* note 197, at 3.

[201] The "choppy water" referred to here by the Author relates to a certain terminological ambiguity when it comes to the word "consideration" in the context of whether a deed will be recognized and honored as having legal effect. For a detailed discussion in this regard, see "Annex A: Blackstone" set forth at the end of this book.

contracts, either express or implied, there must be something given in exchange, something that is mutual or reciprocal,"[202] and "therefore our law has adopted the maxim of the civil law, that *ex nudo pacto non oritur actio*."[203] The consequence of the foregoing is that

> [a] consideration of some sort or other is so absolutely necessary to the forming of a contact, that a *nudum pactum*, or agreement to do or pay any thing on one side, without any compensation on the other, is totally void in law; and a man cannot be compelled to perform it.[204]

This forceful, unambiguous statement by Blackstone of the law of contract is the direct, literal, absolute antithesis of Williston's later purported "doctrine of promissory estoppel."

4.4 *Consistent and Continuing Doctrinal Bedrock*

Nor, until Williston's invention of "promissory estoppel" in the 1920s, was there variance in the fundamental requirement of reciprocity, of mutual exchange.

For example, W. W. Story, son of Supreme Court Justice Joseph Story, writing in his own major treatise on contract law in 1844, stated that "reciprocity of consideration" is "necessary to constitute a parol [i.e., not under seal] agreement."[205] Likewise, "[p]romises, which are wholly gratuitous, are void, for want of consideration; for, however obligatory they may be in morals or in honor ... they are not regarded by the law as legal and valuable considerations."[206]

Similarly Joseph Chitty's comprehensive treatise on contract law in 1851:

> *Ex nudo pacto non oritur actio*. The earliest records of our law show that this maxim was always recognised in this country. But it is a principle not peculiar to English law. It obtained, generally speaking, in the civil law; and, indeed, we have borrowed from the Roman jurists the term *nudum pactum*, as applied to promises without consideration. . . . A gratuitous undertaking may form the basis of a moral obligation, – it may be binding in honor, – but it does not create any legal responsibility.[207]

[202] 2 Blackstone, *supra* note 3, at 444.

[203] *Id.* at 444.

[204] *Id.* at 445.

This is of course consistent with the discussion in *Slade's Case*, in which it was stated that an enforceable contract is "a mutual agreement between the parties for something to be performed by the defendant in consideration of some benefit which must depart from the plaintiff, or of some labour or prejudice which must be sustained by the plaintiff." *See* text accompanying note 189, *supra*.

[205] 1 William Wetmore Story, A Treatise on the Law of Contracts Not Under Seal 1 (Boston, Charles C. Little & James Brown 1844).

[206] *Id.* at 84.

[207] Joseph Chitty, Jr., A Practical Treatise on the Law of Contracts Not Under Seal; and Upon the Usual Defences to Actions Thereon 25–26 (Springfield, George & Charles Merriam 8th Am. ed., from 4th London ed., 1851).

In the same vein, C. C. Langdell, the Dean of Harvard Law School who was credited with inventing the case method of legal study, wrote in his 1880 treatise: "It is a familiar rule of law that contracts not under seal require a consideration to make them binding."[208]

And, of course, this principle was contemporaneously confirmed by Oliver Wendell Holmes, likewise of Harvard Law School and later a Supreme Court Justice, in his famous book *The Common Law* in 1881:

> Our law does not enforce every promise which a man may make. Promises ... by word of mouth or simple writing [i.e., not under seal], are not binding unless there is a consideration for them. That is, ... unless the promisee has either conferred a benefit on the promisor, or incurred a detriment, as the inducement to the promise.[209]

Expounding upon this rule, O. W. Holmes further wrote:

> [I]t is the essence of a consideration, that, by the terms of the agreement, it is given and accepted as the motive or inducement of the promise. Conversely, the promise must be made and accepted as the conventional motive or inducement for furnishing the consideration. The root of the whole matter is the relation of reciprocal conventional inducement, each for the other, between consideration and promise.[210]

There is here no chink in the doctrinal armor through which promissory estoppel – that is, the purported enforcement of promise in the total absence of any consideration therefor – might penetrate.

[208] Christopher Columbus Langdell, A Summary of the Law of Contracts 58 (Boston, Little, Brown, & Co. 2d ed. 1880).

[209] Oliver Wendell Holmes, Jr., *supra* note 194, at 253.

[210] *Id.* at 293–94.

Part II

The Invention

Artificial Creation of the Doctrine of Promissory Estoppel

> Error, indeed, is never set forth in its naked deformity, lest, being thus exposed, it should at once be detected. But it is craftily decked out in an attractive dress, so as, by its outward form, to make it appear to the inexperienced … more true than the truth itself.[211]
>
> —Irenaeus of Lyons

5 TERRA INCOGNITA

And then came Williston.

Already prominent as a professor at Harvard Law School and nationally preeminent figure in his field,[212] Samuel Williston took it upon himself in the 1920s to effect a fundamental shift in the tectonic plates of American contract law. As discussed at length in the Introduction, he proposed to make executory promises potentially legally binding, and thus subject to liability for nonfulfillment, despite the absence of mutual assent and despite the absence of mutual consideration. The mere uncompensated act of "promising" to do, or to abstain from doing, something in the future – indeed, the mere act of making any manner of forward-looking, future-oriented statement of intent or contemplation – was to expose the "promisor" to potential law suit if the promisor were to change their mind. Williston dubbed this purported new rule of promissory liability "promissory estoppel,"[213] and claimed

[211] Irenaeus of Lyons, Adversus Haereses [Against Heresies] bk. I, preface (c. 175–185 A.D.), *in* Ante-Nicene Fathers 315, 315 (A. Cleveland Coxe ed., Alexander Roberts & James Donaldson trans., Buffalo, N.Y., Christian Literature Publ'g Co. 1885). The passage stems from Irenaeus writing in regard to and against the gnostics.

[212] *See, e.g.*, Erwin N. Griswold, *In Memoriam: Samuel Williston*, 49 ABA J. 362 (1963); Austin W. Scott, *Samuel Williston*, 76 Harv. L. Rev. 1330 (1963).

[213] *See* 1 Williston Treatise, *supra* note 8, § 139, at 308.

to situate it within the realm of contract,[214] despite its naked, point-blank, radical abnegation of the two fundamental criteria for the formation and legal recognition of contract.

The enormity, the raw ambition, of this project is arresting.

6 NEWFOUND, ARTIFICIALLY CREATED, STRICT LIABILITY TORT

Setting aside for a moment the matter of formal, sealed deeds, to which this discussion shall later recur, Western civilization had consistently rejected the imposition of strict liability for uncompensated unfulfilled promise. As has been seen, contract liability, which is strict,[215] would only be imposed where both parties had voluntarily entered into a mutual exchange transaction. As distinct from contract, tort law in the context of a contractual transaction, though not requiring a promise to have been compensated, imposed as a prerequisite to the imposition of liability that the promisor have acted wrongfully,[216] either through harmful tortious negligence committed during the course of performance, or through tortious fraud in making the promise itself, known as "promissory fraud."[217]

To impose strict – that is, not tortiously wrongful in the ordinary sense – liability for unfulfilled uncompensated informal promise was, in fact, to create a newfound species of strict liability tort.

[214] *See* FIRST RESTATEMENT, *supra* note 2, § 90.

[215] *See, e.g.*, DAN B. DOBBS, THE LAW OF TORTS 5 (West 2000):

> Breach of contract is not in itself a tort. . . . Contract law is at least formally strict liability law. Most of tort law, on the other hand, is at least formally fault-based. Specifically, a person is often liable for a contract breach even if he is not at fault and made every effort to perform the contract as promised. But one is not ordinarily liable under tort law even for conduct that causes horrible injuries unless he is at fault in some way. The reasoning and formal themes of tort law thus differ enormously from those of contract law.

See also RESTATEMENT (SECOND), *supra* note 2, § 235(2): "When performance of a duty under a contract is due any nonperformance is a breach." There is no requirement here that negligence have been committed, simple nonperformance suffices, whatever the reason.

[216] *See, e.g.*, DOBBS, *supra* note 215, at 5.

[217] Randy E. Barnett & Mary E. Becker, *Beyond Reliance: Promissory Estoppel, Contract Formalities, and Misrepresentations*, 15 HOFSTRA L. REV. 443, 492 (1987):

> For over a hundred years, . . . common law courts have repeatedly held that tort liability for promissory misrepresentation requires that the promise be a lie when made. The tort standard has become fairly rigid, and promissory estoppel is a relatively new, and certainly more flexible basis for liability.

Making a contractual promise to perform, when it is already consciously known to the promisor at the moment of promise that they have no intention whatsoever to perform in the future, can be characterized as "promissory fraud," a tort. For general discussion, see, e.g., Ian Ayres & Gregory Klass, *Promissory Fraud*, 78-May N.Y. ST. B.J. 26 (2006). *See also* RESTATEMENT (SECOND) OF TORTS § 530(1) cmt. c (AM. LAW INST. 1977) ("Since a promise necessarily carries with it the implied assertion of an intention to perform it follows that a promise made without such an intention is fraudulent and actionable in deceit. . . .").

Given that promissory estoppel, as now discussed at length, radically rejects the two central, fundamental prerequisites for the formation of contract, it is manifest that the purported doctrine cannot properly be characterized as contract.

By contrast, to see that promissory estoppel indeed constitutes a tort, specifically a strict liability tort for unfulfilled uncompensated promise, consider by way of comparison the elements of California's tort of promissory fraud:

> (1) a promise made regarding a material fact without any intention of performing it; (2) the existence of the intent not to perform at the time the promise was made; (3) intent to deceive or induce the promisee to enter into a transaction; (4) reasonable reliance by the promisee; (5) nonperformance by the party making the promise; and (6) resulting damage to the promise[e].[218]

As one sees from review of the foregoing elements of promissory fraud, they parallel the elements of Section 90's definition of promissory estoppel, with the sole addition of the requirement of fraudulent intent.[219] This fraudulent intent is reflected in the scienter requirements that the promise have been made "without any intention of performing it," that such "intent not to perform" existed "at the time the promise was made," and that such promise was made with the "intent to deceive or induce the promisee to enter into a transaction." If we remove these scienter specifications of fraudulent intent, what remains is, in essence, promissory estoppel.

Promissory estoppel is thus a newfound, artificially created, strict liability tort for unfulfilled uncompensated informal promise – a strict liability tort masquerading as contract.

This was ground upon which the law had heretofore, for very good reason, declined to enter.[220] It was terra incognita.

7 TECHNICAL CONTOURS OF THE CONCEPT

The vehicle used by Williston to advance his objective was, as discussed earlier, the Restatement of the Law of Contracts – herein the First Restatement for simplicity of reference – to be drafted under the auspices of the newly organized American Law

[218] Behnke v. State Farm Gen. Ins. Co., 196 Cal. App. 4th 1443, 1453 (2011).

See also CAL. CIV. CODE §§ 1572(4), 1710(4); Berkey v. Halm, 224 P.2d 885 (1950); Lawrence v. Gayetty, 20 P. 382 (1889).

[219] See RESTATEMENT (SECOND), *supra* note 2, at § 90(1).

[220] See Barnett & Becker, *supra* note 217, at 491–92; RESTATEMENT (SECOND) OF TORTS, *supra* note 217, § 552C cmt. e (for strict liability to apply to contractual misrepresentation, "there must be a misrepresentation of fact.... *[Strict liability for contractual misrepresentation] does not apply to misrepresentations of ... intention....*") (emphasis added); DOBBS, *supra* note 215, at 5 (in tort, "misrepresentations are not actionable unless they state 'past or existing facts'"; "defendant's present intent is a factual matter distinct from promises ..., so a false statement of present intention is actionable if it meets all the other requirement for establishing fraud.").

As to liability for unfulfilled formal promise – one thinks here of the Roman *stipulatio* and the Anglo-Norman sealed deed – see the discussion *supra* Chapters 1 and 3.1.2.2.

Institute (ALI), expressly founded for this purpose. In deference to his academic stature, Williston was placed at the head of the drafting committee as Reporter for the First Restatement. At his side as deputy was placed Professor Arthur Corbin of Yale.

From this influential perch, Williston now put pen to paper to craft his novel, artificial principle of promissory liability. To reprise, Section 90 of the First Restatement appeared under a heading that read "Informal Contracts Without Assent or Consideration," a rubric on its face utterly alien – indeed directly antithetical – to contract law. As already set forth earlier, the text in principal part was simple and direct:

> § 90. Promise Reasonably Inducing Action or Forbearance
>
> (1) A promise which the promisor should reasonably expect to induce action or forbearance on the part of the promisee or a third person and which does induce such action or forbearance is binding if injustice can be avoided only by enforcement of the promise. . . .[221]

That Williston was fully aware of the radical implications of his proposal, one has only to look to his own major treatise on contract law published just a few short years prior. Though still operating within the precinct of classical contract law, one senses in Williston's writing that the early germ of ambition had begun to sprout. One feels that he may already have been straining at the leash of established precedent. In a critical footnote in that treatise, he made the following confession. The proposition that one might enforce a promise upon which another has reasonably relied, even though the promisor in no way requested such reliance, Williston wrote, "is by no means without intrinsic merit, but it should be recognized that if generally applied *it would much extend liability on promises, and* that at present *it is opposed to the great weight of authority.*"[222]

Yet, just several short years later, Williston crossed the Rubicon.[223]

[221] Restatement (Second), *supra* note 2, § 90(1).

[222] 1 Williston Treatise, *supra* note 8, § 139, at 313 (emphasis added).

[223] Over the course of subsequent decades, there has been speculation as to the precise role played at the time by Williston's strong deputy, Professor Arthur Corbin of Yale, in Williston's decision to declare *alea iacta est*.

In the early 1970s, Professor Grant Gilmore, likewise of Yale, recounted personal discussions he had earlier had with Corbin in which Corbin was cast as effectively a coequal, if not the principal, proponent and driver of the new doctrine in debates with colleagues at the ALI. Gilmore, *supra* note 13, at 63. That account by Gilmore has gained wide currency. The extent to which those personal recollections of Gilmore and Corbin are precisely accurate, however, is unknown. Professor Sidney DeLong of Seattle University has written, no doubt with a wry smile, that "[t]he little story of how Section 90 came to be has now achieved the status of an originary myth among contracts scholars." Sidney W. DeLong, *The New Requirement of Enforcement Reliance in Commercial Promissory Estoppel*, 1997 Wis. L. Rev. 943, 962 (1997). Professor DeLong continued that "[i]nterested readers may consult the sacred text in Gilmore, Death of Contract. . . .," and that "[d]oubt was recently case on Gilmore's account of Williston's and Corbin's respective roles in this drama by evidence that Williston himself

7.1 *The Elements of a Promissory Estoppel Claim*

For litigational purposes, promissory estoppel as proposed by Williston embodies four elements: (i) promise; (ii) which the promisor should reasonably expect to induce action or forbearance (often referred to as "detrimental reliance"[224]); (iii) detrimental reliance has occurred; and (iv) injustice can only be avoided by enforcement of the promise. It is worthwhile at this juncture to examine each of these elements in sequence, with an eye to how they have been interpreted and implemented by courts over the course of the intervening decades.

7.1.1 "Promise"

We begin with the first element, namely, the requirement that a promise have been made. In ordinary contract law, in order to constitute a promise, a statement must be sufficiently unambiguous and definite for a court reasonably and justly to hold the promisor liable for nonfulfillment.

In promissory estoppel, by contrast, various courts applying Section 90 have held that definiteness of the "promise" is quite simply not required.[225] Rather, any statement that one "should reasonably expect to induce action or forbearance" constitutes a "promise" sufficient for promissory estoppel purposes.[226] Thus, an indication of one's anticipation or future intent, even where the speaker has no

drafted Section 90, as noted in a letter from Arthur L. Corbin to Robert Braucher, the original Reporter for the Second Restatement of Contracts." *Id.* at 962 n.55.

Certainly, the course of Corbin's career and his own major treatise on contract law appearing in 1950 make clear that he was a dedicated advocate of promissory estoppel. *See, e.g.*, Arthur L. Corbin, *Recent Developments in the Law of Contracts*, 50 HARV. L. REV. 449, 454–56 (1936–1937); ARTHUR LINTON CORBIN, 1A CORBIN ON CONTRACTS: A COMPREHENSIVE TREATISE ON THE WORKING RULES OF CONTRACT LAW §§ 193–209 (West Publ'g Co. rev. ed. 1963) (1950). His role as deputy next to Williston in the First Restatement drafting effort locates him likewise at the center of events. Yet, it was Williston who had first coined the term "promissory estoppel" in his major 1920 treatise, who served as Reporter and thus leading figure in the First Restatement, who personally drafted Section 90, and who led the recorded ALI debate on the matter. Accordingly, this book and the discussion herein focus on Williston himself. It is nonetheless clear that Corbin and presumably others served as strong allies in Williston's effort to usher promissory estoppel into doctrinal existence.

Further discussion of the matter may be found in Alden, *Rethinking Promissory Estoppel*, *supra* note 2, at 679–81.

[224] "Detrimental reliance" is action or forbearance in reliance on a promise which, if the promise is not ultimately fulfilled, leaves the promisee in a worse position than they would have been in had the promisee never learned of and relied on the promise in the first place. Such detrimental reliance can include, e.g., expenses incurred, or alternative economic opportunities foregone, in either case based on an assumption that the promise would be fulfilled.

[225] *See, e.g.*, Blinn v. Beatrice Cmty. Hosp. & Health Ctr., 708 N.W.2d 235, 247 (Neb. 2006); Hoffman v. Red Owl Stores, Inc., 133 N.W.2d 267, 275 (Wis. 1965).

[226] *See* Blinn, 708 N.W.2d at 247.

intention to express or be legally bound by a formal commitment,[227] can trigger the imposition of liability.

The implications of this expansionist judicial interpretation of the term "promise" in the promissory estoppel context are of course momentous. It manifestly presents the Pandorean prospect of liability being imposed upon myriad day-to-day communications among individuals. No longer does one have the sealed, separated legal compartments of (i) enforceable mutually agreed mutual exchange; (ii) gifts enforceable because delivery, thus grant, has actually occurred; (iii) unenforceable gratuitous promises to make a gift in the future; and (iv) other promises or statements, likewise unenforceable due to the absence of counterconsideration flowing from the promisee to the promisor. Rather, one can now slide quickly from enforceable categories (i) and (ii) down the slippery slope into enforcing categories (iii) and (iv) on the basis of nearly any forward-looking statement, subject to only the thinnest of doctrinal safeguards, as shall be seen. The imposition of liability is no longer cabined to commercial transactions and consummated family gifts. The bulkhead doors have been blown open. Water may now flood throughout the lower decks.

Nor, from a policy perspective, need the requirement of definiteness for enforcement have been jettisoned in the promissory estoppel context. The philosophy of the definiteness requirement in traditional contract law is that it would be unjust to enforce a commitment that a party simply has not made. A similar reluctance to enforce in promissory estoppel a "promise" that a party has shied away from making in any concrete form would, on its face, appear appropriate.

That courts have shed the limitation of definiteness illustrates powerfully the extent to which they have embarked upon an expedition into the imposition of liability untethered to the voluntary consent of private actors.

7.1.2 Should Reasonably Expect to Induce Detrimental Reliance

This requirement of promissory estoppel reduces, in a word, to foreseeability. A couple points are worthy of note in this regard.

7.1.2.1 FORESEEABILITY IN TORT AS DISTINCT FROM CONTRACT. First, while foreseeability plays an important role in both contract and in tort, its referent in the two cases is slightly distinct.[228] In contract, foreseeability does not go to whether one

[227] *See id.* at 246.

[228] This distinction is succinctly laid out by Professor Ayres et al.:

> [F]oreseeability in contract is about the scope of recovery – the damage calculation. In tort, foreseeability goes to the scope of the duty. If, given the nature of the conduct and the circumstances, the defendant could not reasonably foresee the risk of any harm to the plaintiff or a class of persons similarly situated, there is no duty of care owed to the plaintiff.

has a duty. After all, one has already made an absolute commitment to deliver a certain performance to the counterparty, and has thus undertaken a duty. Rather, foreseeability acts as a limitation on the amount of damage that may appropriately be imposed on a party in breach. One has only agreed, as it were, to be responsible for harm to the counterparty that one could reasonably foresee at the time of contracting if breach were ultimately to occur. The seminal case here is of course *Hadley v. Baxendale*.[229]

By contrast, foreseeability in tort goes to the preliminary issue of whether one even has a duty of care to avoid certain potential harmful consequences to specified others.[230] The classic example is *Palsgraf v. Long Island Railroad*, in which Benjamin Cardozo wrote for the New York Court of Appeals that an actor does not have a duty to a specified plaintiff to exercise care to avoid potential harms to that plaintiff from a Rube Goldberg sequence of events so absent of notice of risk as to lie outside the realm of reasonable foreseeability at the time of the actor's conduct.[231] Cardozo then took it as given, though without holding, that if one does have a duty of care to a specified plaintiff, and harm does arise to that plaintiff from a failure to conduct oneself consonant with that duty, this would "entail liability for any and all consequences, however novel or extraordinary."[232]

Foreseeability of both types would appear logically to apply in the promissory estoppel context. To begin with, in light of Williston and the ALI having claimed to situate promissory estoppel within the realm of contract, the amount of any monetary damage award in promissory estoppel should presumably be subject to the same limitation as other, truly contractual damage awards – namely, only such damages as are, at the time of the "promise," reasonably foreseeable consequences of nonfulfillment of that promise. Foreseeability would go to the damage calculation.[233]

Ian Ayres, Gregory Klass & Rebecca Stone, Studies in Contract Law 1008 (West Academic, Foundation Press 10th ed. 2024) (citations omitted).

[229] Hadley v. Baxendale, 156 Eng. Rep. 145, 9 Exch. 341 (1854).

[230] Palsgraf v. Long Is. R.R. Co., 248 N.Y. 339, 346 (1928):

> The question of liability is always anterior to the question of the measure of the consequences that go with liability. If there is no tort to be redressed, there is no occasion to consider what damage might be recovered if there were a finding of a tort.

[231] *Id.* at 341–44.

[232] *Id.* at 346. Oliver Wendell Holmes had made a similar point several decades earlier:

> [I]f the defendant's servant did commit an unjustifiable battery upon the plaintiff's person, the defendant must answer for the actual consequences of that wrong to her as she was, and cannot cut down her damages by showing that the effect would have been less upon a normal person. (citation omitted) The measure of a defendant's duty in determining whether a wrong has been committed is one thing; the measure of liability when a wrong has been committed is another.

Spade v. Lynn & Boston R.R., 172 Mass. 488, 491 (1899).

[233] Whether recovery for promissory estoppel claims should encompass full, normal contract damages, i.e., expectancy damages including lost profit, or whether recovery should be limited to, e.g., expenses incurred or other concrete reliance harm, has been a point of debate and

In addition, and rather to the obviously tortious aspect of promissory estoppel, foreseeability as facially stated in Section 90 clearly goes to the preliminary issue of whether any liability may be imposed whatsoever. Unless "the promisor should reasonably expect to induce action or forbearance on the part of the promisee or a third person," no liability in promissory estoppel will lie. Foreseeability would go to the likelihood, the possibility, of action or forbearance by the promisee.[234] To borrow the language of tort, under promissory estoppel the promisor has no duty to the promisee to carry through on the promise unless the promisor should reasonably expect to induce detrimental reliance.

7.1.2.2 REASONABLENESS OF RELIANCE. The second point worth discussing is whether the "promisee's" reliance must have been reasonable as a prerequisite to recovery. There are differing potential views of Section 90 in this regard.

To begin with, a fairly straight literal reading shows that Section 90 simply requires that the reliance be foreseeable. This might initially be surprising to some, but a careful examination of the text of Section 90 shows that the grammatical placement of the word "reasonably" in Section 90 refers to whether it is reasonable to expect. In other words, whether it is reasonable to foresee.

At this juncture, however, a choice of interpretation presents itself. One could follow a grammatically broader, but substantively narrower, interpretation by insisting that the "promisor" can only be held responsible for foreseeing reasonable reliance by the "promisee," not unreasonable reliance. There are plenty of courts that have taken this tack. Williston himself on at least one occasion, if not more, in describing his proposed doctrine of promissory estoppel, likewise read in a reasonableness-of-reliance requirement. To the extent that a reasonableness-of-reliance requirement is read in as a gloss or necessary corollary by courts, this provides some check upon the scope of potential liability.

disagreement over the years. Williston himself intended that full expectancy damages be available. Certain later observers have focused on the fact that promissory estoppel is nominally predicated upon detrimental reliance, and argued that damages should be limited as they would if a claim sounded in reliance rather than expectancy. The latter camp's view was reflected in the addition of a sentence to revised Section 90 in the Restatement (Second), published in 1981, to the effect that "[t]he remedy granted for breach may be limited as justice requires." RESTATEMENT (SECOND), *supra* note 2, § 90(1).

This book's facial challenge to the historical, philosophical, economic, and moral bases for the artificial doctrinal invention of promissory estoppel in toto, renders detailed inquiry into the optimal measure of damages for a promissory estoppel recovery award a matter of secondary importance, if not altogether moot, for current purposes. Accordingly, the issue will not be further explored here.

234 The Author is not as personally convinced as others appear to be that these two arguably distinct types of foreseeability can, in fact, always be as neatly disentangled and segregated as here laid out. Given, however, that precisely such distinction and description has been explicitly articulated and embraced by leading figures in the field of tort, and further discussion would exceed the scope of our current inquiry, the distinction is accepted here for purposes of exposition and discussion.

But precisely because promissory estoppel is wholly invented, there are no long centuries of precedent establishing its contours upon which one might call. Courts are making it up, so to speak, as they go along. Just as there are courts that have read in a reasonableness-of-reliance requirement, there are plenty of courts that have handed down promissory estoppel decisions without discussing reasonableness of reliance, for the obvious reason that it is not facially required by Section 90. And the caselaw experience we have of judges shucking off any requirement of definiteness in imposing promissory estoppel liability illustrates amply the open-ended, unbounded potential for the section to be applied without regard to reasonableness of reliance.

One may these days from time to time be faced with persons who might very well – or are even inclined to – rely on and sue others on the basis of "promises" they have not paid for. Even if such reliance is unfair, unjustified, and objectionable from the perspective of the person making a forward-looking statement of intent or anticipation. There exist those who feel entitled to rely on others' statements as binding, immutable commitments, even though the person relying has not paid or rendered any other consideration in exchange therefor, and then to perceive themselves to have been jilted, to have been wronged, to have been cheated of their rightful due, by the "promisor" changing their mind. It is entirely foreseeable in such a circumstance that a reasonable person making a statement could or should expect that the "promisee" might choose to rely.

This is of particular concern in light of the significant philosophical and legal shift in American culture over the past half century away from personal responsibility and toward an ethos of entitlement and victimhood where others are held responsible and compelled to pay for one's own misfortune, one's own mistakes, one's own failures, malfeasances, and nonfeasances, one's own choices. Oliver Wendell Holmes reflected the voice and thinking of a prior, more robust age, when he wrote in 1899 concerning the assumption of risk limitation on tort liability (a limitation that has now, for all practical purposes, been effaced from American law), that "a man cannot shift his misfortunes to his neighbor's shoulders."[235] Those days are now long past.

If ever there did, there no longer exists in many different contexts any broad-based social consensus on what should be considered reasonable in a plaintiff's own conduct and sensitivities. Thus, even before a court that reads in a reasonableness-of-reliance requirement, the unfortunate "promisor" may find themselves being held liable in circumstances where the promisor does not believe such a result to be fair or just. And the court might very well not choose to discuss reasonableness of reliance at all.

This concern obtains despite the obvious argument that it is inherently unreasonable to consider oneself entitled to sue a "promisor" for damages for nonfulfillment

[235] Spade, *supra* note 232, at 747.

of a "promise," where the plaintiff has neither rendered nor promised anything in return to the promisor. From a moral perspective, why should the plaintiff have any claim whatsoever against the "promisor's" assets? This subject is reprised later when the book turns to the moral foundations of contract law. Suffice it to say for current purposes that, to the extent the courts or legislature of a state have adopted promissory estoppel in that jurisdiction, they have by that very act alone brushed aside prima facie the idea that one private actor trying to take another's assets for nonfulfillment of an uncompensated, gratuitous "promise" is inherently unreasonable.

7.1.3 Detrimental Reliance Must Actually Have Occurred

Section 90 requires that the promise "does induce such action or forbearance."[236] Obvious examples along these lines would be the incurrence of expenses, or deliberately foregoing to pursue an alternative business transaction with an unrelated third party. Merely having heard the promise and, as a consequence, expecting or anticipating that the promise will be fulfilled – but without actually taking or forbearing action as a result thereof – is not sufficient.[237] This is, of course, an important limitation against completely wild assertions of liability for literally any forward-looking statement under the sun.

7.1.4 Injustice Can Only Be Avoided by Enforcement

This final element in a promissory estoppel claim was deliberately crafted by Williston to provide judges with maximum, essentially unfettered, discretion to apply their own sense of justice in deciding whether to impose liability. In the ALI's debate on the proposed doctrine of promissory estoppel, Williston stated: "Unquestionably, the word 'injustice,' … leaves a certain leeway … to the judge. … As to the specific inquiry what injustice means, *it means something indefinite* and *the meaning is purposely left somewhat indefinite*."[238] As such, it is tantamount to judicial fiat rather than an actual rule of law, properly understood. This was by design, not accident, in the invention of promissory estoppel and the drafting of Section 90.

While one might hope that a given judge would apply discretion in a reasonably uniform manner across different defendants without regard to political or personal bias, there are no mandatory standards against which to test that exercise of

[236] Restatement (Second), *supra* note 2, § 90(1).

[237] *See, e.g.*, Congregation Kadimah Toras-Moshe v. DeLeo, 450 N.E.2d 691, 693 (Mass. 1989) ("The inclusion of the promised $25,000 in the budget, by itself, merely reduced to writing the Congregation's expectation that it would have additional funds. A hope or expectation … is not equivalent to … reliance. …").

[238] ALI Debate on Section 90, *supra* note 30, at 86 (emphasis added).

discretion. The closest one gets to criteria for application of this element is a comment to Section 90 – only added later in the Restatement (Second) published in 1981, as described below – which suggests that a judge's decision as to whether enforcement is required to avoid injustice "may depend on the reasonableness of the promisee's reliance, on its definite and substantial character in relation to the remedy sought, of the formality with which the promise is made. . . ."[239] This is not a list of factors that must be considered and addressed, but merely a set of nonexclusive suggestions from the drafters of the Restatement (Second).[240]

7.2 *Further Expansion of Scope: Reliance by Third-Person Nonpromisees*

Skipping ahead momentarily in our historical timeline for purposes of cohesive substantive exegesis of the doctrine in its now current form, during the 1960s and 1970s a revision of the First Restatement was undertaken that further expanded the scope of potential liability under promissory estoppel.[241] The Restatement (Second) of Contracts, published in 1981, introduced the assertion that liability in promissory estoppel can run not only to the person to whom a "promise" is actually addressed but instead to a third person who becomes aware of the "promise" and chooses to rely detrimentally thereon, provided that such reliance is reasonably foreseeable.[242]

[239] RESTATEMENT (SECOND), *supra* note 2, § 90 cmt. b (emphasis added). The comment also mentions as possible factors for a judge's consideration "the extent to which the evidentiary, cautionary, deterrent, and channeling functions of form are met by the commercial setting or otherwise, and on the extent to which such other policies as the enforcement of bargains and the prevention of unjust enrichment are relevant." *Id.* Further, the comment specifies that "[t]he force of particular factors varies in different types of cases: thus reliance need not be of substantial character in charitable subscription cases, but must in cases of firm offers and guarantees." *Id.* This "must" in the final clause is the only apparently mandatory factor for inclusion in those specific, limited, firm offer and guarantee circumstances.

Of particular note is the fact that the list of suggested factors does not suggest attention to whether the "promisor" was intentionally trying to induce reliance, as distinct from merely being able to foresee that reliance might occur. From a doctrinal perspective, this is a tremendously important inquiry, and will be discussed at length *infra*.

[240] The degree of focused analysis brought to bear on the injustice element in actual court practice is not clear. Professor Marco Jimenez, after surveying more than 300 promissory estoppel cases decided in the 1980s, noted that "surprisingly few judges require a plaintiff to show that the equitable principle of 'justice' has been satisfied." Marco J. Jimenez, *The Many Faces of Promissory Estoppel: An Empirical Analysis under the Restatement (Second) of Contracts*, 57 UCLA L. REV. 669, 670 (2010).

[241] The Restatement (Second) of Contracts was published in 1981, but had been the product of debate and drafting within the ALI since the early 1960s. Initially, the Reporter for the Restatement (Second) was Professor Robert Braucher of Harvard Law School, serving in that capacity from 1963 to 1971, but upon Braucher's nomination to the Massachusetts Supreme Judicial Court, his place as Reporter was thereupon filled by Professor E. Allan Farnsworth of Columbia Law School. *See* E. Allan Farnsworth, *Ingredients in the Redaction of the* Restatement (Second) of Contracts, 81 COLUM. L. REV. 1, 3 (1981).

[242] RESTATEMENT (SECOND), *supra* note 2, § 90(1).

As amended by the Restatement (Second), Section 90 consequently reads in relevant part:

> (1) A promise which the promisor should reasonably expect to induce action or forbearance on the part of the promisee *or a third person*. . . .[243]

Whether this language is truly as unbounded as it facially appears is open to question. Read simply, it is of potentially staggering breadth. However, in the comment relative to this language we find the following passage: "If a promise is made to one party for the benefit of another, it is often foreseeable that the beneficiary will rely on the promise."[244] The scenario presented by this hypothesis in the comment is, in effect, akin to enforcement of an actual, true contract by an intended third-party beneficiary thereof, just stripped of the requirement of mutual exchange necessary to the formation of true contract. The third-person nonpromisee asserting a promissory estoppel claim would stand in the same position structurally as an intended third-party beneficiary of a true contract. Pursuant to this comment, certain cases interpreting the "third person" language in Section 90 have read in a requirement – at least in practical effect in rendering judgment in a particular case whether or not formally stated as absolutely mandatory in all cases – that the nonpromisee third party have indeed been an intended beneficiary of the promise.[245]

Certain other changes to Section 90 effectuated by the Restatement (Second) have attracted some scholarly attention, yet are ancillary to the principal danger posed by promissory estoppel, either because they do not go into the issue of whether any liability should attach in the first place or are limited in their application to highly specialized circumstances.

First, a sentence was added to the effect that "[t]he remedy granted for breach may be limited as justice requires." *Id.* As briefly averred to earlier, Williston's initial concept had been that a promissory estoppel claim should be treated in a manner fully equivalent to any either breach of contract claim predicated upon an actual mutual exchange. That is, a successful plaintiff could recover full expectancy damages, the objective of which is to place the plaintiff in the economic position the plaintiff would have enjoyed had the promise been carried out. Over the years, certain other commentators had suggested that promissory estoppel awards should perhaps in many instances be limited to reliance damages, the objective of which is to place the plaintiff in the economic position the plaintiff would have been in had the promise never been made in the first place.

Second, the drafters of the Restatement (Second) decided that a promise to make a gift to a charitable institution should be enforceable even if the institution has not in fact relied on the promise whatsoever. The mere act of speaking the promise is irrevocable, the speaker is legally bound and cannot back out, even though what is at issue is an anticipated gift rather than any kind of mutual exchange. This is reflected in a new subsection (2) to Section 90: "A charitable subscription . . . is binding under Subsection (1) without proof that the promise induced action or forbearance." *Id.* § 90(2).

These two modifications to Section 90 in the Restatement (Second) will not be further explored here.

243 *Id.* § 90(1) (emphasis added).

244 *Id.* § 90(1) cmt. c.

245 *See, e.g.*, Donald B. Murphy Contractors, Inc. v. King County, 49 P.3d 912 (Wash. Ct. App. 2002):

That is, however, a limiting interpretive gloss voluntarily imposed by those courts. Nowhere does the comment, in fact, require that a nonpromisee be an intended beneficiary of the promise in order to trigger the "third person" proviso. The third-person language can just as easily be read as merely illustrative of the most likely scenario contemplated by the drafters, rather than as a limiting, sole permissible application.

Indeed, that the cited passage from the comment is in fact merely illustrative, rather than setting a limit, is clearly demonstrated by a subsequent sentence therein, to wit: "Justifiable reliance *by third persons who are not beneficiaries* is less likely, but may sometimes reinforce the claim of the promisee or beneficiary."[246] That is, justifiable reliance by third-person nonpromisees who are not intended beneficiaries of the promise may also lead to damages under Section 90, even though the drafters envision that scenario as "less likely."

Depending on how broadly courts choose to interpret and apply that comment over time, the potential implications of the "third person" nonpromisee addition to Section 90 are manifest.

To date, judging by cases that have come to the Author's attention, litigants and courts have been restrained in their claims under and application of Section 90's assertion of liability running to nonpromisees.[247] Yet, as has occurred in other areas

> Murphy [the subcontractor] further contends that the County is estopped to deny its promise [to the general contractor] to procure insurance. But the County made no direct promise to Murphy. Murphy relies on comment (c) to section 90 of the Restatement (Second) of Contracts for the proposition that a promissory estoppel claim may lie where a third party relies on a promise to another. Murphy has not shown, however, that the promisee's [Author: nonpromisee's] reliance may be found where the promisee [Author: nonpromisee] lacks third-party beneficiary status. Because the contracting parties did not intend to benefit Murphy, reliance by Murphy on the promise to procure insurance was not justifiable. The promissory estoppel claim was properly dismissed.

Id. at 915 (citation omitted).

Likewise, see, e.g., Zollinger v. Carrol, 49 P.3d 402 (Idaho 2002):

> Only if [the guarantor] Zollinger can show that a contractual relationship existed between Carrol and Truxal and ECSI, for his benefit, and that it was foreseeable that he would rely on that agreement, are the predicates for Zollinger's promissory estoppel claim established.
>
> ....
>
> We conclude that the district court correctly ruled that because Zollinger was neither a promisee nor third-party beneficiary of the shareholder agreements, his alleged actions in reliance on the promises contained in the agreements do not entitle him to relief on his claim of promissory estoppel.

Id. at 405 (citations omitted).

[246] RESTATEMENT (SECOND), *supra* note 2, § 90(1) cmt. c.

[247] A significant area of potential application of liability to third-person nonpromisees under Section 90 are industrial plant closures. Consider a situation in which a major regional employer firm that has come under severe market and financial stress communicates through large meetings with employees and interviews with the press its anticipation with regard to whether certain production facilities will need to be closed due to economic hardship. If the

of the law, a new articulation of liability often has a disturbing capacity to expand greatly with the passage of years.[248] Only time will tell.

8 THE OBJECTIVE AND THE MARKETING

Returning now in historical timeline to the 1920s, when promissory estoppel was initially articulated and built into the First Restatement, it is of central importance to the subject to examine Williston's justification for his novel, radical doctrine, and the statements he made to market the concept to his colleagues in the ALI. This section of the book sets forth the essential structure of Williston's articulated rationale. Part III of the book, *infra*, then undertakes a detailed, forensic critique and rebuttal of Williston's claims to precedential basis for, and reasoning in favor of, promissory estoppel.

company is not sufficiently pessimistic in its prognoses, but then ultimately announces a closure, suit could theoretically be brought not only by adversely affected employees but also by a wide variety of arguably adversely affected parties throughout the region. Claims could be alleged predicated upon alternative employment not accepted or pursued in reliance on the company's hope of remaining open; loss in residential home value when parties that could have sold at higher prices before announcement of the plant closure, chose not to sell in timely manner, in reliance on public statements made by the company; loss in investment value to businesses and property purchasers who invested or purchased in the region in reliance on company predictions of remaining viable. And the list goes on and on. Nothing in Section 90 as written provides any kind of clear limiting principle upon the scope of such potential lawsuits and imposition of liability therefor.

Precisely these types of plant closures and litigated communications occurred some decades ago in the American "Rust Belt" states clustered around the Great Lakes, for example. Summarized in broad terms, the resultant spate of promissory estoppel claims, brought particularly in the Sixth Circuit, affirmed that promissory estoppel liability is entirely possible under federal common law as applied in connection with collective bargaining situations. But those suits focused on employee claims for lost wages, and are of perhaps limited precedential value where they arise in the context of collective bargaining agreements (where the union is technically the contractual counterparty with the employer, but the employees represented by the union are clearly the intended beneficiaries of the collective bargaining agreement) and related communications affected by federal statutes. For examples of cases relating to such employment disputes, see, e.g., Local 1330, United Steel Workers of America v. U.S. Steel Corp., 631 F.2d 1264 (1980); Abbington v. Dayton Malleable, Inc., 561 F. Supp. 1290 (S.D. Ohio 1983), *aff'd without reported opinion*, 738 F.2d 438 (Table) (6th Cir. 1984); Anderson v. AT&T Corp., 147 F.3d 467 (6th Cir. 1998). For an example of a promissory estoppel suit brought by a municipality against an employer predicated upon a plant relocation, see, Charter Twp. of Ypsilanti v. General Motors Corp., 506 N.W.2d 556 (Mich. Ct. App. 1993).

[248] A classic example of such inflation is the anti-mafia statute known as "RICO" (the Racketeer Influenced and Corrupt Organizations Act, 18 U.S.C. §§ 1961–1968), which is now routinely used by civil litigators against targets that bear literally no similarity to organized underworld crime. The Author is aware of this through direct personal knowledge in practice. For a published case example of such, see Hill v. Gateway 2000, Inc., 105 F.3d 1147, 1148 (7th Cir. 1997) (in suit against early personal home computer manufacturer Gateway, plaintiff "arguing ... that the product's shortcomings make Gateway a racketeer ..., leading to treble damages under RICO....").

Critical points of reference here are as follows.

At effective inception, as briefly touched upon earlier, in 1920 Williston brought forth his major treatise on contract law.[249] Therein he played with the idea, almost as a casual aside, of shifting the entire basis of promissory enforcement from mutual exchange to unrequested reliance, claiming ancient and fundamental historical pedigree for the latter.[250] It is here that Williston for the first time dubbed his envisioned enforcement on the basis of unrequested reliance "promissory estoppel."[251] He invented the term.

Next, as part of his effort to justify and market such a radical realignment to his colleagues, in his capacity as official Reporter for the First Restatement, Williston presented in 1926 certain explanatory "Commentaries"[252] prefatory to the upcoming ALI debate on his draft restatement of contract law.[253] These Commentaries took as their point of departure Williston's claim that the historic foundation of contract law lay not in mutual exchange but rather unrequested reliance, and boldly threw it down as a conceptual gauntlet.[254]

To tie this claim of medieval historicity with the modern era, in both his 1920 treatise and his 1926 ALI Commentaries, Williston asserted that certain categories of existing caselaw, along with a handful of idiosyncratic, isolated cases, were in their essence predicated upon promissory estoppel, though not, of course, under such freshly minted moniker.[255]

Finally, the transcript of the face-to-face debate later in 1926 among Williston and his ALI colleagues documented both the concerns of those colleagues, as well as the specific, less overtly ambitious manner in which Williston defended his draft.[256] In that ALI debate, Williston sought to present draft Section 90 as, in truth, no real innovation whatsoever, but merely an attempt for simplicity of exposition to gather under one roof a litany of preexisting exceptions to the consideration requirement.[257] Yet, even here a glint of Williston's true, broader, ultimate objective –

[249] *See* 1 Williston Treatise, *supra* note 8. As observed in note 8, the copyright and preface are both dated 1920, although the formal publication date is listed as 1924. To best track the development of Williston's own thinking temporally, this work shall be referred to as Williston's "1920 treatise" in the principal text of this book.

[250] *Id.* § 139, at 313.

[251] *Id.* § 139, at 308.

[252] *See* Williston, *First Restatement Commentaries*, *supra* note 29.

[253] ALI Debate on Section 90, *supra* note 30.

[254] Williston, *First Restatement Commentaries*, *supra* note 29, at 14.

One will notice that these Commentaries, as well as the ALI debate, refer not to Section 90 but rather Section 88. The reason for this is that during the drafting process, Williston's proposal was originally designated as Section 88, but due to later additions ultimately appeared as Section 90. Throughout the principal text of this book, reference shall therefore be to Section 90 to avoid confusion.

[255] *Id.* at 14–20.

[256] *See* ALI Debate on Section 90, *supra* note 30.

[257] *See id.* at 86, 107, 108.

already made clear in his 1920 treatise and 1926 ALI Commentaries – shines through.[258] The modesty of Williston's oral presentation and discussion with his colleagues is belied by the immodesty of the actual text of Section 90, which throws open the door to Williston's desired shift in the very foundations of promissory enforcement.

In what follows, both here and in Part III of this book, Williston's claims of precedential authority for promissory estoppel shall follow the overall historical development of Anglo-American contract law. The first to be addressed are Williston's most profound, far-reaching, and ambitious claims, namely, those regarding the true origins of contract law. Second to be taken up are his assertions regarding certain caselaw categories and isolated cases as evidence of preexisting, innominate promissory estoppel in action.

The past was erased, the erasure was forgotten, the lie became truth.[259]

—George Orwell

8.1 *The Origins of Contract Law*

In his massive 1920 treatise, Williston included a roughly seven-page section, heavily footnoted, entitled "Estoppel as a substitute for consideration."[260] It is here that he introduced to American legal academia his concept of promissory estoppel, with these words:

> It is generally true that one who has led another to act in reasonable reliance on his representations of fact, cannot afterwards in litigation between the two deny the truth of the representations, and *some courts have sought to apply this principle to the formation of contracts, where, relying on a gratuitous promise, the promisee has suffered detriment*. It is to be noticed, however, that such a case does not come within the ordinary definition of estoppel. If there is any representation of an existing fact, it is only that the promisor at the time of making the promise intends to fulfil it. As to such intention there is usually no misrepresentation and if there is, it is not that which has injured the promisee. In other words, he relies on a promise and not on a misstatement of fact; and the term "promissory" estoppel or something equivalent should be used to mark the distinction.[261]

[258] Williston stated that the principle of Section 90 "cannot be made more definite. The variety of circumstances that may arise [justifying application of promissory estoppel] is such that it is *impossible to enumerate them all*." *Id.* at 100 (emphasis added).

[259] GEORGE ORWELL [ERIC ARTHUR BLAIR], 1984 [originally published as NINETEEN EIGHTY-FOUR], at 75 (New York, Penguin Group (USA) (Signet Classics) reprint 1950) (1949).

[260] 1 WILLISTON TREATISE, *supra* note 8, § 139, at 307–14.

[261] *Id.* at 307–8 (emphasis added).

"Promissory estoppel" was born.

Though the passage quoted enters upon the distinction between "equitable estoppel" and "promissory estoppel," sets the stage for his discussion of modern cases that he asserted gave precedent for the latter,[262] and notes the difference from promissory fraud,[263] several pages deeper in Williston posited the true genesis, the fountainhead, of promissory estoppel in the very origins of Anglo-American contract law itself:

> [I]t may fairly be argued that *the fundamental basis of simple contracts historically was action in justifiable reliance on a promise—rather than the more modern notion of purchase of a promise for a price*, and that it is a consistent development from this early basis to define valid consideration as any legal benefit to the promisor or legal detriment to the promisee given or suffered by the latter in reasonable reliance on the promise. Such a definition *eliminates the necessity of a request by the promisor* for the consideration.[264]

The purpose of Part I of this book was to ground the discussion throughout in the actual history of contract law development in the Anglo-American world, from which the inaccuracy of Williston's statement is facially apparent. This shall be expounded upon *infra*.

Williston conceded and confessed the radical nature of what he proposed:

> The proposition is by no means without intrinsic merit, but it should be recognized that if generally applied *it would much extend liability on promises, and* that at present it *is opposed to the great weight of authority.*[265]

At this juncture in 1920, there was no more than Williston's bare bones, single-sentence assertion as to the historical genesis of Anglo-American contract law.

In his 1926 ALI Commentaries, Williston then fleshed out his historical claim with the following explanation – still extraordinarily brief, indeed cursory, relative to the momentous alteration of contract law envisaged:

> The action of *Assumpsit was originally based on reliance by the plaintiff on a promise rather than on a bargain.* It was not until the old action of Debt was swallowed and extended by the action of assumpsit that the idea of exchanging consideration as the price of a promise became the predominant one. Professor Ames [Williston's mentor and predecessor at Harvard Law School] in his History of Assumpsit (Lectures on Legal History, page 142), summing up a preceding argument, says:

[262] All of this shall be addressed, and Williston's claims to precedential authority critiqued, in significant detail *infra*.

[263] The existing concept and law regarding "promissory fraud," as distinct from promissory estoppel, has already been discussed *supra*.

[264] *Id.* at 313 (emphasis added).

[265] *Id.* (emphasis added).

"The gist of the action being the deceit in breaking a promise on the faith of which the plaintiff had been induced to part with his money or other property" etc.

Mr. Ames further says (page 143):

"That equity gave relief, before 1500, to a plaintiff who had incurred detriment on the faith of the defendant's promise, is reasonably clear, although there are but three reported cases."

and (page 144):

"Both in equity and at law, *therefore, a remediable breach of a* parol *promise was originally conceived of as* a deceit; that is, *a tort*. Assumpsit was in several instances distinguished from contract."[266]

Again, these assertions are subject to extensive analysis and refutation in Part III of this book. But the essence of the claims is clear: The origin of promissory enforcement was tort. Specifically, a tort that required only reliance by the plaintiff on a promise, not a mutual exchange transaction.

The enormity of Williston's ultimate objective is thus likewise clear: To shift the very foundation, the core philosophy, the moral premise, of promissory enforcement off of mutual exchange, and onto unrequested reliance by the promisee. That is, off of contract, and onto tort.

8.2 *More Recent Categories and Cases*

Given the extraordinary brevity, without detailed analytic support, of Williston's sweeping claim as to the origins of Anglo-American contract law, more meat on the bone was presumably required to bring his ALI colleagues to the table. Here, Williston fielded the argument that there already existed a whole series of caselaw categories and isolated individual cases that – without using his own newly introduced appellation – were nonetheless predicated upon the principle of promissory estoppel. Promises were enforced in the absence of consideration therefor. If, Williston argued, the purpose of the First Restatement was to state the rules of contract law in abridged, summary format, then the way to address these categories and cases was obviously to designate and describe a succinct new rule of decision sufficiently broad, sufficiently unencumbered, to embrace them all. Hence, Section 90.

We see this argument put in play in his 1926 ALI Commentaries, immediately preparatory to the ALI debate scheduled to occur less than two months later:

If the law is to be simplified and clarified, it can be done only by coordinating the decisions under general rules not by stating empirically a succession of specific

[266] Williston, *First Restatement Commentaries*, *supra* note 29, at 14 (emphasis added).

cases without any binding thread of principle. In fact there is a binding thread in all the classes of cases which have been enumerated, namely, the justifiable reliance of the promisee.[267]

We see Williston repeat this same proposition in the ALI debate:

> You can enumerate all the classes of cases which I have enumerated and have a number of special instances, and then another instance will come up and it will not be covered by the Restatement. If the law is to be simplified, it seems to me it must be done by coordinating the classes of cases rather than by enumerating a lot of special instances. That is the reason why I defend Section [90].[268]

8.2.1 Circumventing a Major Objection: Implied Unilateral Contract

The initial, and massive, hurdle faced by Williston in open debate was Mr. Morawetz's trenchant objection that much of what Section 90 proposed to address was already fully enforceable under traditional, classical principles of contract law as implied unilateral contract:[269]

> In order that this section may apply the promisor must reasonably expect to induce certain definite action to be taken. Now, it seems to me that instead of dealing with this matter under the head of consideration, it would go more appropriately under the head of offers. What happens in these cases is that the law holds that if a man makes a promise to induce another to do a certain act, he will be held to have made an offer of a unilateral promise to take effect upon the performance of the act.[270]

267 *Id.* at 19–20.

268 ALI Debate on Section 90, *supra* note 30, at 107. The original text of the transcript referred, of course, to Section 88, later renumbered as Section 90. Williston also quoted, *id.* at 108, the passage from his own ALI Commentaries cited *supra*.

269 Morawetz was, to the best of the Author's knowledge based on review of the record, apparently the first to make this point explicitly and clearly. In subsequent decades, others have likewise made the same observation. *See* Barnett & Becker, *supra* note 217, at 455–57; Jean Fleming Powers, *Promissory Estoppel and Wagging the Dog*, 59 Ark. L. Rev. 841, 856–57 (2007); Alden, *Rethinking Promissory Estoppel*, *supra* note 2, at 683–85.

The Author has in fact made this one of the central theses and programmatic elements in returning contract law to its proper, traditional foundation and contours. *See* Alden, *Reversing the Reliance Revolution*, *supra* note 2, at 1614, 1659–67, 1673. Implied unilateral contract is a doctrinal point of major significance in the context of promissory estoppel.

270 ALI Debate on Section 90, *supra* note 30, at 88.

"Unilateral contract" is a term well known in classical contract law. In essence, one party promises to act or forbear in some manner, if the promisee completes a certain act or forbearance from their side. This is a so-called offer for a unilateral contract. The contract actually forms at the moment of promisee's completion of the requested performance.

Since the promisee in such a situation may be economically or otherwise exposed to risk during the period of time when promisee is endeavoring to complete such performance, the common law has implied upon the promisor a constructive subsidiary promise not to revoke the offer of a unilateral contract for the time for performance stated in the offer or, in the absence of such specification, for a reasonable time. This is, in effect, an option during such

The reason the discussion here concerns implied, as distinct from express, unilateral contract is straightforward. If the reciprocal act or forbearance by promisee, upon completion of which promisor has conditioned promisor's own obligation, has been explicitly stated by promisor in words – thus expressly – one would have an express unilateral contract. Judicial enforcement of such would be clear and obvious. If, by contrast, the promisor has made a promise in the hope of inducing a certain act or forbearance by promisee, but has not articulated in words precisely what it is that promisor seeks nor that promisor's own obligation is to be contingent upon completion of such act or performance, then we are dealing with implied unilateral contract. A court will, under well-known, well-trodden principles of traditional, classical contract law imply upon the promisor the articulation and contingency that promisor did not reduce to actual words. The core of the matter is promisor's desire to induce promisee's act or forbearance, without expressly stating a request for the same.[271] This is, of course, what Morawetz was referring to in the quoted passage.

The significance of all this is that where existing, traditional, classical contract law already provides an obvious, universally understood and accepted pathway to enforcement, there is absolutely no need whatsoever for doctrinal innovation in the form of promissory estoppel.

Though later in the debate Williston was to tip his hand as to the breadth of his ambitions for Section 90, as discussed *infra*, his specific response here to Morawetz's objection concerning implied unilateral contract was, in effect, minimalist:

> I want to cover more in Section [90] than offers. I understand perfectly well what you have in mind, as offers for unilateral contracts, and they are covered under offers; but this section covers a case where there is a promise to give and the promisor knows that the promisee will rely upon the proposed gift in certain definite ways.[272]

period, in which the promisor is the optionor, and the promisee is the optionee who may choose to accept the offer underlying the option by completing the requested performance.

These rules were addressed in Sections 12 and 45 of the First Restatement, as well as Section 45 of the Restatement (Second), though for reasons not clear the Restatement (Second) attempts to avoid use of the term "unilateral contract" almost entirely, relegating that specific terminology to a brief comment on the section. *See* First Restatement, *supra* note 2, §§ 12, 45; Restatement (Second), *supra* note 2, § 45; *id.* at § 45 cmt. a.

[271] There is one additional critical requirement in finding the presence of an implied unilateral contract, namely, that promisee will only benefit from fulfillment of promisor's promise if the promisee in fact takes the specific action or forbearance in detrimental reliance sought by promisor. That is, the promisor promises to do something, and promisee takes action or forbearance in reliance thereon, which the promisee views as beneficial to self, but in so doing, by virtue of that action or forbearance, has brought benefit to the promisor. That is, promisee's benefit only occurs if promisee brings benefit to the promisor. This creates a conditional "only if, then" structure necessary to a mutual exchange transaction. For further detailed discussion of this point, see *infra* note 556 and accompanying text.

[272] ALI Debate on Section 90, *supra* note 30, at 89.

To distinguish promissory estoppel from implied unilateral contract, Williston thus confined his rejoinder here to gift promises – that are typically, though of course not always, intrafamily – where the donor is not seeking to induce some specific act or forbearance by the donee.[273] This is a discrete, limited type of fact pattern. It does not obviate the vast mass of all other situations in which traditional, classical implied unilateral contract could already address the matter conclusively. As to those, Section 90 could easily be applied by a court if it so chose, which would unnecessarily poach on the established ancestral territory of classical contract law. In this regard, Section 90 is already, without more, facially overbroad.

As will be explored in detail *infra*, the intrafamily donative promise in fact played a crucial role in the marketing of promissory estoppel at the end of the day.

8.2.2 Categories and Cases Predicated upon Promissory Estoppel?

The caselaw categories and isolated cases that Williston mustered to push his attack on the requirement of consideration were as follows. His assertions with respect to these are presented here. Critique in each respect is rendered in Part III.

8.2.2.1 GIFTS. As we have just seen with his response to Morawetz's implied unilateral contract objection, Williston emphasized that he wished Section 90 to address promises to make gifts. In his 1920 treatise and in his Commentaries, Williston cited several different types and situations of gifts in this regard – general intrafamily donation, marriage settlements, and charitable donations.

As explored in detail in Part III, the most important, paradigmatic situation cited by Williston was the classic intrafamily donative promise, exemplified by the 1898 Nebraska case *Ricketts v. Scothorn*.[274] In *Ricketts*, a grandfather gratuitously promised, by means of a written promissory note, to give $2,000 to his granddaughter in order that "you have not got to work any more."[275] In reliance thereon, she temporarily left her job, though later resumed employment.[276] This fact pattern served as the one, core, true example of promissory estoppel in action given as an illustration to Section 90 in the First Restatement.[277] This is the acid test.

[273] Alternatively, intrafamily gift promises might well involve a desire on the donor's part to induce certain specific reliance by the family member promisee, but courts might decline to impose legal liability on intimate, familial, or social relations not ordinarily expected to involve the legal system per se. Thus, even though a court might on technical grounds be able to find contract, the court might choose not to, on grounds that contractual liability is generally expected in commercial settings, but not necessarily in all other aspects of life. This point will be reprised briefly *infra*, in Chapter 14.1.

[274] 77 N.W. 365 (Neb. 1898).

[275] *Id.* at 366.

[276] *Id.*

[277] FIRST RESTATEMENT, *supra* note 2, § 90 illus. 2.

A distinct category of intrafamily donative promise given as an example by Williston was a promise "made in expectation of the marriage of the promisee on the faith of which marriage takes place. . . ."[278] Williston conceded that "[t]here is of course no difficulty in the case of an actual bargain in which it is agreed that in consideration of marriage a certain performance is promised, but the cases in question are not cases of bargains; they are gratuitous promises on which justifiable reliance has been placed."[279]

Stepping outside the intrafamily setting, Williston noted that promises to make gifts to charitable institutions have often been enforced even in the absence of consideration therefor.[280] The critical distinction between a gift to a private person and a gift to a charitable institution, of course, is that the latter donation presumptively benefits the broader public. This has led to a judicial preference for enforcement in derogation of the ordinary rules of contract law and property law (recalling here that the law of gifts is taxonomically considered to fall within property law).

Williston also mentioned gratuitous promises to transfer land, in reliance on which the promisee made improvements to the land.[281] Presumably the vast majority, if not nearly all, such cases would involve either intrafamily donative transfers, or donations to charitable institutions, for example, a church.

8.2.2.2 GRATUITOUS BAILMENT. Strangely – given its presumable rarity as a source of litigation in real life – Williston elevated gratuitous bailment cases, in which the bailee fails to protect and preserve the bailor's property, to one of his innominate promissory estoppel categories.[282] "Frequently these cases can be supported on the ground of tort, but not always."[283]

8.2.2.3 WAIVER. The final discrete category that Williston viewed as predicated upon promissory estoppel was waiver, namely, the unilateral, uncompensated relinquishment of a legal right by one who is already party to a contract:[284]

[278] Williston, *First Restatement Commentaries*, *supra* note 29, at 19.

[279] *Id.*

[280] *See* 1 WILLISTON TREATISE, *supra* note 8, § 139, at 308; Williston, *First Restatement Commentaries*, *supra* note 29, at 16–17; ALI Debate on Section 90, *supra* note 30, at 106.

[281] *See* 1 WILLISTON TREATISE, *supra* note 8, § 139, at 311–12; Williston, *First Restatement Commentaries*, *supra* note 29, at 15–16; ALI Debate on Section 90, *supra* note 30, at 90, 99, 104.

[282] *See* Williston, *First Restatement Commentaries*, *supra* note 29, at 18; ALI Debate on Section 90, *supra* note 30, at 106–7.

[283] Williston, *First Restatement Commentaries*, *supra* note 29, at 18.

[284] *See, e.g.*, Clark v. West, 86 N.E. 1, 5 (N.Y. 1908) (citations omitted):

> A "waiver" has been defined to be the intentional relinquishment of a known right. It is voluntary and implies an election to dispense with something of value, or forego some advantage which the party waiving it might at its option have demanded or insisted upon . . .

> A large body of cases ordinarily classified under the heading of "Waiver" in reality involve nothing but promises held binding on the promisor. . . . A frequent illustration is where after a contract to buy and sell goods to be delivered on a certain day, the buyer assents to delivery on a later day. Relying on this, if the seller fails to tender them on the day originally fixed and makes tender on the latter day, the buyer must take the goods. Yet there is no consideration for his promise to accept at a day later than that fixed in the contract. There is nothing but reliance on his promise to do so. The law is clear that in any case where a party to a contract agrees to give up a possible future defence or forgo the advantage of a condition of an existing contract provided for his benefit, the promise is binding if the promisee relying thereon changes his position.[285]

8.2.2.4 MISCELLANEOUS ISOLATED CASES. In addition to the categories discussed in which Williston saw preexisting, innominate promissory estoppel, he also cited a collection of miscellaneous, isolated cases that he likewise so interpreted. Those individual interpretations are examined and critiqued seriatim in Part III. Suffice it to say for present purposes that many, if not all, stand on shaky ground or otherwise provide little persuasive power.

8.3 *Reaction of ALI Colleagues and Williston's Response Thereto*

Just as he had earlier in the debate pointed out that much of what could be described as falling within promissory estoppel could be addressed through existing, traditional contract law applicable to implied unilateral contracts, Morawetz – though not fundamentally challenging Williston or his draft Section 90 – raised objection that Section 90 as drafted had an uncertain, inchoate frontier:

> I am not quarrelling with the idea of this Section, but I do think the section is not clear. The purpose of these Restatements is to clarify the law, to make it more certain. It seems to me that this Section would have the contrary effect. If I were a judge on reading this section I should not know where to draw the line.[286]

To this Williston responded simply, and in a manner that illustrated the indeed almost unbounded scope of his proposed new doctrine: "It cannot be made more definite. The variety of circumstances that may arise is such that it is impossible to enumerate them all."[287] This statement revealed starkly Williston's true ultimate intention, his true ambition, with Section 90.

That case also discussed the distinction between waiver, which involves intentional relinquishment, as distinct from equitable estoppel, in which a party's conduct or statements preclude them on equitable grounds from asserting a right, without regard to whether there was an actual intention to relinquish that right. *See id.* (citations omitted).

[285] Williston, *First Restatement Commentaries*, *supra* note 29, at 19.

[286] ALI Debate on Section 90, *supra* note 30, at 100.

[287] *Id.*

Similar but stronger was the reaction by Ira Hildebrand of Texas, who said, "I do not believe that we should substitute 'promissory estoppel' for consideration. If Section [90] is approved the law of Contracts becomes too indefinite,"[288] and that "I think we should hold to the old landmarks on this proposition and say only where I call for that action [i.e., promisee's act or forbearance] as a consideration for my offer should the contract be binding."[289] Williston's response was to refer to the various categories described earlier, namely, charitable subscriptions, gratuitous bailment, waiver, and marriage settlements.[290] He stated again his proposition that only a rule as broad as the proposed Section 90 would suffice to cover all of these categories simultaneously, and that such a catch-all, universal, unbounded provision would be prima facie desirable rather than distinctly harmful.[291]

The "guardrails," as it were, that Williston held forth as sufficient to corral wide-ranging application of Section 90 were threefold, all of which have been mentioned previously.

First, he cited the "injustice" requirement: "Unquestionably, the word 'injustice,' . . . leaves a certain leeway one way or the other to the judge. . . . As to the specific inquiry what injustice means, it means something indefinite and the meaning is purposely left somewhat indefinite."[292] He reiterated the observation later: "Injustice is a word that is more or less indefinite anyway. . . ."[293] But to say that the injustice requirement means "something indefinite" is to concede that Section 90 was designed to confer unfettered discretion on the individual judge. This is not, of course, a rule of law, but a declaration of arbitrary personal fiat. It is entirely standardless. It is inchoate, and deliberately so. One's fate as a defendant rests entirely, at least as regards this element, on the personal character, views, predilections, biases, favoritisms and animosities, of the judge. It is no guardrail at all.

Second, Williston cited the foreseeability requirement.[294] This is, as discussed *supra*, no more in fact than the same type of foreseeability requirement one sees in tort. Which is, of course, precisely what promissory estoppel truly is. It is not much of a guardrail, if any, but it forms the essence of the "moral" foundation for enforcement. But it is a grievously incomplete moral foundation for enforcement, as will be discussed *infra*.

Third and finally, Williston cited the requirement that the reliance be "definite and substantial."[295] Again, this is a thin reed to grasp at for restraint of the wild, charging horses of potential enforcement at the heart of Section 90, but there it is.

[288] *Id.* at 105.
[289] *Id.* at 106.
[290] *Id.* at 106–7.
[291] *Id.* at 107–8.
[292] *Id.* at 86.
[293] *Id.* at 92.
[294] *Id.* at 89.
[295] *Id.* at 90–93.

Or rather, was. The Restatement (Second) chose to eliminate the "definite and substantial" requirement.[296]

Williston sought to assuage the concerns of some members of the ALI as to Section 90's breadth:

> Now, there is no broad doctrine that wherever a man makes a promise, a gratuitous promise, and the other relies upon it, the promisee can recover on the promise, and we do not dare in Section [90] make any such broad statement that wherever a gratuitous promise is made and the promisee relies on it to his injury, he may enforce it; that is going far beyond the law and far beyond what we should dare to say.[297]

Such language certainly sounds palliative upon first impression. But the foregoing three guardrails were the only ones actually discussed and actually built into the text of the section. Such a gratuitous promise upon which another chooses to rely is now – following the Restatement (Second)'s elimination of the already vague and insubstantial "definite and substantial" limitation – entirely enforceable under Section 90 subject to no further requirements than that the reliance be foreseeable and that a judge decide to enforce in order to avoid the judge's own unfettered, standardless conception of injustice.

8.4 *Williston's Advocacy in Summation*

In abbreviated form, Williston's argumentative theses in advocacy of adopting "promissory estoppel" thus came to the following: Contract law used to be this way anyway. There exist a smattering of idiosyncratic categories and cases in more recent times that applied the essential concept of promissory estoppel in innominate form. That to "simplify" contract law, it is advisable to depart from an approach permitting a limited number of discrete, contained exceptions to the consideration requirement, in favor of a statement so broad that it can be applied across any such situations, plus in future so many unnamed others that they cannot possibly be enumerated. And that such stunning breadth should not be feared, as the firebreaks

[296] *See* Restatement (Second), *supra* note 2, § 90. Williston had viewed the "definite and substantial" requirement as giving at least some substantive content to the undefined "injustice" requirement:

> Injustice is a word that is more or less indefinite anyway, and I wished as far as possible to characterize it. Certainly, I should dislike very much to leave out the word "substantial," and I think the word, "definite" ought to be left in. Those words narrow the Section undoubtedly. If you leave them out, you make the Section broader and I think add to its vagueness.

ALI Debate on Section 90, *supra* note 30, at 92–93.

[297] ALI Debate on Section 90, *supra* note 30, at 97.

of foreseeability, "definite and substantial" reliance, and avoidance of "injustice," will prevent a wildfire from burning through the structure of contract law.

9 APPLICATION IN PRACTICE

Since its invention in the First Restatement, the doctrine of promissory estoppel has by now, over the course of the intervening decades, been widely adopted throughout the United States, at both the state and federal levels. Though there exist some distinctions among the various states in the extent to which Section 90 as written has been adopted, in their own particular interpretive glosses of the new doctrine, and in how it is applied across various factual situations, it is fair to say that promissory estoppel is now a generally accepted feature of American contract law.[298]

[298] A particularly passionate proponent of promissory estoppel was Professor Eric Mills Holmes of Willamette Law School in Oregon, who in the mid-1990s conducted a nationwide (all 50 states) survey of court decisions to determine how prevalent the doctrine of promissory estoppel had become in practical application since its initial invention in the 1920s. Professor E. M. Holmes stated his results as follows: "[T]his article establishes for the first time that *all American jurisdictions* (including American Samoa, Guam, Puerto Rico, and the Virgin Islands) have adopted and apply a doctrine of 'promissory estoppel' grounded in Section 90 of the Contracts Restatements." Eric Mills Holmes, *The Four Phases of Promissory Estoppel*, 20 SEATTLE U. L. REV. 45, 47 (1996) (emphasis added) (citation omitted). In a discursive companion article, E. M. Holmes went on to summarize the decisions in each state upon which that conclusion rested. Eric Mills Holmes, *Restatement of Promissory Estoppel*, 32 WILLAMETTE L. REV. 263 (1996).

It is important to take E. M. Holmes' bold, simple statement in this regard with more than a grain of salt. Credit here to Professor David Epstein of Richmond University School of Law for flagging to the Author's attention that Virginia has not, in fact, formally adopted promissory estoppel. Correspondence between Professor Epstein and Cambridge Univ. Press (anonymized version on file with Author in email received Aug. 19, 2022, from Cambridge Univ. Press).

If one examines Professor E. M. Holmes' granular explication of his conclusion with respect to Virginia, E. M. Holmes conceded that "Virginia courts doggedly refuse to admit, candidly and definitely, that they in fact apply the doctrine of 'promissory' estoppel." E. M. Holmes, *Restatement of Promissory Estoppel*, *supra*, at 478. This, of course, confirms the accuracy of Professor Epstein's observation.

Yet, E. M. Holmes continued:

> Virginia courts seem reluctant to . . . concede the true basis of their promissory estoppel decisions. Nonetheless, these decisions achieve a 'just result' by either stating 'estoppel' or 'equitable,' rather than 'promissory' estoppel, or by torturing an illusory bargained-for consideration as grounds for the decision.

Id. at 478–79. Based on his read and discussion of relevant Virginia caselaw, E. M. Holmes stated in summation that

> one can cautiously state that Virginia courts have raised promissory estoppel to a sufficient cognitive level in modern decisions to conclude: Virginia recognizes the doctrine of promissory estoppel as stated in the Restatement (Second) of Contract Section 90 and . . . will apply the doctrine. . . .

Id. at 483.

Though some states have rejected or sought to limit the doctrine, others, such as California, Wisconsin and Nebraska, are quite friendly to it. Similarly, though in certain factual situations application of promissory estoppel has often been resisted – such as "promises" of employment (where there is concern that application of promissory estoppel would tend to undermine the at-will presumption in American employment law) – in certain other areas it has been widely embraced – such as subcontractor bids, where promissory estoppel has quite literally supplanted traditional contract as the new paradigm presumptively to be applied.

Promissory estoppel has for decades now routinely been taught in law school curricula without question or challenge, as accepted writ. Generations of American lawyers have grown up assuming and believing that it is legitimate and long-established doctrine.

10 THE DESTABILIZATION OF CONTRACT LAW

The upshot of all this is that contract law, as now taught in American law schools, has a strangely bifurcated, indeed schizophrenic, character.

At its least deleterious, one is taught the principles of traditional contract law, then separately the principle of promissory estoppel, and ne'er the twain shall meet. At exam time, a student can analyze a given fact pattern according to the actual rules of contract law, but then, like a jack-in-the-box suddenly springing up out of nowhere, analyze the same fact pattern under promissory estoppel, possibly with the same ultimate result, possibly with a different one.

At its worst, the competing principles are never properly disaggregated and segregated from each other, thus leading to severe doctrinal conflation and conceptual confusion. When is mutual consideration required, and when not? How can the circle be squared? This situation is exacerbated by the fact that Williston's doctrinal innovations did not confine themselves to Section 90 alone – he sought to redefine, rearrange, and rewire the rules of contract law in manifold manner in order to provide a comfortable nest for the cuckoo's egg of promissory estoppel.

E. M. Holmes similarly mentioned North Carolina as a state "masquerading promissory estoppel" in its decisions. *Id.* at 497.

Whether or not one agrees with E. M. Holmes' exegesis and interpretation of particular cases, the point remains that as to any given state at issue, direct personal review of the caselaw decisions in that state is required to ascertain whether, to what extent, in which factual situations, and with what codicils, conditions, and modifications, that state has in fact adopted promissory estoppel.

That being said, any lawyer, judge, or law professor familiar with American contract caselaw can easily and immediately attest to the fact that promissory estoppel analyses are undertaken and decisions rendered in a wide array of jurisdictions across the country on a routine basis. The ubiquity of cases illustrative of this statement renders concise citation thereof neither possible as a practical matter within the space limitations of this book – shy of E. M. Holmes' massive all 50 states review spanning some roughly 200 pages of summarizing text – nor necessary for present purposes.

Unless meticulous explanation of the invention of promissory estoppel and the doctrinal heresy it represents is undertaken, students routinely demonstrate a failure to understand when a promise should be viewed as binding, and when not. The fault is not theirs. It is the fault of an internally contradictory set of rules presented to them as a coherent body of law. All of this is known to the Author from direct personal experience, both as a student once upon a decade, and as a law professor now.

10.1 *Grant Gilmore and "The Death of Contract"*

As could and should of course have been expected, several decades after publication of the First Restatement, commentators began to observe that the theoretical and doctrinal fundament of contract law – supporting the entire edifice – had in fact been critically destabilized.

Most prominent of those commentators, most articulate in his diagnosis, and most far-reaching in his prognostication, was Grant Gilmore of Yale Law School. In 1970, Gilmore gave a series of lectures at Ohio State which he subsequently used as the basis for his famous book *The Death of Contract*, published in 1974.[299] Though, as shall be shown, Gilmore was careless to the point of recklessness or indeed utter disingenuity in his historical assertions, leading to grave error (or deliberate deception), he was brilliantly articulate, had an acerbic wit, and incisively discerned the true nature and doctrinal ramifications of promissory estoppel. Several passages from *The Death of Contract*, in a section of that book ominously entitled "Decline and Fall," open a window into his thinking.[300]

As to the indeterminate contours of the doctrine:

> Section 90 is almost the only section of the *Restatement of Contracts* which has no Comment at all. Four hypothetical cases, none of them, so far as I know, based on a real case, are offered as "illustrations," presumably to indicate the range which the section was meant to have. An attentive study of the four illustrations will lead any analyst to the despairing conclusion, which is of course reinforced by the mysterious text of § 90 itself, that no one had any idea what the damn thing meant.[301]

What was clear is that promissory estoppel is directly antithetical to the core requirements of traditional contract law, namely, mutual agreement and mutual

[299] *See* GILMORE, *supra* note 13.

[300] *Id.* at 55 et seq.

[301] *Id.* at 64–65 (citation omitted). It is magnificent writing style, genuinely humorous, but inaccurate as to the illustrations not having been based on actual, real-world cases. As will be discussed *infra*, the first three of the total of four illustrations show factual situations where Williston intended promissory estoppel to apply; the final illustration is intended to show the contrary. Of those first three, illustration 1 is presumably based on Faxon v. Faxon, 28 Mich. 159, 159 (1873), and illustration 2 is manifestly based on Ricketts v. Scothorn, 77 N.W. 365 (Neb. 1898), in each instance with only minor alterations to the facts of those cases.

consideration. It purports to impose liability for unfulfilled "promise" even where those requirements have not been met:

> A remarkable passage in the Restatement (Second) § 90 Commentary explains how most "contract" cases, if not all of them, can be brought under § 90 so that resort to § 75 and consideration theory will rarely, if ever, be necessary. By passing through the magic gate of § 90, it seems, we can rid ourselves of all the technical limitations of contract theory.[302]

As a result, "the promissory estoppel principle of § 90 . . . has, in effect, swallowed up the bargain principle of § 75."[303]

Gilmore brought out the contradiction between preexisting contract law and the newly minted doctrine of promissory estoppel in all clarity:

> We have become accustomed to the idea . . . that the universe includes both matter and anti-matter. Perhaps what we have here is Restatement and anti-Restatement, or Contract and anti-Contract. We can be sure that [Oliver Wendell] Holmes, who relished a good paradox, would have laughed aloud at the sequence of § 75 [the mutual assent to a mutual exchange "bargain" requirement] and § 90 [promissory estoppel]. The one thing that is clear is that these two contradictory propositions cannot live comfortably together: in the end one must swallow the other up.[304]

As a result of this fundamental, irreconcilable tension, this artificial grafting of anti-Contract into the body of Contract, "[d]uring the past forty years we have seen the effective dismantling of the formal system of classical contract theory. We have witnessed what it does not seem too farfetched to describe as an explosion of liability."[305]

[302] GILMORE, *supra* note 13, at 90 (citation omitted). The specific passage in the comments to Section 90 referred to by Gilmore reads as follows: "This Section . . . states a basic principle which often renders inquiry unnecessary as to the precise scope of the policy of enforcing bargains." RESTATEMENT (SECOND), *supra* note 2, § 90, cmt. a.

[303] GILMORE, *supra* note 13, at 72.

First Restatement Section 75 defined the term "consideration" as an act, a forbearance, an alteration of legal relation, or a return promise, "bargained for and given in exchange for the promise." FIRST RESTATEMENT, *supra* note 2, § 75(1). The "bargain principle" referred to by Gilmore was also anchored in First Restatement Section 19(b): "The requirements of the law for the formation of an informal contract are . . . [a] manifestation of assent . . . by every promisor to the consideration for his promise. . . ."). *Id.* § 19(b).

In the Restatement (Second), the bargain principle is found not only in Section 75 ("[A] promise which is bargained for is consideration if, but only if, the promised performance would be consideration.") but more directly in Section 17(a) ("[t]he formation of a contract requires a bargain in which there is a manifestation of mutual assent to the exchange and a consideration") and Section 71 ("(1) To constitute consideration, a performance of a return promise must be bargained for. (2) A performance or return promise is bargained for if it is sought by the promisor in exchange for his promise and is given by the promisee in exchange for that promise."). RESTATEMENT (SECOND), *supra* note 2, §§ 17(a), 71, 75.

[304] GILMORE, *supra* note 13, at 61.

[305] *Id.* at 65.

Gilmore pressed the idea that traditional contract law is itself somehow descended from tort. That it constitutes a special application, a subset, as it were, of tort law. As has already been explored at length in this book, this assertion is historically unfounded. But under the impact of promissory estoppel:

> We are fast approaching the point . . . where any detriment reasonably incurred by a plaintiff in reliance on a defendant's assurances must be recompensed. When that point is reached, there is really no longer any viable distinction between liability in contact and liability in tort. We may take the fact that damages in contract have become indistinguishable from damages in tort as obscurely reflecting an instinctive, almost unconscious realization that the two fields, which had been artificially set apart, are gradually merging and becoming one.[306]

The historically and doctrinally objectionable assertions in this passage are manifest. As a minor point, his casual statement that damages in contract have become indistinguishable from damages in tort fails utterly to recognize that mental distress, pain and suffering, and punitive damages, while potential features of a monetary award in tort, are as a general rule not available in contract, for good and compelling reasons.[307] However, the major point, the critical error, is his claim that the two fields of contract and tort had been artificially separated. This reflects either ignorance of, or worse, refusal to acknowledge, the actual doctrinal development of both fields throughout the entire medieval and Renaissance periods of English legal history up through Slade's case in 1602. But Gilmore's central thesis is evident.

In summation, Gilmore stated:

> Speaking descriptively, we might say that what is happening is that "contract" is being reabsorbed into the mainstream of "tort." Until the general theory of contract was hurriedly run up late in the nineteenth century, tort had always been our residual category of civil liability. As the contract rules dissolve, it is becoming so again. It should be pointed out that the theory of tort into which contract is being reabsorbed is itself a much more expansive theory of liability than was the theory of tort from which contract was artificially separated a hundred years ago.
>
> . . . Classical contract theory might well be described as an attempt to stake out an enclave within the general domain of tort.[308]

As the history explored earlier in this book demonstrates, nothing could be further from the truth. As laid out in the first part of this book – and aside from "formal

[306] *Id.* at 88 (citation omitted). In the elided portion of this citation indicated by ellipsis, Gilmore referred to arriving also at a point "where, to prevent unjust enrichment, any benefit received by a defendant must be paid for unless it was clearly meant as a gift. . . ." *Id.* (citation omitted).

[307] For a discussion of the general rules in this regard, see E. Allan Farnsworth, Contracts § 12.17, at 934–35; § 12.8, at 874–75 (Boston, Little, Brown & Co. 2d ed. 1990). The comparative rarity of exceptional cases that deviate from the norm only serves to highlight general applicability of the standard rules.

[308] Gilmore, *supra* note 13, at 87 (citations omitted).

contract" due to its high admonitory and evidential character[309] – the fundamental nature of contract as consisting of mutually agreed mutual exchange had existed from the Romans, through the medieval period, through the Renaissance, through the Age of Revolutions and the early modern period, through the 1800s. This continued right up until the invention in the 1920s – and even here solely in the United States and not in the rest of the Anglosphere – of promissory estoppel. Gilmore's glib claim that some primordial soup of tort somehow preexisted contract, that contract was somehow derived from and crystallized out of tort, that "contract was artificially separated a hundred years ago"[310] from tort, and that the foundational doctrinal requirements of contract were somehow only "hurriedly run up late in the nineteenth century,"[311] is utterly alien to the actual historical record.

But never let facts stand in the way of good rhetoric.

10.2 "*Contorts*"

Consonant not only with his views but also with his evident ambition to efface the contours of contract and assist in its doctrinal demise, Gilmore suggested a novel but ultimately ill-fated pedagogical experiment – a newly conceived first year law school course to be entitled "Contorts":

> We seem to be in the presence of the phenomenon which, in the history of comparative religion, is called syncretism – that is, according to Webster, "the reconciliation or union of conflicting beliefs." I have occasionally suggested to my students that a desirable reform in legal education would be to merge the first-year courses in Contracts and Torts into a single course which we could call Contorts. Perhaps the same suggestion would be a good one when the time comes for the third round of Restatements.[312]

While enjoying a brief blush of popularity among some in the professoriate, this *soi-disant* Contorts course no longer features in the American legal academic landscape. Yet, though "Contorts" the course may apparently have been a bridge too far,

[309] And even here, as discussed earlier in this book, many if not most if not perhaps nearly all "formal contracts" sounding in debt upon obligation or covenant, may in fact have rested upon mutual exchange – merely that the existence of quid pro quo for the formal promise was not required explicitly to be stated as a necessary prerequisite to enforcement, due again to their high admonitory and evidential character arising from the procedures followed to enter in upon formal contract with its written parchment scrolls, ribbons, melted red wax, and personal seal dies, in a presumably largely illiterate age.

[310] *Id.* at 87.

[311] *Id.*

[312] *Id.* at 89–90.

this in no way impeded the doctrine of promissory estoppel and its collateral implications from storming and conquering the American judicial landscape.[313]

10.3 *Colleagues Chime In*

Nor was Gilmore alone in his doctrinal and interpretive views. A number of other academic commentators, quite likely inspired at least in part by his example, joined Gilmore rhetorically in proclaiming, as it were, the ongoing sack of Rome.

Professor Patrick Atiyah seconded this sentiment in speaking of the "classical model, even while its basis is crumbling on all sides,"[314] and "The Failure of Classical Law."[315] And Professors Michael Metzger and Michael Phillips elegantly drew upon Karl Marx's dark portrayal of the rising communist threat to the free market world order:[316]

> A specter is haunting the law of contracts. The doctrine of promissory estoppel has evolved from relatively modest beginnings as a "consideration substitute" in donative promise cases to a force that threatens to engulf a major portion of contract law.... To the extent that this evolution continues, the future of many traditional contract rules, such as the parol evidence rule, is doubtful.[317]

[313] Beyond the scope of this book are distinct, more recent usages of the term "contort" in reference to breach of contract disputes which might additionally or alternatively involve either traditional, or entirely novel and highly disputed, tort claims. For discussion, see, e.g., Jim Walter Homes v. Reed, 711 S.W.2d 617 (Tex. 1986); Southwestern Bell Tel. Co. v. DeLanney, 809 S.W.2d 493 (Tex. 1991); Erin Hopkins, *Contort vs. Tort: Are We There Yet?*, 49-Aug. HOUS. LAW. 16 (2011); Matthew J. Barrett, *"Contort": Tortious Breach of the Implied Covenant of Good Faith and Fair Dealing in Noninsurance Commercial Contracts – Its Existence and Desirability*, 60 NOTRE DAME L. REV. 510 (1984–85).

[314] P. S. ATIYAH, THE RISE AND FALL OF FREEDOM OF CONTRACT 691 (1979).

[315] *Id.* at 693.

[316] KARL MARX & FRIEDRICH ENGELS, MANIFEST DER KOMMUNISTISCHEN PARTEI [MANIFESTO OF THE COMMUNIST PARTY] 3 (London, J. C. Burghard 1848) ("Ein Gespenst geht um in Europa – das Gespenst des Kommunismus." ["A specter is haunting Europe – the specter of communism."])

[317] Michael B. Metzger & Michael J. Phillips, *Promissory Estoppel and Third Parties*, 42 SW. L.J. 931, 967 (1988).

Part III

The Critique

The report of my death was an exaggeration.[318]
—Mark Twain

These dire prognoses by Gilmore and his fellow physicians as to the imminent demise of contract law bring the patient now into the operating room. Surgical excision of the metastatic doctrinal cancer commences here, with a detailed forensic investigation into, and rebuttal of, the historical and precedential claims asserted by the janissaries of promissory estoppel.

11 CLAIMS TO HISTORICAL PRECEDENT

What made the propagandistic effort to sell the newfound doctrine of promissory estoppel to the professoriate, the judiciary, and the bar, so devastatingly effective was the intellectual sleight of hand employed. An alien incursion into the body of contract law might have excited a normal and salutary immune response. But if the inoculation were disguised as something not actually alien at all, the body might fail to recognize it for the pathogen it truly was.

Two main elements of *maskirovka*[319] were employed. First, Williston asserted that during the medieval and later development of contract law, enforcement was predicated doctrinally upon unfulfilled promise, without regard to whether that promise had been compensated – that is, without regard to the presence or absence of reciprocity, of mutual exchange. Second, he asserted the existence of a vast array of exceptions to the consideration requirement in more modern caselaw.

[318] Statement by Mark Twain [Samuel Langhorne Clemens], during interview in London, England (June 1, 1897), *in* Frank Marshall White, *Mark Twain Amused*, N.Y. JOURNAL, June 2, 1897, at 1, *reprinted in* MARK TWAIN: THE COMPLETE INTERVIEWS, interview 121, at 317 (Gary Scharnhorst ed., Tuscaloosa, Univ. Ala. Press 2006).

[319] In the original Russian, *maskirovka* [маскировка] is "masking," "disguise," or "camouflage." OXFORD RUSSIAN DICTIONARY 213 (Oxford Univ. Press 4th ed. 2007).

That is, Williston in essence claimed that contract law in its genesis really was promissory estoppel, and that the entire structure of modern contract law was riddled with pockets of innominate promissory estoppel. This hypodermic syringe contains nothing really novel or concerning at all. Just take the shot.

11.1 *The Medieval and Renaissance Period*

The core assertion by Williston as to the development of contract law in medieval and later times focused on assumpsit.

To reprise in brief the discussion earlier in this book, assumpsit was a specific form of claim that had originally sprouted from the seedbed of the tort of trespass. While the royal writ of trespass initially addressed massive physical violence, over the course of time it was incrementally expanded to embrace economic harms. Tortious allegations of this kind required more particularized description, referred to as trespass on the special case, and ultimately simply an action on the "case." Assumpsit was one of the types of claim that could be made in an action on the case, alleging that someone had promised to perform some act, had failed so to perform or had done so in a manner causing harm, and that damages should therefore be imposed.

Were the story to begin and end there, perhaps Williston might have had a leg to stand on. But such was not the case. He ignored, perhaps out of ignorance, or perhaps – as will become evident in the discussion later on – quite likely deliberately, the two central facts of how and why assumpsit developed as it did.

First, assumpsit came to be used in cases of contractual nonfeasance precisely in order creatively to circumvent a defendant's otherwise available, nearly unassailable, defense of "wager of law." That is, assumpsit was used as a procedural workaround.

Second, contemporaneous with that extension of assumpsit into purely contractual nonfeasance – as distinct from tortious negligence – such use of assumpsit was coupled with a requirement that there have been reciprocity, a mutual exchange.

That is, assumpsit could be used as a writ sounding in tort when negligence or fraud was present. Or as a writ sounding in contract when reciprocity – that is, mutual exchange – was present. But Williston's entire premise, to be discussed later, that assumpsit could be used successfully to impose liability in the absence of either tortious or contractual predicate, as promissory estoppel purports to do, is not borne out by the historical record.

11.1.1 Samuel Williston and James Barr Ames

One of Williston's own teachers at Harvard Law School was Professor James Barr Ames, a legal historian who served as dean of the school for many years.[320] It was

[320] Professor Ames joined the Harvard Law School faculty in the early 1870s, and served as Dean from 1985 to 1910. JAMES BARR AMES, LECTURES ON LEGAL HISTORY AND MISCELLANEOUS LEGAL ESSAYS 5–7 (Cambridge, Harvard Univ. Press 1913).

upon certain statements made by Ames that Williston founded his case for assumpsit having constituted, in effect, proto promissory estoppel.

At the outset, a striking feature of Williston's assertions in this respect should be noted, namely, the extreme paucity of Williston's historical analysis or evidentiary support for a claim of historicity manifestly intended to revolutionize the entire field of contract law. This should almost always be considered a "red flag" in discussions of legal and intellectual history, and such assertions treated with appropriate caution.

Williston's historical exegesis of the early development of contract law and assumpsit comprises the following brief remarks of his own, and three short, clearly carefully selected and – in modern parlance, "curated" – quotes from Ames' well-known lecture series on legal history:

> The action of Assumpsit was originally based on reliance by the plaintiff on a promise rather than on a bargain. It was not until the old action of Debt was swallowed and extended by the action of assumpsit that the idea of exchanging consideration as the price of a promise became the predominant one. Professor Ames in his History of Assumpsit (Lectures on Legal History, page 142), summing up a preceding argument, says:
>
> > "The gist of the action being the deceit in breaking a promise on the faith of which the plaintiff had been induced to part with his money or other property" etc.
>
> Mr. Ames further says (page 143):
>
> > "That equity gave relief, before 1500, to a plaintiff who had incurred detriment on the faith of the defendant's promise, is reasonably clear, although there are but three reported cases."
>
> and (page 144):
>
> > "Both in equity and at law, therefore, a remediable breach of a parol promise was originally conceived of as a deceit; that is, a tort. Assumpsit was in several instances distinguished from contract."[321]

That's it. The whole thing. Upon these sweeping statements – as so interpreted by Williston – and without description of further investigation or support, contract law was to be upended.

The lectures set forth in this written source, collectively entitled "Points in Legal History," were originally conducted as a series by Ames in 1886–87, and many were also published in Harvard Law Review or the Green Bag. *Id.* at v.

[321] Williston, *First Restatement Commentaries*, *supra* note 29, at 14 (with minor, nonsubstantive formatting correction of indentational error in original as applied to the words "and (page 144):").

Williston's page references to Ames are to the full collection of Ames' lecture series set forth in AMES, *supra* note 320.

It therefore becomes absolutely crucial to inquire into the perspicacity of Ames' statements, and indeed, whether Ames' statements have been fairly and accurately relayed by Williston. Here, very serious objections arise.

11.1.1.1 FIRST AMES QUOTE: MUTUAL EXCHANGE CASES. To take the first quote from Ames, one immediately notes the cryptic "etc." supplied by Williston at the end of the quoted text. And it is wise to have noted that apparently innocuous abridgement and its potential implications. The "etc." in fact stands place for the following additional words in the original text of Ames' lecture: "it was obviously *immaterial whether the promisor or a third person got the benefit* of what the plaintiff gave up."[322] Moreover, the partially quoted sentence in fact was the lead sentence in an exegetical paragraph that Ames summed up with the following conclusion: "From that day to this a detriment has always been deemed a valid consideration for a promise if incurred at the promisor's request."[323]

To make the obvious point, if a detriment has been incurred at the promisor's request, the situation in hand is one that features reciprocity: whatever was promised, in exchange for the requested detriment. Both mutual assent and mutual consideration are present. That is, contract, properly understood. Ames' point was that the specific benefit arising from the detriment so incurred could run, at promisor's request, to a third party specified by the promisor, without vitiating the exchange character of the transaction and thus its contractual enforceability.

Thus, Williston, by elegant elision, took a statement by Ames concerning the enforceability of contract predicated upon mutual exchange, and presented it to his audience as a statement to the effect that no mutual exchange is necessary. That is, a statement having nothing whatsoever to do with the fundamental premise of promissory estoppel was transmogrified into one of the very cornerstones upon which the new doctrine was to be justified. It is difficult to see how this citation to Ames' writing could have been made in intellectual good faith.

11.1.1.2 SECOND AMES QUOTE: PROMISSORY FRAUD CASES. The second passage from Ames' lecture series cited by Williston commenced of course with the weighty words, "That equity gave relief, before 1500, to a plaintiff who had incurred detriment on the faith of the defendant's promise, is reasonably clear...."[324] In the context of an attempted justification of promissory estoppel, this statement, taken alone and out of context, is clearly pregnant with potential significance.

One notes at the end of the passage from Ames cited by Williston the limiting words, "although there are but three reported cases."[325] As it turns out, careful

322 AMES, *supra* note 320, at 142; James Barr Ames, *The History of Assumpsit*, 2 HARV. L. REV. 14 (1888) (emphasis added).

323 AMES, *supra* note 320, at 143 (citation omitted); Ames, *supra* note 322, at 14 (citation omitted).

324 AMES, *supra* note 320, at 143; Ames, *supra* note 322, at 14.

325 AMES, *supra* note 320, at 143 (citation omitted); Ames, *supra* note 322, at 14.

examination reveals that Ames addressed these equity – that is, Chancery, rather than common law – cases in two sequential lectures, respectively entitled "Simple Contracts Prior to Assumpsit," followed immediately by "Express Assumpsit."[326] Moreover, the evidential basis for Ames' statement is even broader than just those three cases mentioned in the later occurring "Express Assumpsit" lecture. The statement about relief for the plaintiff who had incurred detriment on the faith of the defendant's promise is made in both lectures in substantively the same language, and both lectures either cross-reference each other or refer to the same underlying cases on point.[327] As it turns out, the earlier occurring "Contracts Prior to Assumpsit" lecture mentions not only the three cases referred to in the later "Express Assumpsit" lecture cited by Williston but also three additional cases along the same lines, for a total of six.[328] The two lectures in which Ames discussed these cases, all to similar substantive effect, explicitly cross-referencing each other or the same underlying cases, must therefore be read together in this context as a unified whole.

Even with this additional caselaw support, however, given that there are only a total of six Chancery cases referred to and discussed by Ames in this connection, actually reading what Ames had to say about them in greater detail turns out to be worth the effort.[329] What one quickly discovers is that these cases – with only one possible exception, open to arguable interpretation – all appear to have concerned promissory fraud, rather than promissory estoppel. That is, they involved conscious, deliberate deceit on the part of the promisor – the hallmark of promissory fraud – rather than simple nonperformance,the hallmark of promissory estoppel. This point is critical.

Nor is this merely a latter-day interpretation by the Author of Ames' intended point. Ames himself explicitly described these cases as predicated upon fraud:

> It was so obviously just that one who had *intentionally misled* another to his detriment should make good the loss, that we need not go further afield for an explanation of the Chancellor's readiness to give a remedy upon such parol agreements.[330]

So that the reader can review directly what Ames spoke of in his lectures, without simply having to take the Author's word for it, here is his discussion of those six cases:

> In one of them, in 1378, the defendant promised to convey certain land to the plaintiff, who, trusting in the promise, paid out money in traveling to London and consulting counsel; and upon the defendant's refusal to convey, prayed for a

[326] Ames, *supra* note 320, at 122–48.
[327] *Id.* at 126, 143 n.6.
[328] *Id.* (citation omitted): "Three such instances, between 1377 and 1468, are mentioned in the next lecture. Those instances may be supplemented by three similar cases which were brought to light by Mr. S. R. Bird."
[329] *Id.* at 126–27, 144; Ames, *supra* note 322, at 14–15.
[330] Ames, *supra* note 320, at 127 (emphasis added).

subpoena to compel the defendant to answer of his "*disceit.*" *The bill sounds in tort rather than in contract,* and inasmuch as even *cestuis que use* could not compel a conveyance by their feoffees to use at this time, its object was doubtless not specific performance, but reimbursement for the expenses incurred. *Appilgarth v. Sergeantson* (1438) was also a bill for *restitutio in integrum, savoring strongly of tort.* It was brought against a defendant who had obtained the plaintiff's money by promising to marry her, and who had then married another in "*grete deceit.*" The remaining case, thirty years later, having induced the plaintiff to become the procurator of his benefice, by a promise to save him harmless for the occupancy, *secretly* resigned his benefice, and the plaintiff, being afterwards vexed for the occupancy, obtained relief by subpoena.[331]

In *Gardyner v. Keche* (1452–1454), Margaret and Alice Gardyner promised to pay the defendant £22, "*meaning but craft and disceyt,*" married another woman, "*to the great disceyt* of the said suppliants, and ageyne all good reason and conscience." The defendant was compelled to answer the bill. In *Leinster v. Narborough* (*circa* 1480), the defendant being betrothed to the plaintiff's daughter-in-law, but desiring to go to Padua to study law, requested the plaintiff to maintain his *fiancée,* and a maidservant to attend upon her during his absence, and promised to repay upon his return all costs and charges incurred by the plaintiff in that behalf. The defendant returning after ten years declined to fulfill his promise, and the plaintiff filed his bill for reimbursement, and was successful. In *James v. Morgan* (1504–1515), the defendant promised the plaintiff 100 marks if he would marry his daughter Elizabeth. The plaintiff accordingly "resorted to the said Elizabeth to his great costs and charges," and "thorow the desavebull comforde" of the defendant and his daughter delivered to the latter jewels, ribbons, and many other small tokens. Elizabeth having married another man through the "*crafty and false meane*" of the defendant, the plaintiff by his bill sought to recover the value of his tokens, and also the "gret costs and charges thorow his manyfold journeys."[332]

As is reasonably manifest, all of these cases, as so described in the text, involved fraud. The only truly possible exception might be the *Leinster* case involving the man who welched out on paying for expenses incurred on the home front while he spent ten years in Italy, though even there the fact pattern is redolent of potentially conscious mendacity. And that is certainly how Ames saw things, as he considered all six cases to fall under one single, unified rubric, which he summed up as follows: "Chancery gave relief upon parol agreements only upon the ground of compelling reparation *for what was regarded as a tort* to the plaintiff, or upon the principle of preventing the unjust enrichment of the defendant. . . .[333]

[331] AMES, *supra* note 320, at 143–44 (emphasis added, other than with respect to the Latin phrases and the word "grete," which are italicized in the original) (citations omitted); Ames, *supra* note 322, at 14 (emphasis added as just indicated) (citations omitted).

[332] AMES, *supra* note 320, at 126 (emphasis added, other than with respect to the words "circa" and "fiancée," which are italicized in the original) (citation omitted).

[333] *Id.* at 128 (emphasis added).

To drive the point home, then: The second Ames quote cited by Williston does not deal with or provide support for the doctrine of promissory estoppel. Rather, it merely illustrates the manner in which Chancery addressed promissory fraud, either in tort or in restitution "savoring strongly of tort."[334]

11.1.1.3 THIRD AMES QUOTE: RECIPROCITY REQUIRED. Like the second Ames quote, the third likewise appears, on its face, pregnant with potential support for Williston's – and later Gilmore's – theses. Yet again, however, there occur omissions of massive significance.

To reprise, the third passage as quoted by Williston read: "Both in equity and law, therefore, a remediable breach of a parol promise was originally conceived of as a deceit; that is, a tort. Assumpsit was in several instances distinguished from contract."

Taken in context of the whole lecture, which is absolutely worth reading in its entirety to achieve full perspective, what Ames herewith summarized were the following lines of cases. To begin with, the "deceit" cases in Chancery ("equity") that, as we have just seen, involved promissory fraud, rather than promissory estoppel. Next, early common law assumpsit cases in which the claim was predicated upon negligence – thus tort – and where no mutual exchange, no reciprocity, was thus requisite to maintain the claim. And, finally, later common law assumpsit cases in which no negligence was present, but where the claim was laid in assumpsit because the plaintiff had no deed necessary to bring the claim in covenant, and was used as a procedural workaround to circumvent the absence of a defendant's wager of law defense that would have been available had the claim been brought in debt sur contract.

These first two categories are of no further consequence for our discussion here, as they in no way, shape, or form constitute precedent for promissory estoppel. They involve genuinely tortious conduct, recognized as such at that time and ever since.

It is with the third category we must concern ourselves. These are the later common law assumpsit cases where there was no negligence. There was no tortious malfeasance, but rather simple nonfeasance. If one cannot allege negligence, might one be able to allege fraud, in order to invoke assumpsit?

Here, we must return to the extended discussion earlier in this book of the seminal precedent in this regard, *Doige's Case* of 1442.[335] In that case, buyer paid seller for certain land, and the seller, "craftily scheming to defraud" the seller, sold the land to a third party. Seller had no deed requisite for a claim in covenant, and thus brought the case in deceit. The court reasoned that since the seller could have sued the buyer in debt if buyer had failed to pay, and that every contract involves mutual obligation, that is, mutual exchange, therefore the suit in deceit must be allowed. Thus, the true doctrinal basis of the case in fact rested in contractual

[334] AMES, *supra* note 320, at 143–44; Ames, *supra* note 322, at 14.

[335] *Doige's Case*, *supra* note 143, and accompanying text.

reciprocity, despite being formally, procedurally brought as a tort claim. Following that case, it became routine for practitioners to allege fraud and deceit pretextually – entirely in the absence of any proof or particularized demonstration thereof – simply for the purpose of invoking the more advantageous procedure of assumpsit as compared to either covenant or debt sur contract.[336] And as they did so, given that the true basis of the claim lay in reciprocity, in mutual exchange, thus in contract, rather than tort, the merely pretextual allegation of fraud and deceit became standard boilerplate, recognized and accepted as a legal fiction. And it is from the truly exchange-based, contractual nature of the underlying claim that the requirement for reciprocity, for mutual consideration, as a prerequisite to such use of assumpsit was repeatedly articulated and ultimately formalized in the years following.

Accordingly, we see Ames, literally immediately after the text quoted by Williston, continue with the following concession, fatal to Williston's promissory estoppel implication: "By a natural transition, however, actions upon parol promises came to be regarded as actions *ex contractu*."[337] Hence, the reciprocity requirement read into assumpsit actions not predicated upon negligence. After discussing the state of the law in the early 1500s – that is, after *Doige's Case* – as already cited earlier in this book's analysis of the first Ames quote – Ames said: "From that day to this a detriment has always been deemed a valid consideration for a promise if incurred at the promisor's request."[338] This phrase, "if incurred at the promisor's request," is the absolute crux of the matter, as it denotes the mutual exchange character of a transaction – promised action or forbearance by promisor in exchange for action or forbearance by promisee – that is, reciprocity. Deep, detailed examination of the evolution of assumpsit to address simple nonfeasance cases thus puts to rest the idea that there ever existed some notional halcyon, idyllic period of medieval promissory estoppel.

11.1.1.4 THE "ORIGIN" OF CONSIDERATION. To step back for a moment, from the three very brief Ames passages cited by Williston, to one of Ames' broader objectives in his lecture, one sees that Ames was interested in the so-called origin or source of consideration.

The very inquiry, however, is not well conceived from the outset. "Consideration" was a term first used in the 1500s, and terminologically cemented firmly in place by the end of that century.[339] It meant nothing other than that which one does, or

[336] Baker, *Origins of the "Doctrine" of Consideration*, *supra* note 158, at 356: "[T]he main reason for the delictual approach was to find a justification for using actions on the case instead of 'general' writs of debt or covenant...."

[337] AMES, *supra* note 320, at 144 (citation omitted); Ames, *supra* note 322, at 15 (citation omitted).

[338] AMES, *supra* note 320, at 143 (citation omitted); Ames, *supra* note 322, at 14 (citation omitted).

[339] *See supra* Chapter 3.2.4.2.

forbears to do, in exchange for, as payment for, some act or forbearance promised by the other party. That's it. It's that simple.

The term "consideration" is nothing more than a convenient, easy-to-use "handle," as it were, when discussing whether mutual exchange, reciprocity, existed in a given situation. It's simply a name given to preexisting, entirely familiar concept. It is not some strange, alien, inscrutable intellectual construct of unknown origin shrouded in mystery. There is no special, occult magic to the term.

And as we have seen – from Roman times; through the elite colonization of England by the Normans and the continental European, hence Roman law educated, scholars they brought to Westminster; through Bracton's treatise on English substantive law, all written in Latin and often using identical terminology as had appeared in the late Roman Digest of Justinian; through the English judges speaking solemnly over the centuries in Latin phraseology of the requirement in contract of *quid pro quo*, and intoning the formula that *ex nudo pacto nulla oritur actio*; and ultimately through the use of the term "consideration" to describe what one side provides as one half of an exchange transaction, and "mutual consideration" to describe both sides of the exchange transaction – the principle and requirement of reciprocity was the constant backdrop to enforcement of informal, "parol," contract. The creative use of assumpsit to dodge certain procedural features of covenant and debt sur contract did not change that. The contractual use of assumpsit had to conform itself to the requirements of contract, not the other way around.

Ames, however, made reference to an academic debate of the day as to the origin of the term "consideration," commencing his lecture on "Express Assumpsit" with this passage:

> The mystery of consideration has possessed a peculiar fascination for writers upon the English Law of Contract. No fewer than three distinct theories of its origin have been put forward within the last eight years. According to one view [Oliver Wendell Holmes], "the requirement of consideration in all parol contracts is simply a modified generalization of *quid pro quo* to raise a debt by parol." On the other hand [Salmond], consideration is described as a modification of the Roman principle of *causa*, adopted by equity, and transferred thence into the common law." A third learned writer [Hare] derives the action of assumpsit from the action on the case for deceit, the damage to the plaintiff in that action being the forerunner of the "detriment to the promisee," which constitutes the consideration of all parol contracts.[340]

Based on the entire discussion in this book, it is clear that Oliver Wendell Holmes' theory, as described by Ames, is essentially correct. The requirement of

[340] Ames, *supra* note 320, at 129 (citations omitted); Ames, *supra* note 322, at 1 (citations omitted). Ames in his footnotes to this passage credited these three distinct theories, as he saw them, to (i) Oliver Wendell Holmes and C. C. Langdell, Ames' predecessor as Dean of Harvard Law School; (ii) Professor and Justice Sir John Salmond of New Zealand; and (iii) Judge John Innes Clark Hare.

mutual consideration to form an enforceable contract is literally identical to a requirement of quid pro quo to do the same.

As to Salmond's theory, the description by Ames raises the possibility that there might perhaps be some misapprehension either as to the meaning of the Latin word *causa*, as used by the Romans in contract law, or the nature of its use by English canonists in the Middle Ages. To recall, the single example in the Digest of Justinian to explain the meaning of the term *causa* as a requirement of enforceable contract, is that it denotes a reciprocal obligation by the promisee.[341] That is, mutual exchange, reciprocity. A promise without *causa* was, in the Digest of Justinian, a naked promise, *nudum pactum*, one without reciprocal obligation by the promisee, and thus unenforceable.[342] To the extent that medieval church canon law may have attempted to fundamentally alter the true substantive meaning of *causa* from mutual exchange, into naked, uncompensated promise, the canonists had departed from Roman law.[343] But that departure by the canonists was not adopted by the English courts as the law of contract.[344] To speak of *causa* in its true, original Roman sense, it signifies quid pro quo, reciprocity, mutual exchange.

As to himself, although Ames initially wrote that "[t]o the present writer it seems impossible to refer consideration to a single source,"[345] it is nonetheless clear that he favored the third enumerated view, namely, Hare's thesis. Ames wrote in partial summation of his lecture: "The view here advanced as to the origin of special assumpsit, although reached by an independent process, accords with, it will be seen, and confirms, it is hoped, the theory first advanced by Judge HARE."[346]

To reprise, Ames stated that Hare "derives the action of assumpsit from the action on the case for deceit, the damage to the plaintiff in that action being the forerunner of the 'detriment to the promisee,' which constitutes the consideration of all parol contracts."[347] Here, we have arrived at what appears to be clear error in analysis, as best explained by the great John Baker of Cambridge:

> [W]e must face the near impossibility of linking either the delictual history or the substantive principle with the "doctrine" of consideration in the way suggested by Hare and Ames. The elements of deceit and consequential loss were never incorporated in the consideration clause, but were destined to wither away as fictions. And in the cases that established "detriment to the promisee" as good consideration, the consideration in question had nothing in common with the earlier deceit cases: it was a reciprocal future act, or a promise to act, by the plaintiff.[348]

[341] *See supra* notes 50–53 and accompanying text.
[342] *Id.*
[343] *See supra* Chapter 2.1.
[344] *See id.*
[345] AMES, *supra* note 320, at 129 (citation omitted); Ames, *supra* note 322, at 1 (citation omitted).
[346] AMES, *supra* note 320, at 145; Ames, *supra* note 322, at 16.
[347] AMES, *supra* note 320, at 129 (citation omitted); Ames, *supra* note 322, at 1 (citation omitted).
[348] Baker, *Origins of the "Doctrine" of Consideration*, *supra* note 158, at 357.

11.1.1.5 WILLISTON'S MEDIEVAL AND RENAISSANCE CLAIM COLLAPSES. This concludes the forensic investigation into Williston's reliance on three brief, deracinated quotes from one single source as the totality of his supposed support for promissory estoppel having existed in the Middle Ages and Renaissance period. The investigation here has established that none of the three passages from Ames quoted by Williston provides such support.

And this claim of ancient historicity was the principal, weight-bearing column for Williston's assertion that promissory estoppel should be seen as having legitimacy, an ancient pedigree, rather than merely constituting some ill-advised conceptual parvenu. When one blows out the supporting pillars, the structure collapses.

11.1.2 Arthur Corbin

As noted earlier, Williston's strong right hand during the ALI's First Restatement drafting process was Arthur Corbin of Yale, who served as a formally designated advisor to Williston and as reporter for the restatement's "Remedies" chapter.[349] In 1950, Corbin also published his own massive treatise on contract law, much like Williston had done back in 1920.[350] Corbin acted as a strong ally and confrere of Williston in advocating the new doctrine of promissory estoppel.[351]

Corbin was even more bold, more unambiguous, and thus even more clearly wrong in his statements as to Anglo-American legal history than Williston. Compounding the erroneous statements was an equally cavalier attitude to providing actual historical precedent and analysis for his assertions. As Corbin proclaimed in his treatise:

> It is now quite clear that an informal promise may be enforceable by reason of action in reliance upon it, even though that action was not bargained for by the promisor and was not performed as an agreed exchange for the promise. This is demonstrated by the decisions of the courts of common law from the very beginnings of the action of assumpsit. . . .[352]

This assertion is at odds with the entire historical exegesis set forth in this book. "Black is white, and white is black." Boldly stating an untruth does not render it true.

In like vein:

> The action of assumpsit, a variation of the action of trespass on the special case, was the first action used and intended for the enforcement of informal promises. The breach of a promise was regarded as a sort of deceit; and the remedy was compensatory damages for the injury caused by the promisee's action in reasonable

[349] FIRST RESTATEMENT, *supra* note 2, at ix–x.

[350] *See supra* note 223.

[351] As to speculation on the extent and nature of Corbin's role in the genesis and early marketing of promissory estoppel, see *id.*

[352] 1A CORBIN, *supra* note 223, at 193.

> reliance. This was one of the germs from which the doctrine of consideration sprung; and from that day to this the courts have been familiar with the idea of reliance on a promise as a reason for enforcement. There is certainly no historical inconsistency in the rule stated by the America Law Institute in section 90.[353]

This statement likewise misstates the historical record, which shows only that reliance – a "detriment" – which has been bargained for by the promisor, and is thus part of a mutual exchange, is enforceable in contract.

Corbin's passage also bears the obvious error of stating that assumpsit "was the first action used and intended for the enforcement of informal promises."[354] Nothing could be further from the truth. The principal writ for enforcing informal promises – that is, those not evidenced and thus "formalized" by a deed – had long been debt sur contract, as copiously discussed earlier in this book.[355] Assumpsit was brought into play precisely as procedural legerdemain to evade the affirmative defense of wager of law available in debt sur contract.

Enough said.

11.1.3 Grant Gilmore

Nor do we fare much better with the historical record when we get to Grant Gilmore in the 1970s. To recall, Gilmore stated in *The Death of Contract*:

> Until the general theory of contract was hurriedly run up late in the nineteenth century, tort had always been our residual category of civil liability. As the contract rules dissolve, it is becoming so again. It should be pointed out that the theory of tort into which contract is being reabsorbed is itself a much more expansive theory of liability than was the theory of tort from which contract was artificially separated a hundred years ago.[356]

A reader might well be forgiven for understanding Gilmore's statement that "the general theory of contract was hurriedly run up late in the nineteenth century" to imply that contract was somehow unformed, inchoate, prior to such time. As this entire book demonstrates, that is not the case.

A defender of Gilmore might hang their hat on the word "general," pointing to the particularized, thus arguably not "general," forms of contractual writs during the Middle Ages, namely, debt sur contract, debt sur obligation, and covenant. But even then, by *Slade's Case* in 1602, the law of informal contract had for most purposes in practical effect become centralized under assumpsit, subject to the requirement that there have been consideration given for any promise to be enforced.

[353] *Id.* at 198–99 (citing Ames, *supra* note 320).
[354] *Id.*
[355] *See supra* Chapter 3.1.2.1.
[356] Gilmore, *supra* note 13, at 87 (citations omitted).

Perhaps they might point to the various further elaborations of contract law, especially those related to offer and acceptance, during the 1800s, as a basis for concluding that Gilmore's statement was not misleading. But the fact remains that for centuries prior to the late 1800s referred to by Gilmore, the essential contractual prerequisites of agreement – thus mutual assent – and reciprocity – thus mutual consideration – had been laid down. This is the beating heart of contract. Moreover, as explained by Professor David Ibbetson: "Many of the rules found in the classical model of contract of the nineteenth-century writers were worked out in this period; *and nearly all of these were deductions from the general principle of reciprocity*."[357] A reader might well be forgiven for understanding Gilmore's statement to imply that contract law only truly crystallized conceptually in the late 1800s. Such an implication would not be accurate. Doctrinally speaking, in the 1800s work may have been done on the cabinetry and laying the carpet, but centuries before that the foundation had been laid, the frame of the structure erected, and the roof put on.

Further, and significantly, Gilmore's statement overlooks the complex development of tort law itself, which likewise occurred over the course of many centuries and did not predate contract law.[358] If anything, the evolution and expansion of tort from its origins in physical harm into economic and other harms,[359] and the "rise of negligence,"[360] is far more dramatic than the changes, more of procedural form than essential substantive and conceptual framework, that occurred in contract.

Finally, his assertion that contract was "artificially separated" from tort "a hundred years ago," that is, in the mid to late 1800s, is historically incomprehensible. Contract and tort have always been separate. The instrumentalization of assumpsit to circumvent wager of law did not alter this verity one bit. As explained by Professor Ibbetson at Cambridge University, the home of our culture's leading legal historians: "*In medieval law informal contracts were enforceable only if they were reciprocal: the debtor must have received something in exchange*, quid pro quo."[361] He continued: "*[T]he introduction of the action of assumpsit did not herald any wholesale shift from*

[357] IBBETSON, *supra* note 37, at 143 (emphasis added).

[358] *See id.* In his book, Professor Ibbetson renders an excellent account and exegesis of the historical development of not only contract, but also tort.

[359] *See id.* at 66.

[360] *See id.* at 169:

> The law of torts at the beginning of the nineteenth century was still recognizably medieval. It was characterized by a division between the action of trespass and the action on the case, the latter of which was subdivided into a number of nominate forms and a large residuary group linked together by nothing stronger than that the defendant was alleged to have caused loss to the plaintiff. In the nineteenth century a substantial part of this residuary group coalesced as the tort of negligence. This brought about a wholesale realignment of the law of torts, as this tort, defined by reference to the quality of the defendant's conduct, cut across the previously existing categorization of torts.

[361] *Id.* at 141 (emphasis added).

the exchange model of contract that had prevailed in the fourteenth and fifteenth centuries. . . ."[362]

Thus, we see in the wake of *Slade's Case* of 1602 the following clear and definitive doctrinal statement from the King's Bench in the 1618 case of *Hurford v. Pile*:

> A person who promises cannot countermand and recall his own promise, because *every assumpsit is made by the mutual agreement of both parties and on reciprocal considerations, and through this creates a contract* . . . and because of this the person who assumes cannot make a countermand, for a bargain is a bargain and a contract is a contract. . . .[363]

As accordingly demonstrated, "by the beginning of the seventeenth century at the latest *assumpsit* had to all intents and purposes *adopted the structure of contractual liability found in the medieval law*."[364] Consequently, wrote Ibbetson, "two phenomena" with respect to assumpsit may be observed:

> First of all is the fact that the courts did not treat all actions of assumpsit as equivalent, all based on the wrong of breach of promise. On the contrary, they were willing to look beyond the formal façade of the action at the substance that lay beneath, and they did not baulk at characterizing it as contractual. Secondly, from quite early in the sixteenth century the contractual underpinning of liability in assumpsit was moulding the form that the action was taking, so that by the beginning of the seventeenth it was clear that *the action could in fact be divided into two distinct types: a contractual type* where the plaintiff complained of non-performance, *and a tortious type* where the action was grounded on mis-performance.[365]

What we have, then, with Gilmore's characterization of the historical record of contract and tort, is nothing more than smoke, mirrors, and misdirection.

11.1.4 Eric Mills Holmes

This brings us to the rather extraordinary fealty to the new doctrine of promissory estoppel evinced by Professor Eric Mills Holmes of Willamette University in more recent times. In the past several decades, Professor E. M. Holmes profiled himself as perhaps the most passionate and dedicated recent proponent of the doctrine.

E. M. Holmes took the claims and intimations of his predecessor paladins of promissory estoppel and refined and amplified them to the extent that he has now completely inverted the actual history of contract law and its core doctrines. This

[362] *Id.* at 145 (emphasis added).

[363] Cro. Jac. 483; Ro. 21, 39 (*sub nom. Winter v. Foweracres*); HLS MS 105f f.291; LI MS Misc. 791d ff.80ᵛ, 85ᵛ (emphasis added); *cited and discussed by* IBBETSON, *supra* note 37, at 139–40.

[364] IBBETSON, *supra* note 37, at 135 (emphasis added).

[365] *Id.* at 134–35 (emphasis added).

inversion may be observed in the following series of passages from two law review articles he published in 1996.

Claiming an "ancient genealogy in common law and equity" for promissory estoppel, E. M. Holmes wrote that

> the doctrine now labeled "promissory estoppel" is not a modern, twentieth-century development arising from Section 90 of the Restatements. Rather, it is a venerable, ancient form of relief with historical origins in both the common law action of assumpsit and early equity decisions. . . . "[P]romissory estoppel" is an ancient form of consideration pre-dating the modern bargain theory of consideration by about five centuries.
>
> In light of the doctrine's history, it could be labeled consideration or, perhaps, reliance consideration, instead of "promissory estoppel."[366]

To drive his historical assertion home, he continued: "With the triumph of assumpsit over equity in the 1500s, what we now refer to as 'promissory estoppel' relief was generally granted at common law."[367] This claim by E. M. Holmes is, of course, as we have seen, fiction.

Explaining his newfound concept of "reliance consideration" in further detail, E. M. Holmes wrote:

> Based on its origins in ancient equity and assumpsit, judicial relief for detrimental reliance on promises in modern times generally should be classified as consideration. Accordingly, this would eliminate the need for new terminology such as promissory estoppel. However, because of the advent of bargained-for consideration in nineteenth-century America as the presumed primary legal basis for validating and enforcing informal promises, the reliance consideration classification did not happen.[368]

And in summation he averred:

> Reliance consideration ultimately was usurped by bargained-for consideration. By the end of the nineteenth century, the notion of a bargained-for exchange (i.e., the promise and the detriment must by mutual inducements) became the sole great flywheel of consideration. If it had not, there currently would be three forms of consideration: bargained-for consideration, detrimental-reliance consideration, and past-benefit or moral consideration. But that did not happen because reliance consideration was subsumed within the bargain principle of exchange that underlies modern consideration. Consequently, twentieth-century courts, in the common-law tradition, gradually severed reliance consideration from other forms of consideration and labeled it "promissory estoppel." Presently, reliance consideration has its own autonomous sphere of influence as an evolving equitable

[366] Eric Mills Holmes, *Restatement of Promissory Estoppel*, *supra* note 298, at 271–72 (citations omitted).

[367] *Id.* at 271 n.10.

[368] *Id.* at 273 (citations omitted).

principle for enforcing the right to rely on certain promises and for designing relief to afford corrective justice between parties.[369]

The problem with all this, of course, is that "reliance consideration," definitionally described by E. M. Holmes as promissory estoppel and thus as detrimental reliance that has been neither requested nor deliberately induced by the promisor, never existed in earlier history as a doctrine or concept in Anglo-American contract law. The moniker is his own personal invention, and by his own description stands for nothing more than promissory estoppel itself.

What E. M. Holmes wrote in these passages presents itself as based on deep knowledge of the relevant history, it certainly sounds mellifluous, and essentially none of it is actually true. It is as if one had stepped through the looking glass into a topsy-turvy world where down is up and up is down.

In fact, it is rather reminiscent of Winston working in the Ministry of Truth to rewrite history ex post facto – that which actually occurred, the actual doctrines and cases of contract law, the actual statements of judges, advocates and commentators of the time, have been dropped "into the memory hole to be devoured by the flames," and "the past was brought up to date."[370] We see "history being written not in terms of what happened but of what ought to have happened according to various 'party lines'."[371]

What could have brought E. M. Holmes to engage in such an inversion of the actual historical record? The question of personal motive must remain speculative. For forensic purposes, recourse shall be made to the sources he cited as authority, specifically to those where he moved from general citations of entire books or portions of books, to particular blocks of quoted text from those sources into which we can sink our investigatory teeth.[372]

[369] *Id.* at 275–76 (citations omitted).

[370] ORWELL, 1984, *supra* note 259, at 3, 39–40. For "[w]ho controls the past … controls the future. …" *Id.* at 34.

[371] GEORGE ORWELL [ERIC ARTHUR BLAIR], HOMAGE TO CATALONIA 234 (Penguin Books reprint 1980) (1938).

[372] In his 1996 *Restatement of Promissory Estoppel* article, E. M. Holmes refers to a goodly number of books or portions of books written by other authors as authority for promissory estoppel. *See* E. M. Holmes, *Restatement of Promissory Estoppel*, *supra* note 298, at 271 nn. 9–10. Even casual inspection of that list, however, reveals names of other academics quite familiar to the Author – such as Professors Plucknett and Stoljar – whose views in no way support promissory estoppel, and whose thinking in relevant respect is very much along the same general lines as Professors Baker and Ibbetson of Cambridge in their exegeses of the relevant history.

As it would exceed the reasonable page limitations of this book forensically to dissect each and every book or book portion cited by E. M. Holmes, the inquiry here will limit itself to those sources where E. M. Holmes has in his article quoted a block of text from a source, which sources thus effectively provide the principal claimed or alleged support for E. M. Holmes' theses. These quoted blocks of text are from Professors Baker, Ames, and Plucknett. *Id.*

11.1.4.1 QUOTE FROM BAKER. The first such instance is from John Baker, in alleged support of E. M. Holmes' assertion in the main text that "the doctrine now labeled 'promissory estoppel' is not a modern, twentieth-century development arising from Section 90 of the Restatements" but is, rather, "a venerable, ancient form of relief with historical origins in … the common law action of assumpsit. …"[373]

E. M. Holmes stated the following, as support for the foregoing bold and sweeping assertion, quoting in large part from Baker:

> The idea of using assumpsit "was not so much that the promise should be enforced, for the promise in itself was not actionable, but that the damage incurred in reliance on the word of another should be restored. … It was also a principle of moral philosophy, closely akin to the modern doctrine of promissory estoppel."[374]

Certainly on its face, this might sound suggestive as perhaps constituting support for E. M. Holmes. But here caution is advised, just as one must carefully watch any street magician as he quickly shuffles the three shells around, under only one of which lies the red ball.

To track the red ball with precision, the following forensic analysis is necessary. E. M. Holmes had just point-blank asserted that promissory estoppel "is not a modern, twentieth-century development" but instead "a venerable, ancient form of relief."[375] That is, E. M. Holmes claimed that a naked, uncompensated promise – *nudum pactum* – was enforceable in times past. As it turns out, Baker did not make such a statement in his book, *An Introduction to English Legal History*.[376] Quite the converse.

What Baker was speaking to in the text quoted by E. M. Holmes was the philosophical question of why there should be a remedy at all for a broken executory promise.[377] The relevance of this question at that point in Baker's text is that Baker was addressing a particular significant step forward in contract law. That step was when the strict requirement that plaintiff have first prepaid in order to bring a contractual action in assumpsit for nonfeasance was dropped in the latter half of the 1500s, in favor of permitting the enforcement of wholly executory mutual promises as well.[378] This was, in effect, a philosophical movement from solely the debt-based concept of the plaintiff having given something to the counterparty and demanding return therefor, to adding the covenant-based concept of the mutual exchange of promises, where each party has made a solemn promise to perform a certain way, as

[373] *Id.* at 271.

[374] *Id.* at 271 n.9 (quoting BAKER, *supra* note 92, at 339). E. M. Holmes' own citation is to the third edition of Professor Baker's book, but the identical passage also appears in the fourth edition, which for simplicity has been given here as the relevant reference, with page indication to the fourth edition.

[375] E. M. Holmes, *Restatement of Promissory Estoppel*, *supra* note 298, at 271.

[376] BAKER, *supra* note 92.

[377] *Id.* at 338–39.

[378] *Id.* at 337–41.

sufficient grounds to impose liability. That doctrinal step forward looked to the reliance that each contracting party places on the counterparty's promised counter-performance. But this was still in the context of a mutual exchange – each party has promised some performance to the other. There is not some naked, uncompensated promise to be enforced on either side.

Thus we see, in the very pages from which E. M. Holmes drew this quote from Baker, repeated statements by Baker of the requirement of reciprocity, of mutual exchange, for the contractual use of assumpsit.[379] In the paragraphs leading up to the quote in question, Baker addressed *Doige's Case* of 1442 with the following words: "Although *Doige's Case* was framed as a bill of deceit.... [T]he prevailing judicial opinions treated the claim as contractual. Bargains were in their nature reciprocal.... This is contractual language, the language of *quid pro quo*...."[380] In the paragraphs after the quote, we see in Baker's text the requirement of reciprocity stated repeatedly with respect to the 1500s – now using the term "consideration" to denote that which one gives in exchange for a promise.[381] For example, "[i]n 1565 Plowden explained that 'because words are often spoken or uttered by a man without great advisement or deliberation, the law has provided that a contract by words shall not bind without consideration'."[382] Similarly:

> By 1598 *a binding contract* could be *defined*, in terms still acceptable today, *as "a mutual agreement* between the parties *for something to be performed by the defendant in consideration of some benefit which must depart from the plaintiff, or of some labour or prejudice which must be sustained by the plaintiff*".[383]

As decisively laid down for all posterity by *Slade's Case* in 1602, which squarely addressed the enforceability of wholly executory mutual promises:

> First, that every contract executory implies in itself a promise or *assumpsit*.
> Secondly, that although an action of debt lies upon such a contract to recover the duty, the plaintiff may nevertheless have an action on the case upon the *assumpsit*.[384]

As the decision in *Slade's Case* was explained ex post by Coke:

> It was resolved that every contract executory imports in itself an *assumpsit*. For when one agrees to pay money or to deliver something, he thereby assumes or promises to pay or deliver it. Therefore, when one sells any goods to another, and agrees to deliver them at a day to come, and the other in consideration thereof agrees to pay so much money at such and such a day, in that case both parties may

379 *Id.*
380 *Id.* at 337.
381 *Id.* 339–41.
382 *Id.* at 339.
383 *Id.* at 340 (emphasis added).
384 *Slade's Case*, *supra* note 181, at 437.

> have an action of debt or an action on the case in *assumpsit*, for the mutual executory agreement of both parties imports in itself reciprocal actions on the case as well as actions of debt.[385]

As summed up by Baker, "[a] counter-promise was as good a consideration as an executed act. From this point the English law of contract might truly be said to be consensual; *despite its trespassory guise, liability was based on reciprocal agreement*."[386]

Thus, Baker's brief, isolated reference to promissory estoppel was limited to the philosophy of providing a remedy not only for unrequited value paid but also for disappointed reliance on an executory promise. Vitally, Baker made that comment solely and entirely in the context of the mutual exchange of promises, not naked, uncompensated promise – thus not promissory estoppel. The quote from Baker cannot be cherry-picked out of the explanatory doctrinal setting in which it arose and for which it was intended.

11.1.4.2 ADDITIONAL CITATION TO BAKER. There is a second citation by E. M. Holmes to several pages from an article by Baker that does not involve any direct quotation, and was not used by E. M. Holmes to bolster as important a point in his own assertions.[387] However, in that 1979 article, *From Sanctity of Contract to Reasonable Expectation?*, Baker made a different, distinct statement regarding promissory estoppel that also requires forensic analysis in order fully to cover the ground.

In response to the temper of the times, Baker took up inter alia the subject of Grant Gilmore's essential thesis:

> Has our law of contract dissolved entirely into rules based on status? Has it been absorbed back into tort? Has it, perhaps, been replaced by statutory interpretation? The death of contract has been a talking point in law faculties for some years now, and especially since the publication in 1974 of Professor Gilmore's captivating lectures on the subject.[388]

Baker wrote in this context as to the innovative use of

> the action of *assumpsit*, which was extended by 1500 to remedy the mere failure to perform a covenant. The covenant was not actionable as such without evidence in writing under seal, but the breach might nevertheless be actionable in trespass on the case.[389]

[385] *Id.* at 439–40.

[386] BAKER, *supra* note 92, at 341 (emphasis added).

[387] E. M. Holmes, *Restatement of Promissory Estoppel*, *supra* note 298, at 271 n.9 (citing John H. Baker, *From Sanctity of Contract to Reasonable Expectation?*, *in* CURRENT LEGAL PROBLEMS 1979, at 24–27 (Lord Lloyd of Hampstead et al. eds., Stevens & Sons 1979)).

[388] Baker, *From Sanctity of Contract to Reasonable Expectation?*, *supra* note 387, at 17.

[389] *Id.* at 25.

As explained by Baker, "[t]he problem which occasioned the development of *assumpsit* had been the decision in the thirteenth and fourteenth centuries to restrict actions of covenant at common law to formal agreements under seal."[390]

Baker again addressed contractual assumpsit cases where the plaintiff had made a prepayment to the defendant, but in this instance he spoke to the damages awarded in such cases:

> The plaintiff in such actions did not merely recover back his money; he wanted, and received, compensation for the loss caused by committing his money to a frustrated venture when he could have spent it more wisely. The basis of these *assumpsit* cases, therefore, was nothing but promissory estoppel.[391]

With tremendous and genuine respect for Professor Baker's erudition and expertise in English legal history, the Author must respectfully disagree with this particular characterization of what constitutes "promissory estoppel," a novel and artificial American invention of recent provenance. Whatever may be said about the amount and type of damages in assumpsit cases, this is not the defining or distinctive feature of promissory estoppel. Promissory estoppel purports to assert liability even where there is no consideration for a promise – thus no mutual exchange – and where there is no mutual agreement. It does not follow logically that damages awarded beyond simple return of a prepayment somehow indicates the presence of promissory estoppel. The litmus test for the presence of promissory estoppel is not the type or amount of damages. It is, quite simply, whether there was consideration for a promise to be enforced, whether there was mutual exchange.

That mutual exchange, of course, need not necessarily be explicit and express. As discussed earlier in this book, and as perceptively observed by Morawetz during the American Law Institute (ALI) debates and by Jean Powers in more recent times, when a party makes a promise for the deliberate purpose of inducing detrimental reliance thereon by another, it is entirely possible for a court to find the existence of an implied mutual exchange, an implied unilateral contract, under the existing rules of traditional contract law, without any need to reach for the exotic and unbounded doctrine of promissory estoppel. And we see precisely this same conception and understanding in Baker's summation of this portion of his 1979 article, where he wrote of

> a general principle that a person who has relied on an otherwise unenforceable promise, *which was calculated to induce reliance,* is entitled to redress if the non-enforcement of the promise would leave him worse off than if he had not relied on it.... An expectation arising from a mere voluntary courtesy, not calculated to induce reliance ... is not the kind of expectation which it would be reasonable to expect the law to enforce.[392]

[390] *Id.* at 26.

[391] *Id.*

[392] *Id.* at 29 (emphasis added).

So to return to E. M. Holmes, the portion of Baker's article to which he cited certainly includes a statement that at first blush, without a careful read, appears quite seductive. But upon closer analysis, one sees that the statement does not truly provide substantive support for the premise that promissory estoppel existed in early English legal history.

11.1.4.3 QUOTE FROM AMES. The largest and most significant block of text quoted by E. M. Holmes is from Ames, at this point familiar territory.[393] The quoted text concerns those early equity – that is, Chancery – cases addressed by Ames, likewise quoted in this book, which were predicated upon promissory fraud rather than promissory estoppel.[394] As discussed earlier, such cases do not provide support for promissory estoppel.[395]

11.1.4.4 QUOTE FROM PLUCKNETT/ST. GERMAN. The third textual sentence quoted by E. M. Holmes is that of Plucknett quoting St. German's *Doctor and Student* exegetical colloquies.[396]

It is important in this context to see E. M. Holmes' own doctrinal assertion in his endnote, for which he held out St. German as support:

> With the triumph of assumpsit over equity in the 1500s, what we now refer to as "promissory estoppel" relief was generally granted at common law. By the mid-sixteenth century, "St. Germain [in 2 Doctor and Student, ii. ch. 24] regarded it as settled that 'if he to whom the promise is made have a charge by reason of the promise ... he shall have an action ... though he that made the promise had no worldly profit by it.'" Theodore F. T. Plucknett, A Concise History of the Common Law 643 (5th ed. 1956).[397]

This citation to St. German is misleading, for the following reason. What St. German was explaining is that a valid, enforceable contract may be formed where the promisor requests the counterparty's performance to flow to the direct benefit of a third party. As long as there exists a mutually agreed mutual exchange, for

[393] E. M. Holmes, *Restatement of Promissory Estoppel*, *supra* note 298, at 271 n.10 (citing Ames, *supra* note 322, at 14–15).

[394] *Id. See also supra* Chapter 11.1.1.2.

[395] *See supra* Chapter 11.1.1.2.

[396] E. M. Holmes, *Restatement of Promissory Estoppel*, *supra* note 298, at 271 n.10 (citing PLUCKNETT, *supra* note 57, at 643, in turn citing DOCTOR AND STUDENT, *supra* note 108, at 230, *reprinted with modern spelling in* ENGLISH SOURCES, *supra* note 45, at 484).

St. German's original spelling reads:

> Yf he to whome the promyse ys made: haue a charge by reason of the promyse whyche he hathe also perfourmed: than in that case he shall haue an accyon for that thyng that was promysed thoughe he that made the promyse haue no worldely profyte by yt.

DOCTOR AND STUDENT, *supra* note 108, at 230.

[397] E. M. Holmes, *Restatement of Promissory Estoppel*, *supra* note 298, at 271 n.10.

example, "I will pay you to perform the following service to such other person," the fact that the service is provided for the direct benefit of that third person, rather than to the direct benefit of the promisor, is of no matter. Clearly and obviously, if the promisor has requested such service to flow in that manner, the promisor had some reason for doing so. The counterparty's performance may be to the direct benefit of the third party, but it is, by ineluctable inference, of indirect benefit to the promisor. The promisor presumptively had a rational reason for their request. An easy example of this principle in action is a parent requesting a doctor to provide medical service to the parent's child, for which service the parent promises to pay. The mutually agreed mutual exchange is payment of money for provision of medical service. The direct benefit of the service is to the child. But it is unquestionable that the parent benefits indirectly from having their child receive medical treatment. And the medical doctor has incurred a detriment – the expenditure of effort in rendering treatment – at the request of the parent promisor. Mutual consideration is absolutely present.

That this contractual structure is precisely what St. German had in mind is immediately observed if one simply reads the very next sentence of his text, which was not quoted by E. M. Holmes:

> As if a man say to another, heal such a poor man of his disease, or make such a highway, and I shall give thee this much, and if he do it I think an action lieth at the common law.[398]

11.1.4.5 CONCLUSION AS TO E. M. HOLMES. In conclusion, therefore, careful review of the foregoing underlying source material cited by E. M. Holmes reveals that it does not support his extraordinary and unfounded claim that, "[w]ith the triumph of assumpsit over equity in the 1500s, what we now refer to as 'promissory estoppel' relief was generally granted at common law."[399] The assertion is simply incorrect.

11.1.5 Summation as to Assertions Regarding Assumpsit

Drawing together the foregoing forensic analyses, a genuinely disturbing picture of dysfunction in American legal academia emerges. Repeatedly we see massive misrepresentations of the historical record leading to complete inversion of actual doctrine, supported – if at all – by no more than a handful of cursory quotes from secondary rather than original sources, and these often cherry-picked and selectively

398 DOCTOR AND STUDENT, *supra* note 108, at 230–31.
St. German's original spelling reads:

> As yf a man saye to an other (heele suche a poore man of hys dyssease/ or make suche an hyghewaye/ and I shall gyue the thus moche/ and yf he do yt I thynke an accyon lyeth at the comon lawe.

399 E. M. Holmes, *Restatement of Promissory Estoppel*, *supra* note 298, at 271 n.10.

abridged in a manner at odds with their authors' overall statements taken in full context.

We are all human, each individual's knowledge is necessarily limited in many ways, and we all make mistakes. Such is our shared condition as fallible human beings. But what we have seen here, in the drive to push promissory estoppel upon the American legal system, is something different. The lack of any serious scholarship to back up serious assertions as to the historical record cannot reasonably be explained as simple difference of opinion, or mere negligence. It appears clearly to cross the line into either deliberate deception, or, at minimum, utter recklessness with regard to the truth or falsity of that which is claimed for motivated polemical purpose. This record does not bring credit upon the American legal academy, and is one from which the profession should distance itself for the sake of honor and integrity.

What it means for the particular inquiry here is that promissory estoppel cannot be pawned off as enjoying long and well-anchored lineage. It is an invention, a novum. It is artificial, and must be addressed as such. Fundamental discussion as to whether this novel doctrine is salutary and therefore advisable as a newfound adoption into the structure of American contract law, or whether it is dangerously unbounded in principle and potentially pernicious in both moral and practical effect, must be made on its own terms. That discussion cannot be brushed aside with casual assertions or assumptions of precedential pedigree.

11.2 *Isolated, Idiosyncratic Categories and Cases*

This brings us now to Williston's second major pillar of claimed precedential support for promissory estoppel. This consists of a motley hodgepodge of certain discrete legal categories taken together with a limited number of isolated cases at the U.S. state court level, which Williston interpreted as preexisting exemplars of promissory estoppel in action.

11.2.1 Gifts

First to be addressed is the category of gifts. These play an absolutely central role in the story of promissory estoppel and the ALI's endorsement thereof.

There is of course nothing unusual about gifts as a type or category of transaction. As we all know from our own personal experience, they typically occur where the heart is involved. One gives a gift to a beloved family member or, in a more general eleemosynary spirit, makes a gift for the benefit of a broader nonfamilial group or society as a whole. But they are a distinct, discrete category of transaction, with their own rules and their own bases, both moral and practical, in legal philosophy and policy.

The question for current purposes, however, is how gifts relate to contracts, and why they should have any impact on contract law whatsoever.

To review the bidding, as it were, this book has already addressed at length Blackstone's fundamental exegesis of the distinctions between gifts and contracts as subcategories of property law within his taxonomical structure.[400] Broadly speaking, when one owns property, an inherent characteristic of that ownership is the ability to alienate that property to another. As we all know, a transfer, a grant, of property may be effectuated on a gratuitous, uncompensated basis. Or it may be done as part of a mutual exchange consisting of reciprocal grants of property, such as cash payment for goods. The former is gift, the latter is contract.

Within the realm of gift, the following general rules obtain. First, a gift, the grant of property, is not effective and enforceable until the gift has been delivered by the donor to the donee.[401] Second, a promise to make a gift in the future does not constitute such delivery, and is not enforceable against the contemplated donor if the donor should happen to change their mind prior to delivery, to actual consummation, of the gift.[402]

Why these gift rules should be so is reasonably evident from a moral perspective: The contemplated donee hasn't paid the donor anything for the gift. The donee does not affirmatively promise to do anything of benefit to the donor. To put it in colloquial terms, the donee is simply the fat and happy beneficiary of the donor's contemplated largesse.

Under such circumstances, why in all the world should the contemplated donee be permitted to force a promised gift to occur, where the donor has not yet made delivery? If the donor has changed their mind, and no longer wishes to make the uncompensated gift, to use court and police power to seize the contemplated gift assets and transfer them to the contemplated donee intuitively borders on judicial theft. It is, after all, the donor's property. By what moral right can the contemplated donee compel the donor to proceed, when the donor has changed their mind and the contemplated donee hasn't done anything for the donor? "Give me something for free, or I will take it from you by force." The mere fact that one could fabricate a new and different legal regime imposing liability for unfulfilled gift promises does not mean that one should do so, morally.

To address this obvious ethical objection, Williston bored in on whether the contemplated donor affirmatively knew, or should have known, that the contemplated donee would rely. In relevant part, the ALI debate ran along the following lines.

To set the stage, Williston acknowledged the well-known rules of existing law, and sought to ring-fence the ambit of his proposed new doctrine:

> Now, there is no broad doctrine that wherever a man makes a promise, a gratuitous promise, and the other relies upon it, the promisee can recover on the promise, and

[400] *See generally supra* Chapter 4.3.

[401] *See, e.g.*, 2 BLACKSTONE, *supra* note 3, at 441; FARNSWORTH, *supra* note 307, at 50–51.

[402] *See, e.g.*, FARNSWORTH, *supra* note 307, at 49–50.

> we do not dare in Section [90] make any such broad statement that wherever a gratuitous promise is made and the promisee relies on it to his injury, he may enforce it; that is going far beyond the law and far beyond what we should dare to say.[403]

At the same time, Williston had to concede Morawetz's fundamental point on the other side that a promise made for the purpose of inducing a promisee to act in a certain manner can easily be treated as an implied unilateral contract under preexisting traditional contract law.[404] That is, an exchange transaction involving both sides doing something of benefit for the other. Thus, contract. No new doctrine is required for such circumstances.[405]

Williston therefore faced the challenge of navigating his proposed new doctrine into the narrow channel between the Scylla of there existing no rule requiring enforcement as a matter of course for all uncompensated promises upon which there has been reliance, and the Charybdis of clear and obvious enforcement for promises made for the purpose of inducing particular reliance. Williston sought to do so by focusing on a circumstance where there is more than just a simple uncompensated promise, there is actual knowledge or constructive knowledge that the promisee will rely in a certain manner, but stopping short of the promise having been made in order to induce such reliance:

> I want to cover more in Section [90] than offers. I understand perfectly well what you have in mind, as offers for unilateral contracts, and they are covered under offers; but this section covers a case where there is a promise to give and the promisor knows that the promisee will rely upon the proposed gift in certain definite ways.[406]

403 ALI debate on Section 90, *supra* note 30, at 97.

404 *Id.* at 88–89.

405 Williston also acknowledged the well-known existing legal rule concerning the more aggravated circumstance where promisor makes a promise not only for the presumable purpose of inducing reliance but also knowing full well at the time of the promise that promisor has no intention ever to perform. This is, of course, promissory fraud, already discussed at length *supra*. This point was made during the ALI debate by George Crothers:

> May I not suggest that this falls within Section 709 of the California Civil Code, as one of those acts or statements intended to mislead another, coming under the head of deceit, and would it not be better to leave it under deceit rather than under Contracts . . .?

Id. at 93.

Williston responded:

> I do not regard a promise to do something in the future as deceitful merely because the promise is broken. If a man promises something intending at the time he makes the promise not to perform it, that is deceit, and if the promise is made fraudulently, he may in most jurisdictions be the subject of damages for a tort; but to call a promise deceit merely because the promisor, although intending to keep it when he makes it, afterwards decides not to, is to my mind a misuse of language.

Id.

406 *Id.* at 89.

So what are these promises, as a practical matter of everyday life? As explored earlier, Williston discussed four subcategories: gift promises to charitable institutions; promises made to induce or in anticipation of a contemplated marriage; promises to donate land, followed by improvements made thereto by the contemplated donee; and intrafamily gifts of all other sorts.[407]

11.2.1.1 CHARITABLE GIFTS. As to gifts promised to charitable institutions, already prior to inception of the ALI in the 1920s, certain courts in the United States had embraced a special, limited, idiosyncratic exception to the consideration requirement for the enforcement of promise, applicable solely to this charitable context.[408] The reason for this, of course, lay wholly outside the realm of contract law and arose from a motivated policy decision by courts to ensure through compulsion of law that donations promised – but not yet delivered – to charitable institutions would be in fact ultimately be consummated.[409] All in the broader public interest.

In the special and very limited context of contemplated gifts to charitable institutions, the courts had thus suspended the consideration requirement for promise, at least where the contemplated donee had detrimentally relied on the promise.[410] Viewed in a slightly different way, they had suspended the delivery requirement for

Williston did seek to restrict the potential reach of promissory estoppel by including within draft Section 90 a requirement that the foreseeable reliance be of a "definite and substantial character." FIRST RESTATEMENT, *supra* note 2, § 90. In his view, this would provide some bounds to application of the "injustice" concept to be applied by the court in its otherwise unfettered discretion:

> Injustice is a word that is more or less indefinite anyway, and I wished as far as possible to characterize it. Certainly, I should dislike very much to leave out the word "substantial," and I think the word, "definite" ought to be left in. Those words narrow the Section undoubtedly. If you leave them out, you make the Section broader and I think add to its vagueness. . . . We have not gone so far as to say that any reliance on a gratuitous promise will render the promise enforceable provided injustice cannot be otherwise avoided.

We have confined the Section to the case where a reasonable person would say that the promisor expected the man to do just what he did or that he ought to have expected it.

ALI debate on Section 90, *supra* note 30, at 92–93.

The Restatement (Second) drafting group abandoned this limiting language that Williston had considered important, removing the "definite and substantial character" requirement as to the nature of the foreseeable reliance. RESTATEMENT (SECOND), *supra* note 2, § 90(1).

407 *See supra* Chapter 8.2.2.1.

Williston also mentioned a fourth category, namely, gratuitous promises to transfer land, in reliance on which the promisee made improvements to the land. *See supra* text accompanying note 281. Such promises are highly likely, as a matter of practical observation of human affairs, to be made either to a charitable institution, such as a church, or to a family member. As such, promises of this character may be expected to fall within one or the other of those two respective subcategories and will thus not be treated separately here for analytic purposes.

408 *See, e.g.*, FARNSWORTH, *supra* note 307, at 93–94.

409 *Id.* at 94.

410 *Id.*

gifts. Whichever way characterized, the point of attachment for legal liability to consummate a charitable donation was accelerated to a time before actual delivery of the gift. Moral of the story: When invited to an alumni fundraising dinner by the dean of your alma mater, be careful what you say over cocktails.

However, since this narrow, carefully cabined exception for policy reasons had already been created by the courts, why was it now necessary to suspend the consideration requirement in a much more wide-ranging, indeed nearly boundless, manner, as Section 90 would do? Even if one accepts the courts' premise that their judicially created exception was a justified and ethical rule of law – a premise most definitely open to philosophical challenge – the situation the courts wished to address had thus already been addressed. This does not generate a mandate for an inflation of the exception so massive that it could easily engulf a great portion of the entire field of contract law.

11.2.1.2 GIFTS IN ANTICIPATION OF MARRIAGE. The second subcategory of gift promises mentioned by Williston, namely, those made to induce or in anticipation of a contemplated marriage, is again a narrow, tightly confined species of factual situation. Moreover, it easily breaks down into two buckets, each of which can be easily dealt with.

If the promise to give land, money, or other property is made for the purpose of inducing a couple to marry, we have on our hands an obvious case of either express or implied unilateral contract, if the court so chooses. If, by contrast, no intent to induce marriage is present, then we are dealing with an intrafamily (or contemplated family) gift, to be addressed momentarily. Either way, gift promises in the marriage context will fall under other categories discussed here and may be analyzed as such.[411]

11.2.1.3 GIFTS OF REAL ESTATE WHICH IS THEN IMPROVED. The third subcategory of gift promises mentioned by Williston are those with respect to land, upon which improvements are then made by the contemplated donee prior to actual transfer of title. Presumably, such gifts of real estate in the great majority of cases are made either to charitable institutions such as churches, or to family. As such, they can and should be analyzed in the same manner as gift promises under one or the other of those two rubrics, as appropriate.[412]

11.2.1.4 INTRAFAMILY GIFTS GENERALLY. This brings us to the fourth and perhaps largest subcategory of gifts discussed by Williston, namely, intrafamily gifts in

[411] For further discussion of gift promises in anticipation of marriage, see Alden, *Rethinking Promissory Estoppel*, *supra* note 2, at 687–88.

[412] For further discussion of promises to donate land, followed by improvements thereto made by the contemplated donee, see *id.* at 688.

general. Here again, as in the marriage context, the promised gift may be made to induce reliance by the other family member, and may thus be viewed as express or implied unilateral contract should a court choose to do so. If, however, the promised gift is made simply out of familial love or other motivation, where reliance is foreseeable but neither requested nor implicitly sought, we have now arrived at the core and most important fact pattern clearly identified by Williston as the predicate for adoption of promissory estoppel.

11.2.1.4.1 Ricketts v. Scothorn. As one sees in the caselaw, from time to time disputes occur where someone has promised to make a gift to a family member in the future, but the promisor passes away before actually having delivered the gift – thus before consummation of the gift, which would render it legally effective as an actual grant of property right[413] – and without having made provision therefor by means of legally binding testamentary disposition, such as by will or trust. If the executor of the decedent's estate declines to honor decedent's donative promise, cases have arisen in which the disappointed promisee has brought suit in an attempt to enforce decedent's gratuitous promise.

However, as long established in Anglo-American law, a promise to make a gift in the future is unenforceable.[414] This is for the simple reason that a promise to make a gift in the future is, tautologically, gratuitous, not reflective of a mutual exchange transaction.[415] There is no mutual consideration, thus no contract.[416] There is nothing that the contemplated donee, at the request of the contemplated donor, has promised to do for the donor, or abstain from doing, in return that would give the donee any moral right to insist that the donor carry through on the promise to make the gift. The prospective donor is fully at their liberty to change their mind and simply not consummate the gift if they so choose.[417] What this means operationally

[413] *See, e.g.*, FARNSWORTH, *supra* note 307, at 50.

[414] *See, e.g.*, *id.* at 49–50. This point was also explicitly conceded by the court in the seminal case Ricketts v. Scothorn, discussed at length *infra*:

> The instrument in suit [a promissory note] being given without any valuable consideration, was nothing more than a promise to make a gift in the future of the sum of money therein named. Ordinarily, such promises are not enforceable even when put in the form of a promissory note.

Ricketts v. Scothorn, 77 N.W. 365, 366 (Neb. 1898).

[415] *See, e.g.*, FARNSWORTH, *supra* note 307, at 49.

[416] *Id.* at 49–50.

[417] There exist, of course, excellent and morally utterly defensible reasons for which a prospective donor might change their mind. For example, prior to delivery and thus consummation of the gift the contemplated donee might have betrayed or brought harm to the prospective donor, or caused the prospective donor emotional distress, or demonstrated galling ingratitude. Likewise, the prospective donor might have suffered a change in economic or other circumstance that render the contemplated gift ill-advised or otherwise no longer attractive.

And if there are no specific adverse circumstances leading to a change of mind, the property to be delivered by the prospective donor is, after all, the donor's own money. It does not belong

is that a decedent's genuine desire to make provision for a family member may be frustrated if there is nothing but a bare promise by the decedent – no delivery, no trust, no will – reflecting the intended gift.

Several decades prior to Williston's effort to bring promissory estoppel into being in the 1920s, the state of Nebraska in the 1898 case *Ricketts v. Scothorn*[418] had handed down a judicial decision addressing a fact pattern much along these lines. In *Ricketts*, a grandfather had promised to give his granddaughter $2,000 so "that you have not got to work any more."[419] He did not condition the gift upon any counter-performance, or promise thereof, by her. The court was explicit and pointed in its insistence that no consideration for the promise was present, that the promise was thus entirely gratuitous.[420]

The grandfather could, of course, have simply given his granddaughter the $2,000 up front, in which case she would immediately have become the owner thereof. No later dispute involving the grandfather's estate would have eventually arisen. But apparently the grandfather did not wish to deliver the cash immediately, as this would have required an undesired or infeasible liquidation of certain real property.[421] Hence, his promise to deliver the money in the future.

Before the grandfather had delivered the promised $2,000, he passed away.[422] Interestingly, the grandfather had not been unaware of the concept of a will or incapable of having one put in place. The grandfather's name was John C. Ricketts, and it was Andrew D. Ricketts who served as executor of the grandfather's last will and testament.[423] In such capacity, executor Andrew declined to pay that sum to the promisee granddaughter, Katie Scothorn. It can only be inferred that the grandfather's will contained no mention of the $2,000 he intended Katie to receive. Nor is there mention of the sum having been transferred into any trust. Katie brought suit against Andrew in his capacity as executor, seeking enforcement of the unfulfilled gratuitous promise made by her grandfather before he had passed.[424]

The court ruled in favor of the granddaughter Katie.[425] But on what basis? There was a line of precedent as long as one's arm to the effect that a promise to make a gift in the future is simply unenforceable. What legal legerdemain could the court apply to fox its way past the reader?

to the contemplated donee. The potential donee may hope for, may anticipate, the contemplated gift, but has no right to insist that it be consummated.

418 77 N.W. 365 (Neb. 1898).

419 *Id.* at 366.

420 *Id.*

421 *Id.* ("[H]e stated … that if he could sell his farm in Ohio he would pay the note out of the proceeds.")

422 *Id.*

423 *Id.* at 365.

424 *Id.*

425 *Id.* at 367.

As it turns out, the court's attempted sleight of hand was clumsy and inelegant. The entire decision turns on misapplication of one line of precedent, and misstatement of another.

First, the Nebraska tribunal pointed to decisions involving gratuitous promises to religious, charitable, and educational organizations – as discussed *supra* – in which a number of courts had been willing to set aside the normally foundational and immutable requirement of mutual consideration on grounds of a judicial public policy preference in favor of funds flowing to such institutions.[426] If the organization had detrimentally relied on the promise, such as by committing to third-party contractors for building or renovation plans, before actually having received the anticipated gift, precedent existed for enforcing the promise without any consideration therefor.[427] In other words, at such point the anticipated donor could no longer change their mind, even though the gift had not yet been consummated. These preexisting precedents already applied – in effect though not in name – promissory estoppel, though restricted to and philosophically predicated upon the narrow, discrete public policy context giving rise to them.

However, irrespective of whether one personally favors such a public policy motivated exception to the consideration requirement, it has no bearing upon a gift promise to a private individual. Katie Scothorn was not a religious, charitable, or educational institution serving the needs of the broader public. She was not a church, a hospital, or a university. The entire normative benefit-to-the-broader-public premise of enforcement without consideration in this narrow, idiosyncratic class of cases is simply absent in *Ricketts*.

Second, the court called upon the concept of equitable estoppel to cloak with presumptive precedential pedigree the essentially unprecedented nature of its decision.[428] According to the court, equitable estoppel could be applied to prevent someone who had promised to do something in the future from denying, as it were, that there had been consideration received for such promise, even where this is demonstratively contrary to the actual facts.[429] This would render the uncompensated promise enforceable upon a fiction.

The problem with this claim by the court is that it ran directly opposite to the actual tenets of the doctrine of equitable estoppel, long recognized and explicitly stated by no less than the US Supreme Court just short years prior. The *Mowry* case[430] had involved an insurance agent's representation that the beneficiary of the policy would be notified by the insurer prior to the due date of each premium payment.[431] That representation – in substantive effect a promise – was made prior to

[426] *Id.* at 366.
[427] *Id.*
[428] *Id.* at 366–67.
[429] *Id.*
[430] Union Mut. Life Ins. Co. v. Mowry, 96 U.S. 544 (1877).
[431] *Id.* at 546.

execution of the written insurance policy, which laid out the precise due date of each payment explicitly but contained no supplemental notification covenant by the insurer.[432] Accordingly, no notification was given, a payment whose due date was stated clearly in the policy was missed, the policy lapsed, and the insurer declined the beneficiary's claim under the policy.[433]

The court's decision in *Mowry* turned on a straightforward application of the parol evidence rule, pursuant to which any negotiations or agreements prior to a completely integrated written agreement on point are merged into, and superseded by, the definitive terms of the written contract, which sets forth the entire and exclusive agreement between the parties.[434] Accordingly, the agent's earlier promise regarding prior notification of premium deadlines was not part of the agreement, and the insurer was not estopped to deny the beneficiary's claim upon the lapsed insurance policy.[435] In the course of explaining its reasoning, the US Supreme Court inter alia laid out as a matter of general doctrine – not limited solely to this case – the factual circumstances to which estoppel might apply, and those to which it clearly does not:

> [A]n estoppel from the representations of a party can seldom arise, except where the representation relates to a matter of fact, – to a present or past state of things. *If the representation relate to something to be afterwards brought into existence, it will amount only to a declaration of intention or of opinion, liable to modification or abandonment upon a change of circumstances of which neither party can have any certain knowledge. The only case in which a representation as to the future can be held to operate as an estoppel is where it relates to an intended abandonment of an existing right*, and is made to influence others, and by which they have been induced to act. *An estoppel cannot arise from a promise as to future action with respect to a right to be acquired upon an agreement not yet made.*[436]

This was not new doctrine invented by the US Supreme Court, but simply a statement of long-established common law principle. As applied to *Ricketts*, the grandfather's promise to make a gift in the future thus could not be enforced on a theory and claim of estoppel. Yet, that is precisely what Nebraska did.

What we have, then, with *Ricketts*, is a rogue case. Circumstances would have been different had the court forthrightly admitted that it was blazing a new doctrinal trail directly contrary to the existing common law tradition. A candid intellectual posture would have flagged clearly that there was no valid existing precedent for the court's decision, but that the court believed for reasons sufficient that an exception

[432] *Id.*
[433] *Id.*
[434] *Id.* at 547.
[435] *Id.* at 547–48.
[436] *Id.* at 547 (emphasis added).
As a separate point, the case's reference in the quoted passage to abandonment of an existing right will be addressed *infra*, in this book's discussion of waiver.

to the consideration requirement should be applied to the facts at hand. The *Ricketts* court could have done this as a sui generis, one-time exception, limited to this single, particular case, or more ambitiously could have suggested – for potential adoption by judicial colleagues in other cases – a narrow, confined categorical exception to the consideration requirement for cases satisfying certain factual predicates roughly along the lines present in *Ricketts*. Such an approach would alert readers to the decision's status relative to actual lines of precedent and generally accepted common law rules, and presented a fair tableau for others to consider in future decisions. But by dragging the red herring of charitable subscriptions across the path, and wildly mis- and overapplying the concept of equitable estoppel into factual territory where it clearly does not run, the court effectively practiced dissimulation. *Ricketts* is not merely a rogue case; it is an intellectually dishonest one. This can and must be said here, even if one is personally sympathetic to the result in *Ricketts*.

For those readers who find their hearts on the side of Katie Scothorn rather than the other testamentary beneficiaries – despite the fact that Katie's grandfather presumably had not specified the gift to her in his formal will, and that in reliance on the promised gift she only stepped away from her employment for roughly a year before resuming work[437] – there exist discrete, limited, far more responsible alternative doctrinal innovations that could be crafted to enforce gift promises under similar factual circumstances.

For example, one could create a special, limited exception to the delivery requirement in gift law, as follows. A contemplated donor has promised to make a gift. Throughout their lifetime, the donor has consistently evidenced a continuing intention for the gift ultimately to occur, and has neither by word nor deed demonstrated any desire to renounce the intended gift. The donor then passes away before having delivered the gift, and without having made testamentary disposition therefor pursuant to will or trust. A new rule of "constructive" or "deemed" delivery," if one will, could be adopted, providing that delivery is considered for legal purposes to have occurred immediately upon the contemplated donor's passing, prior to application of the rules of testamentary disposition otherwise applicable. Under a hypothetical rule of this sort, the grandfather's continuing and manifest intention that Katie receive the $2,000 would be honored, and Katie would receive that sum out of the estate prior to the claims of other beneficiaries thereof. A trap for the unwary, for those normal folks in everyday life who do not possess law degrees and may thus be unaware of certain niceties involved in legally effectuating their good faith wishes, would be defanged. This would seem perhaps a reasonable,

[437] Prior to the gift note, Katie Scothorn was employed as a bookkeeper with Mayer Bros. Then, "[f]or something more than a year the plaintiff was without an occupation; but in September, 1892, with the consent of her grandfather, and by his assistance, she secured a position as bookkeeper with Messrs. Funke & Ogden." Ricketts v. Scothorn, 77 N.W. 365, 366 (Neb. 1898).

salutary, and carefully cabined exception to the delivery requirement in gift law, which would not pose a threat to the entire doctrinal structure of the distinct and separate field of contract.[438]

11.2.1.4.2 Restatement Illustrations. The reason this entire subject of promised but as-yet undelivered intrafamily gifts has deserved the foregoing level of attention is that such intrafamily gift promises constitute, in truth, the core and central concrete factual circumstance offered by Williston to illustrate application and justify adoption of promissory estoppel. As will soon be seen *infra*, none of the other categories or isolated cases precedentially cited by Williston really bear weight. And the illustrations of promissory estoppel in action given in the First Restatement were all founded upon real-world cases involving intrafamily promises.[439]

11.2.1.4.2.1 Faxon v. Faxon The first of those illustrations in the First Restatement reads as follows: "A promises B not to foreclose for a specified time, a mortgage which A holds on B's land. B thereafter makes improvements on the land. A's promise binding."[440]

From Williston's various writings, it is clear that he drew this particular illustration from the 1873 Michigan Supreme Court case *Faxon v. Faxon*.[441]

[438] Alternatively, one could revive – either solely for this particular factual predicate or more broadly – the concept of formal contract now generally moribund and vestigial in American law. Thus, one could, for example, specify a rule that would render a "formal" gift promise binding. The requisite degree of formality could be specified to include, for example, that the promise be not just oral but in writing, that it perhaps contain certain "magic language" reciting a clear intention to be legally bound despite the absence of any consideration for the promise, that the writing be executed before a notary public, that the notarized writing perhaps be filed with a local court or other recordkeeping agency.

The problem with this "formal" gift promise approach, of course, is that the greater the efforts taken to avoid the risk of fraud by a claimed donee, or of a donor inadvertently stumbling into an unintended legal obligation, the more the whole procedure comes to resemble precisely the type of legal niceties of which the average, normal citizen might well not be aware. Why not, in that case, simply stick to the existing pathways for testamentary disposition via will or trust? Perhaps there is a Goldilocks zone to be aimed at in this respect, with sufficient formality to obviate the risk of fraud, but not quite the level of formality and procedural safeguards as in the case of a will or trust. If so, this might offer another alternative pathway for those in the position of Katie Scothorn's grandfather.

[439] The First Restatement listed four illustrations in this regard. Only the first three, however, postulate enforcement of the promise. The fourth concludes no enforcement, as the promisee expected the promise to be performed, but did not change position in detrimental reliance thereon. As the fourth example does not demonstrate an affirmative imposition of liability on the basis of promissory estoppel, it is not discussed further here. *See* FIRST RESTATEMENT, *supra* note 2, § 90 illus. 1–4.

[440] *Id.* illus. 1.

[441] 28 Mich. 159 (1873). The case is typically cited as "Faxton v. Faxon," though this appears quite likely to be due to a mere partial typographical error in the heading, though not the body, of the original case reporter. It is a family dispute case, with Theodore acting as the complainant against the defendant, his half-brother Josiah Faxon. There is no discussion in the case of

Reading the case quickly reveals its intrafamily nature. One man lent money to his half-brother, taking back two mortgages.[442] After the half-brother's death, the man prevailed upon the half-brother's son to remain in possession and maintain the land:

> [A]fter Ezra's [half-brother's] death, when Josiah [son thereof] was contemplating removal to another region complainant urged and persuaded him to remain and undertake the care of the land and of the younger children on a promise that the mortgages should never be enforced against them. . . .[443]

The man wrote "cancelled" on each mortgage and initialed the cancellations, though holding onto and retaining the papers, and the mortgage loans were never paid off.[444] The man stressed to his half-brother's son that this was all "for the sake of the family," and the court concluded that "[i]t is quite plain that his [the man's] only motive, as then expressed, was to make such use only of the papers as might be necessary to protect the family in their title."[445] For whatever reason, the man subsequently changed his mind and tried to enforce the mortgages and foreclose on the land.[446]

Depending on how one interprets the court's language, it decided the case either on the basis of unilateral contract or on the basis of waiver. Either way, that is, on the basis of existing traditional contract law, and not some innominate principle of promissory estoppel.

Along the unilateral contract line of analysis, the court wrote:

> The present case is a very strong one in some respects; for a young man was induced to give up his projects for his own advancement, and devote himself to the preservation of property which did not appear worth the sacrifice. . . . A *promise is not gratuitous which is made to procure such efforts and results*. . . .[447]

Along the alternative waiver line of analysis, the court wrote:

> The complainant [the man who lent money to his half-brother] may have estopped himself without any positive agreement, if he *intentionally* led defendants [the son and his mother] to do, or to abstain from doing, any thing involving labor or expenditure to any considerable amount, by giving them to understand they should

anyone bearing the name "Faxton." The case has accordingly been referred to here as Faxon v. Faxon.

The reason to believe that *Faxon* likely served as the basis for illustration number 1 is to be found in Williston, *First Restatement Commentaries*, *supra* note 29, at 15; 1 Williston Treatise, *supra* note 8, at 312 n.39.

442 Faxon v. Faxon, 28 Mich. 159, 159 (1873).

443 *Id.*

444 *Id.* at 160.

445 *Id.*

446 *Id.* at 159.

447 *Id.* at 161–62.

> be relieved from the burden of the mortgages. . . . There is no rule more necessary to enforce good faith than that which compels a person to *abstain from enforcing claims* which he has induced others to suppose he would not rely on.[448]

Only a concurring opinion by one of the judges floats the idea that the man's effort to persuade the son to stay and take care of the land, and the man's promise to cancel the mortgages, were

> rather in the nature of friendly advice than with any view to bind himself, or to influence their action. . . . His assurances, however, have undoubtedly been relied upon and acted upon by defendants, and considering the great lapse of time without any claim under the mortgages on the part of complainant, I am not disposed to dissent from the conclusion of my brethren.[449]

The concurring opinion of this one judge, and not the majority of the court, would thus appear to fall along Williston's narrow navigational line of predicating liability upon knowledge that reliance would occur, without any desire to induce that reliance.

So, stepping back, why the detailed investigation into this case? The reason it is important is that this is one of the three – the only three – illustrations actually given in the First Restatement of how promissory estoppel might operate in practice to enforce a gratuitous promise. And we see that the actual, real-world case upon which the illustration was based was in fact not decided on promissory estoppel whatsoever, but was quite satisfactorily resolved using age-old principles of traditional contract law. The best Williston might have been able to do in defense of this choice of illustration would be to aver that the same result could have been arrived at by the court using promissory estoppel as was done using traditional contract law. And even then, only if the facts were along the lines of the lone concurring opinion, rather than those that appear to have been concluded by the majority opinion.

Even if we take the most generous approach to Williston's use of this case as the basis for his illustration, and assume that the lone concurring opinion's view of the facts and intentions was in fact closer to the truth than the majority's view, we would be left with an illustration suggesting the application of promissory estoppel in practice that is confined to the idiosyncratic, messy, deeply personal and emotionally fraught domain of unfulfilled intrafamily gift promises and litigation arising therefrom. This is the type of highly specific factual setting that, in many areas of caselaw over the ages, leads to particularized, special treatment confined to its specific factual context and thus not allowed to bleed out into and contaminate the entire rest of the body of doctrine. Especially not commercial doctrine at the heart of an advanced and complex economy. That is, even if someone were somehow to agree with Williston that there is somewhere some huge lacuna in

[448] *Id.* at 161.
[449] *Id.* at 162.

preexisting gift and contract law that must be addressed, it could and should be addressed in a modest, limited manner confined to the distinct and distinctive intrafamily donative factual context in which it arises.

11.2.1.4.2.2 *Ricketts Redux* The second illustration in the First Restatement appears to be based on *Ricketts*, with only minor factual twists:

> A promises B to pay him an annuity during B's life. B thereupon resigns a profitable employment, as A expected that he might. B received the annuity for some years, in the meantime becoming disqualified from again obtaining good employment. A' s promise is binding.[450]

The twists, of course, are that in *Ricketts* it was not an annuity but rather a gift promissory note, and that Katie returned to work just over a year later – in precisely the same line of employment as a bookkeeper as before receiving the gift note – and was thus not functionally disqualified from appropriate employment.[451] Williston simply goosed up the detrimental reliance aspect of his illustration to make sure it fit squarely within the stated requirement of Section 90. But the structural similarity is clear. As such, the analysis and critique of the use of *Ricketts* to justify and exemplify the novel doctrine of promissory estoppel is as described *supra*.

11.2.1.4.2.3 *Riff on Hamer v. Sidway* The third illustration in the First Restatement is likewise structurally quite familiar from preexisting caselaw, right down to the dollar number employed in the factual hypothetical:

> A promises B that if B will go to college and complete his course he will give him $5,000. B goes to college and has nearly completed his course when A notifies him of an intention to revoke the promise. A's promise is binding.[452]

This hypothetical is of course very close to the 1891 New York case of *Hamer v. Sidway*, in which an uncle promised a young man $5,000 if he abstained from dissolute pastimes until the age of twenty-one.[453] The young man did so, and the case therefore clearly constitutes an instance of unilateral contract, where acceptance and formation of the contract only occurs upon completion of performance by the promisee.

The principal twist here is that in the First Restatement illustration, the contemplated donor tries to back out of the gift before the contemplated donee has had a chance to complete performance, that is, before the unilateral contract has technically formed. This kind of situation, where there is an offer for a unilateral contract, and performance by the offeree would take some time to complete, creates an obvious risk to the offeree if the offeree commences performance and, before having a chance to complete performance, offeror revokes the offer.

450 First Restatement, *supra* note 2, § 90 illus. 2.

451 Ricketts v. Scothorn, 77 N.W. 365, 366 (Neb. 1898).

452 First Restatement, *supra* note 2, § 90 illus. 3.

453 124 N.Y. 538, 539–40, 27 N.E. 256 (1891).

One way to address this problem and protect the offeree would be to apply Section 90's principle of promissory estoppel, as the illustration suggests could be done. The danger in doing so, of course, lies in Section 90's nearly unbounded character.

As it turns out, however, the First Restatement already provided in parallel to Section 90's principle of promissory estoppel a much more modest and well-confined solution to the problem of offeree's risk. This more conservative and responsible approach was set forth in Section 45 of the First Restatement, entitled "Revocation of Offer for Unilateral Contract; Effect of Part Performance or Tender," reading as follows:

> If an offer for a unilateral contract is made, and part of the consideration requested in the offer is given or tendered by the offeree in response thereto, the offeror is bound by a contract, the duty of immediate performance of which is conditional on the full consideration being given or tendered within the time stated in the offer, or, if no time is stated therein, within a reasonable time.[454]

In explication of the foregoing, the comment to this section stated:

> The main offer includes as a subsidiary promise, necessarily implied, that if part of the requested performance is given, the offeror will not revoke his offer, and that if tender is made it will be accepted. Part performance or tender may thus furnish consideration for the subsidiary promises.[455]

That is, when an offer for a unilateral contract is made, an implied option agreement is found to exist to protect the offeree for some period of time to permit the offeree to complete performance, without risk of offeror revoking the offer. The mutual consideration in this implied option contract is, from the offeror, the implied promise not to revoke for such period, and from the offeree, the investment of time, effort, or resources in part performance of the offered principal, underlying transaction.

The elegance of this approach is manifest and provides a reasonable solution to a real-world problem using the tools of traditional contract law. No resort to promissory estoppel is necessary to protect the offeree's part performance.[456]

[454] First Restatement, *supra* note 2, § 45.

[455] *Id.* § 45 cmt. b.

[456] The comment to First Restatement Section 45 continued by stating that promissory estoppel could also employed in this context: "Moreover, merely acting in justifiable reliance on an offer may in some cases serve as sufficient reason for making a promise binding (see § 90)." *Id.*

Resort to promissory estoppel to protect the offeree would of course be wholly unnecessary to the extent that offeree's efforts or other detriment incurred to date are in fact in part performance of what the offeror is seeking. The main text of First Restatement Section 87(2) already addresses that situation. Only if those efforts or other detriment are unrelated to part performance does this remark in the comment even make sense. And if the efforts or other detriment do not relate to part performance, thus do not serve to perform what the offeror is seeking, is it even appropriate to bind the offeror in any manner whatsoever?

This inquiry will be reprised in the recommendations portion of this book, when a further, later development in the promissory estoppel revolution is taken up and critiqued. That later development is set forth in Section 87(2) of the Restatement (Second), which provides:

11.2.1.4.2.4 Conservatism in Doctrine This conservative, traditionalist approach will be a recurring theme as this book proceeds. Just as with the first Section 90 illustration addressed here, one is powerfully reminded of the point already made *supra* that many so-called promissory estoppel cases have either long been or could easily be satisfactorily addressed as to result within the conceptual framework of preexisting traditional contract law. And where traditional contract law does not provide the plaintiff a remedy, there may be compelling reasons for not doing so. Promissory estoppel thus often serves as no more than an alternative method of reaching the same result as would already obtain under traditional contract law. And to the extent that promissory estoppel reaches beyond preexisting law, or carries the potential to do so, it may constitute an ill-advised doctrinal innovation.

The great, shining example of a situation where the plaintiff would not have prevailed, yet the heartstrings might call for a remedy, is that of Katie Scothorn. Even there, one must disregard the grandfather's formal last will and testament, and disregard the perhaps entirely justified expectations of the other beneficiaries of that will, in order to give Katie the $2,000. But if one does perceive injustice to Katie sufficient to outweigh the interests of the other, formally designated beneficiaries, promissory estoppel would allocate that money to her. Yet, one highly idiosyncratic fact pattern, limited to the intrafamily donative setting, hardly constitutes a clarion call for generally effacing the requirement of mutual consideration for the formation of contract. As already argued, significantly more limited, carefully walled-off and cabined doctrinal exceptions could be created to achieve the desired result in that case, without destabilizing contract law as a whole.

And these three illustrations in the First Restatement were the actual, true basis that prevailed at the end of the day, as the public face and formal justification for the creation of promissory estoppel.

In other words, the adoption of promissory estoppel stands or falls substantially on the basis of one single rogue, unnecessarily doctrinally ambitious, intrafamily donative case. *Res ipsa loquitur*.

For the sake of completeness, the other categories and isolated cases mentioned by Williston will now be discussed.

11.2.2 Gratuitous Bailment

An idiosyncratic category brought into play by Williston as support for promissory estoppel was the field of gratuitous bailment. In his *Commentaries* laying the

> An offer which the offeror should reasonably expect to induce action or forbearance of a substantial character on the part of the offeree before acceptance and which does induce such action or forbearance is binding as an option contract to the extent necessary to avoid injustice.

RESTATEMENT (SECOND), *supra* note 2, § 87(2).

This Restatement (Second) Section 87(2) concept of binding an offeror to a contract where the offeree has not even accepted the offer was based on the 1958 California Supreme Court subcontractor bid case Drennan v. Star Paving Co., 333 P.2d 757 (Cal. 1958). *See* FARNSWORTH, *supra* note 307, at 201–2.

groundwork for the First Restatement, Williston stated that "[f]requently these cases can be supported on the ground of tort but not always. A striking recent case is Siegel v. Spear. . . ."[457]

By way of background, the typical bailment situation in any commercial setting is of course contractual in nature. The bailor pays the bailee to take custody of some item of property and protect it from loss or harm for some period of time. Bailee's duties are contractual in nature and governed by the agreement between the parties. Bailee's failure therefore to protect can provide grounds for strict liability for breach of contract.

By contrast, gratuitous bailment only leads to liability in normal legal theory if the bailee has been negligent, that is, any liability sounds in tort.[458]

If a case were to arise where there is no contractual bailment, and there is no tortious negligence, the imposition of liability would be anomalous and inappropriate under normal legal theory, and might indeed suggest that the principle of promissory estoppel has been applied. This was apparently Williston's line of thinking when he cited *Siegel*[459] as a case in point. *Siegel* involved a furniture merchant bailee who gratuitously promised to store plaintiff's furniture, and separately, likewise gratuitously, promised to obtain insurance thereon. The insurance was not obtained, a fire destroyed the furniture, and the bailor sued.[460]

Siegel is difficult to interpret and instrumentalize as useful precedent, however. To begin with, the court was clear that the bailor paid no compensation at all to the bailee, either for the bailment, or for bailee's promise to arrange insurance on the furniture.[461] Yet, the court went on to say that "we think there was a consideration for the agreement to insure."[462] This conclusion makes no sense doctrinally. Williston was thus undoubtedly correct when he stated, "[t]here is no element of consideration in the case, the bailment being gratuitous. There is simply reliance."[463]

[457] Williston, *First Restatement Commentaries*, *supra* note 29, at 18.

[458] See Richard H. Helmholz, *Bailment Theories and the Liabilities of Bailees: The Elusive Uniform Standard of Reasonable Care*, 41 U. KAN. L. REV. 97 (1992), who wrote that liability in gratuitous bailment situations is founded upon tortious negligence rather than strict liability: "Negligence is the normal rule for cases involving accidental loss or damage to the property of others. . . ." *Id.* at 97, 99. Helmholz also wrote of the "older, but now discredited, view that treated bailments as contractual in nature. . . ." *Id.* at 99.

For a similarly strong, unambiguous statement of current doctrine, see STUART M. SPEISER, CHARLES F. KRAUSE & ALFRED W. GANS, THE AMERICAN LAW OF TORTS 831–32 (West 2009) ("It is firmly established that a bailee's liability arises only from some act of negligence on his part.").

[459] Siegel v. Spear & Co., 234 N.Y. 479, 138 N.E. 414 (1923).

[460] *Id.* at 480–81.

[461] *Id.* at 481–82.

[462] *Id.* at 483.

[463] Williston, *First Restatement Commentaries*, *supra* note 29, at 18. Although he only addressed the bailment and not the insurance aspect of the situation, as can be seen from the quoted text

Further, although the court chose to impose liability on the bailee, the precise grounds and standard therefor were not clear. One might think that perhaps the court's use of the word "consideration" meant that the court viewed the bailee's failure to insure gave rise to strict liability, sounding in contract. Yet, in discussing similar cases where liability had been imposed, findings in those cases of "misfeasance" or "gross negligence" are mentioned in *Siegel*, both sounding in tort.[464]

What we are left with is a case where there is very clearly no consideration at any time for any promise. Where there is no duty arising out of the two distinct promises to take possession and to insure, but where the court finds a duty in "trust" that arises out of actually taking possession of the furniture.[465] Where there was no gross negligence or thus liability as to the bailment itself, but where liability is predicated upon the failure to insure.[466] Where we are uncertain as to the liability standard that was applied to that failure to procure insurance. And where we are therefore entirely uncertain whether liability for failure to perform duties arising from the trust-by-virtue-of-possession sounds in strict liability, suggestive of contract, or some level of negligence, which would constitute tort.

Even if one were with sharpened machete somehow to hack one's way through the conceptual jungle presented by *Siegel*, we are still left with certain irreducible facts about gratuitous bailment as a springboard for overthrowing classical contract law. First, it is an unusual and idiosyncratic niche in the law. Second, in its modern incarnation, liability arising from gratuitous bailment disputes has crystallized into its proper form as tort, clearly predicated upon negligence rather than strict liability.[467] And, third, gratuitous bailment transactions do not constitute the beating heart of modern, thriving commerce. It is a sidelight to the main show. There is no reason for us at this late date to take a domain of manifest and obvious tort and use it to upend the contract law rules that form the legal substrate for our national economy.

11.2.3 Waiver

The next category brought to bear by Williston, like Napoleon training his cannon on Wellington's high ground position at Waterloo, was waiver: "A large body of cases ordinarily classified under the heading of 'Waiver' in reality involve nothing but promises held binding on the promisor."[468]

here, Williston was clear that reliance on a promise does not constitute consideration for that promise.

464 *Siegel*, 234 N.Y. at 483.

465 *Id.*

466 *Id.* at 482–83.

467 *See* Helmholz, *supra* note 458, at 97, 99; Speiser et al., *supra* note 458, at 831–32.

468 Williston, *First Restatement Commentaries*, *supra* note 29, at 19.

In the contractual context, a waiver is generally understood to be the voluntary, gratuitous, unilateral relinquishment of an existing right.[469] Because nothing has been given by the counterparty as consideration for a waiver, the waiver may be freely revoked at any time.[470]

If, however, prior to revocation, the counterparty detrimentally relies on the waiver, then the waiver may no longer be revoked.[471] Williston is of course correct to point out that such a situation in fact constitutes a form of promissory estoppel.

There are, however, certain cardinal characteristics of waiver that sharply limit its scope and applicability and thus clearly distinguish it from the nearly unbounded promissory estoppel of Section 90.

First and foremost, waiver cannot be used to create a contractual relationship – or indeed any contractual obligation whatsoever – that did not already exist by virtue of an extant contractual relationship between the parties founded upon mutual assent.[472] You cannot waive yourself de novo into an otherwise nonexistent obligation.[473]

This means that waiver does not pose the central and overriding risk posed by Section 90's promissory estoppel, namely, roping someone into liability for an

[469] See, e.g., a classic case discussing the doctrine, Clark v. West, 86 N.E. 1, 5 (N.Y. 1908) (citations omitted):

> A waiver has been defined to be the intentional relinquishment of a known right. It is voluntary and implies an election to dispense with something of value, or forego some advantage which the party waiving it might at its option have demanded or insisted upon....

Accord Hoxie v. The Home Ins. Co., 32 Conn. 21, 40 (1864). *See also* John S. Ewart, *Estoppel or Waiver*, 29 Harv. L. Rev. 724, 729 (1916) (waiver "is a purely unilateral act, its favorite definition being 'an intentional relinquishment of a known right'").

Interestingly, Farnsworth has argued that the precise, technical meaning of the term is slightly distinct from the generally accepted definition:

> Although it has often been said that a waiver is "the intentional relinquishment of a known right," this is a misleading definition. What is involved is not the relinquishment of a right and the termination of the reciprocal duty but the excuse of the nonoccurrence of or a delay in the occurrence of a condition of a duty.

Farnsworth, *supra* note 307, at 587 (citations omitted).

[470] Clark v. West, 86 N.E. at 5; Farnsworth, *supra* note 307, at 589–90.

[471] Farnsworth, *supra* note 307, at 589–90 (citations omitted).

[472] *See, e.g.*, Nat. Util. Serv. v. Whirlpool, 325 F.2d 779 (1963). A party

> cannot by waiver of a condition precedent to his own liability create obligation in himself where none previously existed. To create such an obligation requires a new contract and new consideration.... "One cannot 'waive' himself into a duty to make a gift of money...."

Id. at 781 (citations omitted).

This discussion in *Whirlpool* clearly corresponds to Farnsworth's technical definition of the term "waiver." *See* Farnsworth, *supra* note 307, at 587, as discussed *supra* note 456.

[473] *Id.*

uncompensated statement of future anticipation or intent, tying them up like Gulliver when they had not consented to any mutual, contractual obligation in the first place.

Second, courts decline as a matter of doctrine to find waiver of a material term of a contract, one that goes to the heart of the consideration bargained for a party.[474] In other words, waiver will only be found as to immaterial terms of a contract. Those that are not at the heart of the deal, but merely incidental, ancillary thereto.[475]

All this means that waiver is not a prowling tiger just waiting for the moment the zookeeper is incautious to rip and rend its way out of confinement. Rather, it is a well-domesticated housecat, fluffy, purring, and quite possibly declawed entirely.

As a consequence, this book does not take issue with the doctrine of waiver or its current contours. The criticism lodged in this book is against Section 90 and certain intimately related and equally unbounded sections to be discussed *infra*.

11.2.4 Miscellaneous Isolated Cases

Finally, having now exhausted the caselaw categories that Williston viewed as supportive of his new doctrine, we come to a relatively small collection of generally scattered, isolated, individual decisions at the US state court level, which Williston claimed as precedent for promissory estoppel and which fall outside the categories already discussed. As shall be seen, some of these additional cases are unclear or open to dispute as to holding or interpretation. They may be found variously in his 1920 treatise, and later in his written Commentaries in support of his draft First Restatement.[476]

The actual named cases worthy of discussion are *Rerick v. Kern*;[477] *Bassick Manufacturing Co. v. Riley*;[478] *Devecmon v. Shaw*;[479] *Wilson v. Spry*;[480] *Wood*

[474] *See, e.g.*, Clark v. West, 86 N.E. at 5 (citation omitted).

[475] FARNSWORTH, *supra* note 307, at 591 (citations omitted).

[476] One should not be deceived by the larger number of cases chain cited in the footnotes to his 1920 treatise. Many of these are already addressed under the categories analyzed *supra*. Others stand for quite the contrary proposition altogether. Therefore, although a handful of footnotes in the treatise might appear at casual first glance to be lengthy, actually reading Williston's text carefully, and what the various cases are actually being cited for, and printing out and reading the remaining few, reveals the decidedly modest picture presented here in this book. Readers are strongly encouraged personally to pore over the relevant treatise text and review those cases for their own satisfaction on point. *See* 1 WILLISTON TREATISE, *supra* note 8, at 307–14.

[477] 14 Serg. & Rawle 267 (Pa. 1826), *discussed or cited in id.* at 311 n.34; Williston, *First Restatement Commentaries*, *supra* note 29, at 15–16.

[478] 9 F.2d 138 (1925), *discussed or cited in* Williston, *First Restatement Commentaries*, *supra* note 29, at 15–16.

[479] 14 A. 464 (Md. 1888), *discussed or cited in* Williston, *First Restatement Commentaries*, *supra* note 29, at 17.

[480] 223 S.W. 564 (Ark. 1920), *discussed or cited in* Williston, *First Restatement Commentaries*, *supra* note 29, at 17.

v. Danas;[481] and *Estate of Switzer v. Gertenbach*.[482] These few cases deserve to be discussed here for the sake of giving full treatment to Williston's argument, and since they have been specifically identified by Williston, can be read and analyzed directly on one's own.[483] For the sake of brevity, the analyses provided here shall be somewhat abridged and will "cut to the chase," as it were.[484]

11.2.4.1 RERICK V. KERN. *Rerick v. Kern* was an early 1800s Pennsylvania decision that did indeed enforce a gratuitous parol grant of a license to divert and use water from a stream, on grounds that the licensee had incurred substantial expense in reliance on the gratuitous grant.[485] The licensor was not permitted by the court to revoke the license.

The ordinary rule in property law is that a parol license to use real property is revocable.[486] An irrevocable license, as sought by the licensee in *Rerick*, is tantamount to an easement,[487] which would ordinarily be required to be set forth in a written deed.[488] The court in *Rerick* deviated from these traditional property law rules by holding a gratuitous parol license, that is, without a deed, to be irrevocable, thus creating de facto an "easement by estoppel."[489]

This decision was, in effect, predicated on the principle of promissory estoppel, and lay outside the family donative context. Williston was thus entirely justified in citing this case as precedent for his proposal.

[481] 120 N. E. 159 (Mass. 1918), *discussed or cited in* 1 WILLISTON TREATISE, *supra* note 8, at 308 n.25.

[482] 122 Ill. App. 26 (1905), *discussed or cited in* 1 WILLISTON TREATISE, *supra* note 8, at 307 n.22, 308 n.25.

[483] As noted *supra* in the discussion of Gilmore's recounting of his conversations with Arthur Corbin, there may have been certain loose and – as far as reasonable review of the actual record discloses – potentially frankly fabulist talk at the time the promissory estoppel proposal was being considered by the ALI to the effect that there existed an enormous, otherwise unnoticed iceberg of precedential caselaw lurking beneath the surface. Gilmore reports Corbin as having represented to his colleagues that he had a list of "hundreds, perhaps or thousands?" of such precedential cases. *See* GILMORE, *supra* note 13, at 63; text accompanying note 73. Given that the cases on this mysterious alleged list remain unnamed and unspecified, the discussion here will confine itself to the actual written case made in favor of promissory estoppel by Williston in his writings. Blind belief in the existence of such multitude of other cases, without citations to which one might turn, does not provide a reasonable roadmap for forensic investigation.

[484] Additional analysis and discussion may be found in Alden, *Rethinking Promissory Estoppel*, *supra* note 2, at 692–98.

[485] Rerick v. Kern, 14 Serg. & Rawle 267, 267–68, 271–72 (Pa. 1826).

[486] JESSE DUKEMINIER, JAMES E. KRIER, GREGORY S. ALEXANDER, MICHAEL H. SCHILL & LIOR JACOB STRAHILEVITZ, PROPERTY 778 (New York, Wolters Kluwer 10th ed. 2022).

[487] *See* RESTATEMENT (THIRD) OF PROPERTY: SERVITUDES ch. 4, intro. note, at 496 (AM. LAW INST. 2000).

[488] *See* DUKEMINIER ET AL., *supra* note 486, at 778; JOHN G. SPRANKLING & RAYMOND R. COLETTA, PROPERTY: A CONTEMPORARY APPROACH 697 (St. Paul, Minn., West Academic 3d ed. 2015); Henry v. Dalton, 151 A.2d 362, 366 (R.I. 1959).

[489] *See* SPRANKLING & COLETTA, *supra* note 488, at 697.

By way of limitation, however, it is worth noting that *Rerick* and other cases that have followed in its footsteps[490] inhabit the intersection of contract and property law. The latter body of doctrine is well known for its long legacy of distinctive rules driven in part by the particularized characteristics of real property.

Williston was also quite frank in discussing the relative weight of competing precedent in the matter:

> This decision has been followed by other cases holding that a license cannot be revoked in violation of its terms after the licensee has seriously changed his position on the faith of it. It should be noticed that no slight acts or merely technical reliance will serve. *The weight of authority, moreover, is opposed to these decisions* and holds a gratuitous license revocable though action has been taken in reliance upon it.[491]

In light of Williston's candid admission that this line of cases was at odds with the bulk of existing precedent in property law, the doctrinally conservative approach to *Rerick* and progeny is to leave them to their distinctive province. Permit property law to continue to evolve as its own separate ecosphere, along its own principles and practical concerns, and with its own doctrinal predators and prey. Let property law work it out, as it were, over time. It might well be the case that there eventually emerges pushback against such innovations in property law just as one sees here in this book in the domain of contract.

11.2.4.2 BASSICK MFG. CO. V. RILEY. Williston further cited the *Bassick Manufacturing Co. v. Riley* federal case handed down a century later as an example of *Rerick* having cross-contaminated Pennsylvania law as to licenses more generally, outside the real property context.[492] This reference to *Bassick* does not fare well upon careful review. As Williston wrote in his *Commentaries*:

> This doctrine [*Rerick*] has been extended at least in Pennsylvania to other cases than those involving licenses for the use of real estate. In Bassett [sic] Mfg. Co. v. Riley, (1925) 9 F. (2d) 138, the District Court for the Eastern District of Pennsylvania held that where a manufacturer promised a distributor the right of

[490] Williston in his treatise cited seven other cases in this regard. *See* 1 WILLISTON TREATISE, *supra* note 8, at 311 n.35.

[491] *Id.* at 311 (emphasis added). Modern property law cases exist on both sides of the doctrinal dispute here. For the traditional approach, see Henry v. Dalton, 151 A.2d 362, 366 (R.I. 1959) (license to use real property must be evidenced by written deed). For an approach along the lines of the principle of promissory estoppel, see Mund v. English, 684 P.2d 1248 (Or. Ct. App. 1984).

Certain language in *Rerick* also raises the possibility that the anomalous decision in that case may in part have been driven by some degree of personal animus of the court toward the licensor, to whom the court referred in its actual written opinion as "an obstinate man who is not worth as many cents." Rerick v. Kern, 14 Serg. & Rawle 267, 272 (Pa. 1826).

[492] Bassick Mfg. Co. v. Riley, 9 F.2d 138 (1925).

exclusive sale for five years, reliance and expenditure of money might make the promise binding.[493]

Citing *Bassick* as precedent for promissory estoppel would only make sense, however, if the exclusive distributorship and related trademark license at issue were in fact gratuitous, lacking in mutual consideration, and that there was thus nothing present but the distributor/licensee's unrequested detrimental reliance thereon. That does not appear to be what the court in fact concluded:

> The contract ... is more than one of ... license without consideration.... It is a contract ... under which the company and the defendant agrees that it [the licensor company] will sell its products exclusively to him [the distributor/licensee] within certain territory for distribution by him under its terms, *and at the same time, not only grant him the privilege, but require of him the duty,* of distribution of its products under its name.[494]

What the court has described is an implied bilateral contract, with full mutual consideration.[495] It thus does not provide an example of promissory enforcement in the absence of mutual consideration. It does not constitute precedent for promissory estoppel.

11.2.4.3 DEVECMON V. SHAW. *Devecmon v. Shaw* in 1888 likewise fails to provide clear support for promissory estoppel, at least on its face, as the court formally decided the case on the basis of express unilateral contract predicated upon mutual consideration.[496] In the case, a nephew took a trip to Europe, to be financed by his uncle, "at the instance and request" of the uncle.[497] The uncle passed away, and the nephew sued the estate for reimbursement of his travel expenses. The court ordered that the expenses be reimbursed on grounds that the uncle had expressly requested that the nephew take the trip.[498] The nephew so doing constituted, in the court's view, consideration for the uncle's promise to pay therefor.[499]

The case is of course structurally similar in certain regards to the famous and nearly contemporaneous case of *Hamer v. Sidway*, in which an uncle promised to pay his nephew $5,000 if the nephew refrained from drinking, smoking, swearing, and gambling until he was twenty-one years of age.[500] The nephew performed, and

[493] Williston, *First Restatement Commentaries, supra* note 29, at 15–16.

[494] *Bassick*, 9 F.2d at 139 (emphasis added).

[495] This distinguishes *Bassick* in critical respect from *Rerick*. In *Rerick*, there was no recitation that licensee's expenditures in detrimental reliance on the real property license had been at the request of or even to the benefit of licensor. Here, in *Bassick*, the court has made it clear that reciprocal obligations, even if in part implied, were present.

[496] Devecmon v. Shaw, 14 A. 464 (Md. 1888).

[497] *Id.* at 464–65.

[498] *Id.* at 465.

[499] *Id.*

[500] Hamer v. Sidway, 124 N.Y. 538, 27 N.E. 256 (1891).

express unilateral contract was found, despite the argument that the requested performance was arguably in the nephew's best long-term interest.[501] A deal is a deal is a deal, so to speak, and because the abstinence was requested, its performance constituted consideration for the promise to pay.[502]

The distinction between *Devecmon* and *Hamer* is that *Devecmon* is more redolent than *Hamer* of constituting a conditional gift promise to the nephew. In *Hamer*, one can imagine the uncle having a biological and emotional interest in seeing a member of the family do well in life over the long haul, and the request to abstain from wild living was made to increase the likelihood of seeing that desire satisfied. And the nephew in *Hamer* temporarily gave up activities he might otherwise have genuinely wished to indulge in. By contrast, in *Devecmon* there is not, at least on its face, the same prospect of "good, clean living" to lay the foundation for future success of the nephew, and it sure is tough duty for the peripatetics among us to tour around Europe all expenses paid. But who is really to say? Perhaps the uncle thought that the young man would benefit from international experience and worldly sophistication, from the opportunity to learn foreign languages, and affirmatively wanted the nephew to spend time overseas for such reasons akin to *Hamer*. And perhaps the nephew really didn't want to spend time living in foreign cultures, and had no talent for languages, and frankly would have preferred to pursue activities in the United States. It is somewhat speculative either way.

Moreover, the court was explicit and pointed in its analysis that the requested nature of the acts by the nephew rendered performance of them valuable consideration. Whether an arrangement is best characterized as conditional gift promise or unilateral contract can often involve a difficult judgment call. Williston stated summarily and conclusively that *Devecmon* clearly involved a mere conditional gift.[503] But the court formally concluded otherwise, namely, that there was "sufficient consideration" present, and so stated quite explicitly.[504] We are all of course free to speculate as to what the true nature of the intentions may have been, but reasonable minds might perhaps differ.

11.2.4.4 WILSON V. SPRY. Williston's attempt to shoehorn *Wilson v. Spry*[505] into the role of precedent for promissory estoppel was simply mistaken. *Wilson* involved a secondary option to acquire an underlying, principal option to purchase land.[506] An option on an option, so to speak.[507] What Williston wrote was this:

[501] *Id.* at 545–46.
[502] *Id.* at 546.
[503] Williston, *First Restatement Commentaries*, *supra* note 29, at 17.
[504] Devecmon v. Shaw, 14 A. 464, 465 (Md. 1888).
[505] Wilson v. Spry, 223 S.W. 564 (Ark. 1920).
[506] *Id.* at 565, 568.
[507] *Id.* at 568.

> So in Wilson v. Spry (1920), . . . the Supreme Court of Arkansas held that making an expensive examination of land under *a gratuitous option* was sufficient consideration to make the option binding. Obviously there was nothing but reasonable reliance on the promise in the option.[508]

What the court actually held, however, was quite the converse. The secondary "option on the option" contained in relevant part the following language in its written text: "*Mr. Spry [buyer/optionee] to put estimators on at once and complete examination.*"[509] The employment of estimators for this purpose involved expense by the buyer/optionee.[510] The court read this language as stating not just a right, but an affirmative obligation, of the buyer/optionee to have an examination of the land conducted:

> The contract for the option [the "option on an option"] was the then present contract being entered into between the parties, by which Wilson [seller/optionor] on his part bound himself to grant Spry [buyer/optionee] 45 days to examine the lands, and in the meantime bound himself not to sell the lands to another, *and Spry on his part bound himself to put estimators on the land at once and to complete the examination. Here, then, were* parties capable of contracting, a subject-matter, a consideration, and *mutual covenants; in other words, all of the essentials of a complete executory contract* [the "option on an option"] on the part of Wilson [seller/optionor] to sell and on the part of Spry to buy, an option. . . .[511]

As a matter of strict grammatical construction, it would appear that the court had solid grounds for its interpretation of the relevant contract language. When the secondary option on an option stated, "Mr. Spry [buyer/optionee] to put estimators on at once and complete examination," the use here of the infinitive "to put" (and the structurally necessarily implied "to complete") is easily and naturally read as stating an agreement or requirement. That is, not only had optionor bound himself to do something, but so had optionee. There was quid pro quo, a mutual exchange of covenants. Reasonable minds might differ as to interpretation, but it is very difficult to quibble with the court's conclusion, much less summarily brush it aside as an irrelevancy. Thus, predicated on the text of the opinion, *Wilson* states a principle in no way providing precedent for promissory estoppel, Williston's summary assertion to the contrary notwithstanding.

11.2.4.5 WOOD V. DANAS. Similarly, Williston discounted the court's contract-based decision in *Wood v. Danas*[512] in order to claim precedent for promissory estoppel.

[508] Williston, *First Restatement Commentaries*, *supra* note 29, at 17 (emphasis added).
[509] *Wilson*, 223 S.W. at 565 (emphasis added).
[510] *Id.* at 566.
[511] *Id.* at 568 (emphasis added).
[512] Wood v. Danas, 120 N. E. 159 (Mass. 1918).

The case involved the distinctive contractual setting of an at-will employment arrangement,[513] in which both the employer and the employee have the right to terminate the employment at any time. Thus, unlike term employment, at-will employment can be viewed as, in effect, a new contractual arrangement formed each and every day the sun rises and the employee shows up for work afresh. And the terms of the contractual arrangement going forward can thus be modified from day to day – each time one party or the other indicates that they are only willing to proceed forward on new, different employment terms, mutual voluntary continuation of the employment arrangement thereafter is either expressly or implicitly on those new contractual terms.[514]

As things transpired, an employee noticed a dangerous defect on a set of stairs she had to use at work, "complained of" and "reported" the same to the employer, and the employer thereupon promised that "he was going to fix those steps for her. . . ."[515] The employer had not yet made the repairs when, roughly a month later, the employee injured herself on the still defective stairs and thereafter sued.[516] The issue for presentation in the case was whether the employer had breached a contractual covenant.

Williston stated simply that, "no doubt also courts allow juries to find an intent to make a bargain in cases where it is difficult to believe there was more than detrimental reliance on a gratuitous promise."[517]

Yet, the court's analysis was quite different, concluding that the jury could indeed legitimately find the existence of a quid pro quo, a mutual exchange, on the facts:

> On this evidence the jury could say, that the plaintiff [employee] no longer agreed that the defendants [employer] owed her no duty respecting the manifest danger, but insisted that the place should be made safe, and that the employer assented to this and agreed to make the repair. . . .[518]

And further, that

> from the complaint [about the defective stairs] made by the plaintiff [employee] and *the defendants' [employer's] promise to repair and the plaintiff's [employee's] continuation in the defendants' [employer's] employ*, the jury could say that a new contract of service was made by which the defendants [employer] were to repair the stairway which the plaintiff [employee] was to use in the course of her employment, and to make it safe; and it could have been found that there was a valid

[513] *Id.* at 162.

[514] Not addressed here are the impact of subsequent legislative and other developments in the specialized domain of employment law that have arisen in more recent years. The analysis here is purely one of contract law, predicated on the state of the law at the time of the case and Williston's argumentative use thereof.

[515] *Id.* at 160.

[516] *Id.*

[517] 1 Williston Treatise, *supra* note 8, at 308 n.25.

[518] Wood v. Danas, 120 N. E. at 162.

> consideration for this new contract of employment, in the mutual promises of the parties. . . .[519]

Consequently, "this express agreement to repair the steps placed upon the defendants [employer] the duty to make them reasonably safe. . . ."[520]

Thus, again, Williston claimed as support a case that, on its stated reasoning, provides no precedent for promissory estoppel, and where the court in its analysis stood on doctrinally quite solid interpretive ground.

11.2.4.6 ESTATE OF SWITZER V. GERTENBACH. The final isolated case to be discussed is *Estate of Switzer v. Gertenbach*, in which the plaintiff Gertenbach claimed to have performed services for his stepfather Switzer pursuant to a contractual arrangement.[521]

Just as in the earlier *Ricketts* case, *Switzer* did contain a broad statement sounding very much like the principle of promissory estoppel.[522] Likewise, just as in *Ricketts*, *Switzer* cited as principal authority for this proposition a charitable donation case.[523] However, as discussed earlier in connection with *Ricketts*, the suspension of the consideration requirement in charitable donation cases is predicated on policy grounds of advancing the public welfare. Such charitable cases provide no proper precedent for suspension of the consideration requirement in cases not involving donations for the commonweal. The court's statement here in *Switzer* is thus rogue and lacking solid precedential basis in the same manner as the similar statement made in *Ricketts*.

Moreover, the court's statement was not even its holding, but rather apparent dictum.[524] A throwaway misstatement of doctrine, as it were, sound and fury signifying nothing. Rather than deciding the case on the merits of the contractual claim itself, the court reversed and remanded on a statute of limitations issue.[525]

As such, the case hardly provides any firm foundation for promoting promissory estoppel.

11.3 *Summation as to Claims of Precedent*

And thus draws to a close this critique of Williston's grand precedential claims. To summarize:

The assertion that contract was philosophically and doctrinally derived during the Middle Ages and Renaissance from tort is not correct. Instead, a particular form of tort writ was borrowed and instrumentalized for the sole purpose of circumventing the otherwise prohibitive affirmative defense of wager of law. In so doing, that tort

[519] *Id.*

[520] *Id.*

[521] Estate of Switzer v. Gertenbach, 122 Ill. App. 26 (1905).

[522] *Id.* at 29.

[523] *Id.* (citing "Beatty v. Western College, 177 Ill. 280," now generally cited as Miller v. W. Coll. of Toledo, 52 N.E. 432 (Ill. 1898)).

[524] *Id.* at 29, 31–32.

[525] *Id.*

writ was made subject to the fundamental requirement for the enforceability of informal contract, namely reciprocity, also known as quid pro quo, mutual exchange, mutual consideration.

Next, any categories of promissory enforcement in which mutual consideration has not been required are idiosyncratic, easily cabined off and contained, or may easily be addressed by much more modest doctrinal expedients. They do not provide any compelling grounds for adoption of the nearly unbounded liability principal of promissory estoppel as set forth in Section 90.

Finally, the casual, suggestive references to various individual cases cited as preexisting examples of promissory estoppel reduce, at the end of the day, to not much more than smoke and mirrors, lacking in precedential substance.

In other words, promissory estoppel was sold and marketed by Williston and his academic allies on the basis of precedential claims almost utterly lacking in solid foundation.

12 MICROECONOMIC ANALYSIS

The foregoing forensic investigation into the claims of precedent by Williston and his allies has been extensive. The reason for this is that those historical assertions had the effect of preemptively disarming the natural immune response that would ordinarily ensue from an attempted introduction of alien doctrinal tissue into the body of the law. In short, an open, honest inquiry and debate as to the advisability of the proposed new doctrine was short-circuited in its incipient phases.

That inquiry and debate is long overdue.

And shall now be undertaken.

Perhaps the optimal point of departure may be to ask why contract law exists in the first place. What interests, what policies, are advanced by the enforcement of mutually agreed mutual exchanges?

12.1 *Pareto Improving Transactions*

Microeconomic analysis provides a strikingly simple answer: Such transactions are Pareto improving.[526]

At risk of boring those already well-versed in academic economics, and of shocking normal folks into horrified intellectual recoil, here is an attempt to strike a balance that lands in the not-too-hot, not-too-cold exegetical Goldilocks zone.[527]

[526] As to the genesis of this type of analysis, see VILFREDO PARETO, MANUAL OF POLITICAL ECONOMY: A CRITICAL AND VARIORUM EDITION (John S. Chipman et al. eds., Oxford Univ. Press 2014) (1906).

[527] It is possible to represent many concepts in economics using mathematical models and graphs. The Author's own background would permit that, having studied the subject at Harvard and in Berlin. This included advanced mathematics and statistics, and postgraduation employment as a statistician using factor and cluster analyses to reduce the dimensionality of a roughly 350-

At its core, the study of individual choices in the field of microeconomics is rooted in the concept of "utility."[528] Put briefly, utility is a notional, abstract measure of a person's well-being, their sense of fulfillment and happiness, and the absence of fear, anxiety, and the like.[529]

Since these states of mind are not, as a practical matter, susceptible of measurement, very little can be said of any given individual's utility "level."[530] Nor can comparisons of one person's level of utility be meaningfully compared to that of another person – or at most, only advisedly and with extreme epistemological caution.[531]

So why, one might ask, do we bother with the concept at all? The reason is that although very little might be known with certainty about specific utility levels, one point appears intuitively quite appealing. And that is that any rational individual, when faced with a choice, a decision to make, will attempt to improve their own utility, as they perceive it.[532]

12.2 *Pareto Analysis of Traditional Contract Law*

And thus the obvious value of a mutually agreed mutual exchange lies bare before us. Rational actors will only assent to a transaction that they believe, ex ante, will improve their own net utility. The phrase "net utility" is used here, as in any exchange transaction it may generally be expected that one experiences not only an increase in one's own utility arising from the benefit received in the deal but also a certain quantum of "disutility" as a result of having to perform something for the counterparty. For example, if someone buys a bag of apples, they experience an increase in utility from now owning the apples, but some amount of disutility from now having less cash in the bank. A person's net utility from a transaction is the difference between their utility increase and utility decrease as a result thereof. To the extent their calculations are ultimately borne out, a mutually agreed mutual exchange will result in higher levels of net utility for both parties.

dimensional vector space and to search for clusters in the resultant n-space. But the impulse to do so has been resisted, as the Author's impression is that in many instances such models do little more than provide an intimidating quantitative veneer to what are, at the end of the day, plain common sense propositions and intuitions equally well understood by all, mathematical background or no. The *in terrorem* effect of mathematical models can, on many occasions, serve to obfuscate rather than elucidate what are in truth fairly straightforward ideas.

528 For basic first year primers in the overall field, see, e.g., C. E. FERGUSON & J. P. GOULD, MICROECONOMIC THEORY (Richard D. Irwin, Inc. 4th ed. 1975); EDWIN MANSFIELD, MICROECONOMICS: THEORY AND APPLICATIONS (New York, W. W. Norton & Co. 2d ed. 1975); WALTER NICHOLSON, MICROECONOMIC THEORY: BASIC PRINCIPLES AND EXTENSIONS (Dryden Press 1972).

529 *See, e.g.*, NICHOLSON, *supra* note 528, at 43.

530 *See, e.g.*, *id.* at 45–46.

531 *See, e.g.*, MANSFIELD, *supra* note 528, at 436.

532 *See, e.g.*, NICHOLSON, *supra* note 528, at 43.

Hence, unlike a transaction along an already maximized "Pareto efficient" frontier[533] – that is, where the net utility of one party can only be increased at a cost to the net utility of someone else[534] – a mutually agreed mutual exchange results in higher net utility to both parties, and is therefore referred to as "Pareto improving."[535]

Thus the beauty of contract law. It increases the likelihood of mutually agreed mutual exchanges being fully performed, leading to Pareto improvement.[536] The increased likelihood of full performance reduces risk to the parties. This also reduces transaction costs undertaken by parties privately to ensure performance or to minimize the harm resulting from nonperformance. All this increases the likelihood that parties will enter into such Pareto improving transactions in the first place. The security and frequency of mutually agreed mutual exchanges can thus be expected to raise the overall cumulative utility in society as a whole – so-called social welfare – despite the obvious difficulty, if not impossibility, of making interpersonal utility level comparisons.[537] This is the essential economic case for the creation and enforcement of contract law.[538]

533 For a seminal highly mathematical treatment of the matter, see generally discussion in Gerard Debreu, *Valuation Equilibrium and Pareto Optimum*, Proceedings of the National Academy of Sciences of the United States of America 40(7) (1954), at 588–92, *reprinted in* READINGS IN WELFARE ECONOMICS 39–45 (Kenneth J. Arrow & Tibor Scitovsky eds., Richard D. Irwin, Inc. 1969).

534 In the simple hypothetical case of a two-party economy, the Pareto efficient frontier can be represented as a curve or line on a two-dimensional graph with x- and y-axes, each axis representing the net utility of one of the two parties. This can easily be generalized, at least as a hypothetical mathematical model, to an n-party economy, with the Pareto efficient frontier now represented by an $(n - 1)$-dimensional hypersurface in n-space.

535 Technically, a "Pareto improvement" results where the utility of one person can be increased without diminution of the utility of another. It is not strictly required that both parties be better off, though this is of course the normal and expected result where both parties have voluntarily agreed to an exchange transaction.

536 One may notice here the distinctive character of the analysis looking at both benefit (giving rise to utility) as well as detriment (giving rise to disutility), with the ex ante anticipated differential between the two (ex ante anticipated net utility) being the key driver of individuals' decisions to enter into mutual exchange transactions. In many contracts courses, one may hear primarily about detriment rather than benefit. The Author considers this to be a deeply flawed approach to truly understanding contractual relationships. For a detailed discussion in this regard, see "Annex B: Langdell" set forth at the end of this book.

537 For another seminal mathematical treatment on this point, see generally Oscar Lange, *The Foundations of Welfare Economics*, ECONOMETRICA 10 (1942), at 215–28, *reprinted in* READINGS IN WELFARE ECONOMICS, *supra* note 533, at 26–38.

538 For application of economic concepts and utility analysis to the field of law generally, see Ronald H. Coase, *The Problem of Social Cost*, 3 J. LAW & ECON. 1 (1960); Guido Calabresi, *Some Thoughts on Risk Distribution and the Law of Torts*, 70 YALE L.J. 499 (1961); RICHARD A. POSNER, ECONOMIC ANALYSIS OF LAW (Boston, Little, Brown & Co. 2d ed. 1977); ANTHONY T. KRONMAN & RICHARD A. POSNER, THE ECONOMICS OF CONTRACT LAW (Boston, Little, Brown & Co. 1979); ROBERT COOTER & THOMAS ULEN, LAW AND ECONOMICS (Boston, Pearson Education, Inc., Addison-Wesley imprint 6th ed. 2000); A. MITCHELL POLINSKY, AN INTRODUCTION TO LAW AND ECONOMICS (New York, Wolters Kluwer 4th ed. 2011).

A good basic overview on utility theory, Pareto improvements, Pareto optimality, Kaldor–Hicks efficiency, and their connection to contract law specifically, is provided by Professor

The conceptual elegance of this analytic framework also illuminates in bright relief a whole range of subordinate contract law doctrines and defenses.[539]

For example, one defense to enforcement is "mistake," namely, a mistaken belief, at the time a contact is entered into, on the part of one or both parties as to the true state of the world materially relevant to the transaction.[540] To the extent a party is operating off of a materially mistaken view of the relevant facts, their ex ante calculation of whether the exchange will increase their utility may be flawed. The resultant transaction might therefore not be Pareto improving, in the sense of improving the utility of both parties to the transaction.

Very much the same can be said of "misrepresentation."[541] Whereas tort is focused on the culpability of the party who has made a false statement – hence tortious fraud requires scienter – contract law is concerned with whether the parties have accurate information upon which to base their ex ante utility calculations. Thus, even an innocent misrepresentation – if material to the counterparty's decisions as to whether to enter into the contract and upon what terms – is grounds for rescission.[542] Failure to provide a rescission right for innocent misrepresentation could lead to the enforcement of transactions that do not increase the utility of both parties and are thus not Pareto improving.

"Duress," of course, falls into the same category of analysis, with the malevolent twist that one party has through improper threat thrown the other party into a Hobson's choice dilemma.[543] The innocent threatened party can choose a mere reduction of their own utility by doing that which is desired by the threatening party,

Jules L. Coleman, *Efficiency, Utility, and Wealth Maximization*, 8 HOFSTRA L. REV. 509 (1980). For his part, Coleman argues:

> We can imagine, then, at least three distinct normative defenses for the Pareto-superior standard, only one of which is utilitarian. These are the utilitarian argument, the contractarian or consent argument, and the libertarian argument. The important point for our present purposes is that one can remain unpersuaded by the utilitarian conception of the good and the right, yet stand prepared to endorse certain institutional arrangements that work to at least some person's benefit and to no one's detriment on the grounds either that rational self-interested persons would consent to such arrangements or that certain of these arrangements respect or are required by a deeper commitment to individual liberty or autonomy.

Id. at 517.

For current purposes of analysis in this book, it is not necessary to delve deeper into the philosophical distinctions drawn by Professor Coleman in his article, or into his particular critique of Professor Richard Posner's views, though certainly the consent and liberty rationales Coleman advances are intuitively highly appealing to the Author.

539 Posner also undertook some decades ago to apply economic analysis to a variety of contract rules and doctrines, including those discussed in this book. *See* POSNER, ECONOMIC ANALYSIS OF LAW, *supra* note 538, at 65–100. The thinking presented here, however, reflects the Author's own independent analysis in each instance, even where the innate logic of the subject might lead to similar or identical conclusions to those advanced by Posner.

540 *See* RESTATEMENT (SECOND), *supra* note 2, §§ 151–58.

541 *See id.* §§ 159–73.

542 *See id.* § 161(4).

543 *See id.* §§ 174–76.

or suffer a truly catastrophic reduction in their own utility if they do not comply and the threat against them is carried out. To enforce a contractual commitment obtained under duress would be to both reward unlawful threats and to impose an ex post economic result that is not Pareto improving.

Whereas the foregoing generally involve circumstances existing at the time a contract is entered into, there is also the excuse of "impracticability" for supervening events occurring thereafter.[544] Again, through the lens of microeconomics, the reason for permitting excuse from the obligation to perform where there has been a massive supervening occurrence that sharply and adversely alters the economics for one party is clear. The objective of contract law is to increase the likelihood that mutually agreed mutual exchange transactions are entered into and are performed fully, as these will increase overall "social" utility. Where an unexpected change in circumstances will lead to a situation where enforcement causes a major loss of utility to one party, this implicit policy objective is no longer served.

For good and obvious reason, the excuse of impracticability will not lightly be granted, as to do so in a casual and frequent manner would vitiate the entire enforcement premise from which the benefits of contract law derive. But in a proper case, where the "disutility" to one party would range from significant to extreme, due to subsequently arising circumstances that were not foreseen at the time of ex ante utility calculations, excuse from performance may be granted. It would make little sense to allow overly rigid enforcement of a rule to cannibalize and defeat the very policy premise upon which the rule was predicated in the first place.

12.3 *Pareto Analysis as Applied to Promissory Estoppel*

And we now arrive at promissory estoppel.

The essential concept of this novel doctrine is that promissory enforcement may be granted where there was no mutual agreement and there is no mutual exchange.[545] It can thus very easily be the case that promissory estoppel will lead to an ex post situation where one party is better off, but the other is distinctly worse off. It is an out-and-out wealth transfer, from one party to the other.

This is particularly so when one party is found to have made a "promise" – which, as we have seen earlier, need not satisfy the contract law requirement of definiteness,[546] and may simply be a statement of intent or anticipation – without trying to induce detrimental reliance by others that would be of benefit to the "promisor." In other words, the promisor isn't seeking to induce someone else to rely and, quite frankly, might prefer that they not do so. But if the reliance is reasonably foreseeable, the "promisor" might be held liable for choosing later not to act on their prior statement of intent or anticipation.[547]

[544] *See id.* §§ 261.
[545] *See supra* text accompanying notes 11–12.
[546] *See supra* Chapter 7.1.1.
[547] *See supra* Chapter 7.1.2.

Under such circumstances, we have a "promisor" who would experience little to no gain in utility from the promisee's reliance whatsoever. And once the promisor is held to account and forced to pay damages pursuant to the doctrine of promissory estoppel, we have a situation where the promisor would ultimately have negative net utility from the interaction.[548]

[548] Utility analysis has also been applied to the legal enforcement of "'gratuitous' promises," aka promissory estoppel situations, by Professor Richard Posner. *See* Richard A. Posner, *Gratuitous Promises in Economics and Law*, 6 J. LEGAL STUDIES 411 (1977), *reprinted in* KRONMAN & POSNER, *supra* note 538, at 46–58.

Posner's analysis, however, is predicated upon a rather extraordinary absolute assumption that enforcement of "gratuitous" promises against the promisor in fact *increases* the *promisor's* (as distinct from just the promisee's) utility.

His point of departure is the friendly, happy, feel-good hypothetical of a deliberately intended gift to a family member:

> [P]eople may indeed derive utility or welfare from increases in the utility or welfare of family members. . . .

Id. at 46.

He immediately extends that hypothetical to gifts to nonfamily members, an extension which is rather more bold:

> . . . or for that matter of strangers. . . .

Id.

So far, we are still in the land of present gift. Posner then turns to gift promises:

> But it cannot explain why a *promise* to make a transfer in the future is made.

Id.

His answer is as follows:

> The approach taken here is that a gratuitous promise, to the extent it actually commits the promisor to the promised course of action . . ., creates utility *for the promisor* over and above *the utility to him of the promised performance*. . . . [I]t does so by increasing the present value of an uncertain future stream of transfer payments.

Id.

Posner then proceeds:

> The economic case for enforcing the gratuitous promise . . . is similar to that for enforcing bilateral promises. The failure to enforce bilateral promises would bias exchanges toward those that take place instantaneously, as distinct from those that are completed only over a period of time. . . . But the symmetry between gratuitous and bilateral promises has been obscured in conventional legal analysis by a tendency to view a promise as a pure cost to the promisor, a limitation on his freedom of action and nothing more. Under this analysis, if the promisor receives nothing from the promisee in return – if, that is, the promise is unsupported by consideration in the conventional sense – the promise confers no benefit on the promisor and there is therefore no social cost in allowing him to break the promise, at least in the absence of any detrimental reliance by the promisee. . . . But this analysis ignores the fact that being legally bound to make an intended transfer may enhance ex ante the value of the transfer [from promisor to promisee] and thereby increase the social product, just as in the case of bilateral promises. . . .

Id. at 48.

Now there may conversely exist circumstances where promissory estoppel leads to a result which "feels" right, which appeals intuitively to our ethical sense of fairness. From long experience with such cases and with typical human reactions thereto, these are generally situations in which the promisor made a promise for the deliberate purpose of inducing the promisee to take, or forbear from taking, action in a manner that in either case is to the benefit of the promisor. Here, enforcement of the promise instinctively feels fair, because ex post both parties would end up with a benefit at the end of the day, and the interchange was deliberately caused by the promisor. Justice feels served.

But note, the essence of the ethical sense here is precisely that ex post result of benefit to both. Very much the same ethical underpinning that furnishes the basis for contract law.

He continues in this vein of viewing the promisor as benefiting from having a gratuitous promise enforced against themselves:

> The question of whether it is economical for society to recognize a promise as legally enforceable thus requires a comparison of the utility of the promise to the promisor with the social cost of enforcing the promise. . . .
>
> Because the size of the promised transfer appears on both sides of the cost-benefit equation, it is difficult to specify with any confidence the effect of size on the net social gain from enforcement. . . . I conclude that the effect is probably positive – i.e., that the case of legal enforcement of gratuitous promises will generally be stronger the larger the promised transfer. In any event, that assumption is employed in the balance of the article.

Id. at 49.

We thus have Posner's truly extraordinary, limiting assumption that the ex ante prospect of enforcement of a gratuitous promise increases the *promisor's* utility. While his assumption might perhaps be defensible in the context of a friendly, fully intended gift promise, typically from one family member to another, such as appeared in the originary *Ricketts* case, his assumption may be completely inapposite in other circumstances. It leaves out of contemplation the aggressive, offensive use of promissory estoppel by plaintiffs in so many other potential factual settings, ones that are not the idyllic, warm-hearted, loving scenario of "grandpa promises a gift to granddaughter." If the promisor did not make the promise for the purpose of inducing promisee's reliance, there is no reason whatsoever to suppose that promisor's utility is increased by enforcement of the gratuitous, uncompensated promise. And in those circumstances where the promisor did intend to induce the reliance, there is no need for promissory estoppel to come into play at all – a court may easily find implied unilateral contract under the rules of traditional contract law.

Moreover, the various laws relative to gratuitous transfers of property – such as the delivery requirement for the effectiveness of gift, and the evidentiary requirements for a person's last will and testament – have been very carefully constructed over the centuries to address the unfortunate human reality of fraud, disputes arising from differing interpretations of words and conduct, changes of heart, and the like. This cuts against calling into existence a doctrine that blows past all the prophylactic strictures of existing law.

Suffice it to say, the utility analysis undertaken by the Author in this book makes no such limiting assumption as has Posner, but is rather predicated upon the full range of potential situations in which a plaintiff may seek to impose liability upon a defendant through means of a promissory estoppel claim.

Nor is that mere coincidence. As it turns out, and as has been seen earlier in this book, a situation in which one party makes a promise for the purpose of inducing another to act or forbear, in a manner to the benefit of the promisor, can very easily be characterized as an implied unilateral contract, well within the precinct of existing traditional contract law.[549] There is no need for promissory estoppel in such situations. The deliberate inducement of an interchange that would leave both better off, and is thus Pareto improving, is the factual predicate both of implied unilateral contract, and of those promissory estoppel cases that intuitively appeal to one's sense of justice and propriety.

The foregoing considerations will play an important role in recommendations to be made later in this book as to how to address different species of "promissory estoppel cases."

13 THE MORAL FOUNDATION OF CONTRACT LAW

13.1 *The Case for Contract*

13.1.1 Derivation from Individual Property Rights

Contract law is founded upon an individualistic philosophy of human society. Much of its early history and doctrine derives deductively from the right of individuals to own private property.

A free society philosophically founded on individual liberty can only exist if it honors and respects the concept of individual ownership of property. This is for the simple reason that human beings will have control and dominion over the physical world around them, and the only alternative to individual control is collective control of some character. Collective control and individual liberty are, as a general matter, inversely related.[550]

Private, individual ownership of property entails the power to use one's assets, which in turn generally comprises inter alia the right to dispose of one's assets as one wishes. This includes the disposition of an asset in exchange for counterperformance by another. Such voluntary exchanges are, of course, contract.

[549] *See supra* Chapter 8.2.1.

[550] The Author proceeds from both the premise and personal experience that individual liberty of thought, speech, and conscience is significantly fostered by freedom from collective control, coercion, and threat of retribution for failure to adhere to thoughts and speech that the collective wishes to impose by force. Collective control over the material means of existence renders the individual at constant risk of precisely such coercion and compulsion. And the Author considers individual liberty of thought, speech, and conscience as conducive to the voluntary exercise of Christian morality.

In so saying, the Author does not intend to criticize or disagree with the concept of "ordered liberty" propounded by the founders of the American republic. Indeed, the very creation and enforcement of property and contract law are essential pillars of such ordered liberty.

This essential verity was recognized by Blackstone, who treated contract law as a subapplication of property law more generally.[551] Per his exegesis, an individual may confer and transfer ownership of property to another.[552] A gratuitous transfer is gift.[553] A transfer in exchange for counterperformance is contract.[554]

If one takes individual liberty to be a foundational good, the foregoing provides philosophical justification for the existence of contract law, at least up through mutually executed, and generally through unilaterally executed, exchange.[555]

The reason for this is manifest. Enforcement of a mutually executed contract – typically a present sale of goods – is no more, really, than recognition of voluntary, reciprocal transfers of property in an exchange between two parties. Cash for goods.

A contract that has so far only been performed, thus executed, on one side, but not yet the other – unilaterally executed exchange – presents a discrete but by no means difficult conceptual step forward. The party who has already transferred cash or other property to another, or performed services for another, now has in a certain sense a legitimate property claim against the payment or other consideration due in exchange therefor.[556] The party who has not yet performed is, in a sense, improperly withholding the consideration constituting such as yet unperformed payment. In effect, improperly withholding what is now notionally the performing party's property. This philosophy can be viewed as underlying the medieval action of debt upon contract, pursuant to which one's right to bring suit was predicated upon the plaintiff first having rendered their own performance.[557] Only then did they have a right to the recompense due, still in the hands of the nonperforming party.

13.1.2 Extension to Future Exchanges

This picture works best, of course, where the counter consideration by the nonperforming party consists of cash or other property – in which the plaintiff can properly be viewed as having a notional property right – as distinct from as yet unperformed services. Whereas the former situation involves present transfers, as it were, of property, this latter situation introduces an aspect that is not property, and is not present, but rather future.

[551] The second volume of Blackstone is entitled "Of the Rights of Things," and covers in comprehensive manner rights in property and the transfer of such rights. One of the subheadings thereunder is chapter 30, which reads, "Of Title by Gift, Grant, and Contract." Therein is contained his summary of English contract law. 2 BLACKSTONE, *supra* note 3, ch. 30, at 440–70.

[552] *Id.* at 440.

[553] *Id.*

[554] *Id.* at 440, 442.

[555] Blackstone described clearly the distinction between "executed" and "executory" contract. *Id.* at 443.

[556] This concept in medieval historical context applicable to the sale of personal property is discussed at some length by Professor Stoljar. *See* STOLJAR, *supra* note 99, at 17–21.

[557] This requirement was set forth in Glanville and discussed many centuries later by inter alia Maitland. *See supra* note 101.

This leap into the future is of course compounded when a contract is bilaterally executory, not yet fully performed on either side.[558]

So upon what does justification for such extension of contract into the future rest? Here comes into play the intuition described analytically in the preceding section in the field of microeconomics.

The enforcement of mutually voluntary executory contract increases, ex ante, the expected utility of both parties. It increases the likelihood of performance by each, and consequently reduces the amount of cost otherwise required to address the risk of counterparty nonperformance. On balance, the creation and enforcement of contract law increases social welfare throughout society. That provides a sufficient moral case for its existence.

13.2 *The Case against Promissory Estoppel*

And that very same microeconomic analysis provides a moral case against promissory estoppel. As discussed earlier, promissory estoppel easily permits the enforcement of "promise" even when the "promisor" was not intending to induce the "promisee's" detrimental reliance.[559] This means that the promisor may well have had nothing whatsoever to gain from the promisee's decision to change position in reliance on the "promise." The ethical premise of promissory estoppel in such cases is thus manifestly that the promisor has, in effect, caused harm to, and thus committed a wrong – in other words, a tort – against the promisee.[560] The only justification for the application of promissory estoppel in such a case, and the consequent governmental expropriation of some portion of promisor's assets, is to right the wrong that has been committed.

But is it in fact ethically responsible to regard the promisor as having committed a wrong against the promisee? Common sense and fundamental fairness militate against such a view.

There are many things in life that all of us hope or wish to receive for free. Such is human nature. And the plaintiff in a promissory estoppel case is quite precisely hoping to receive something for free – the entire predicate for the claim is that the plaintiff paid no consideration for promisor's promise.

But a desire to receive something for free does not provide any kind of moral justification for insisting thereon. And particularly no moral foundation for the invocation of governmental power to claw assets out of another person.

[558] This leap occurred during the latter half of the 1500s, as exemplified by the cases Lucy v. Walwyn (1561), Strangborough v. Warner (1589), and Wichals v. Johns (1599). *See supra* note 170 and accompanying text.

[559] *See supra* Chapter 8.2.1.

[560] *See supra* Chapter 6.

At the irreducible core of every promissory estoppel case lies a voluntary decision by the plaintiff to change their position in reliance upon a hope, an anticipation, an expectation, that something will be given to them for free.

While the child in all of us might sympathize, the adult in us is morally more mature. And at the beating heart of moral maturity is to be found recognition of and respect for the principle that we are all responsible for our individual decisions.

The voluntary, uncompelled decision to rely on a mere hope or anticipation of receiving something for free must ultimately be seen as the moral responsibility of the party who so chooses. They may have made a calculated decision, taken a calculated risk, but the risk need not have existed in the first place, and they properly bear responsibility for the outcome.[561] The "harm" or "injury" to plaintiff that implicitly underlies the doctrine would not have arisen whatsoever, but for plaintiff's voluntary, uncompelled decision to take a risk.

As stated earlier, it takes two to tango.

For any of us to hold someone else accountable and – economically – punishable for our own voluntary, uncompelled choice to incur a risk is very difficult to justify ethically. It borders on, if not crosses boldly over, the *limis* of judicially implemented theft. Philosophically, it is fundamentally un-American.

Herein lies the essential moral case against promissory estoppel.

[561] In a more robust era of American history, this moral principle was reflected and encapsulated in the tort law defense that plaintiff had knowingly and voluntarily "assumed the risk."

Part IV

The Pathway Back

Return to Classical Contract Law

In light of the foregoing, the Author's fundamental contention in this book is that the doctrine of "promissory estoppel," as set forth in Section 90 of the Restatement (Second), should be rejected and rescinded, as an artificial, ill-advised, and destabilizing interloper in the cathedral of classical contract law.

Prefatorily, to assuage any potential concern that so-called promissory estoppel cases might thereafter no longer be decided in satisfactory manner, this book describes a framework for the treatment of such cases within the parameters of traditional contract law.

14 PROPOSED CONCEPTUAL FRAMEWORK FOR DECIDING "PROMISSORY ESTOPPEL CASES"

As Grant Gilmore noted, nearly all contract cases can now be decided on promissory estoppel grounds,[562] much like a smaller mammal being swallowed by a python.[563] Promissory estoppel's nearly unlimited liability principle would permit it to consume contract law for breakfast, and then move on to other prey in the afternoon if courts so chose to release it from captivity. Its potential, theoretical appetite knows few bounds.

It is entirely possible, however, to turn the doctrinal sword around (a reckless shift of metaphors), to apply contract law to cases decided on promissory estoppel grounds.

This exercise would reveal where the judicial results would in fact be substantially the same, and where they would differ. And all on the solid, defensible, responsible basis of traditional contract law, as follows.

At the outset, one can and should eschew entirely the use of promissory estoppel in cases that fall within the heartland of preexisting contract law. Those are situations where

[562] Gilmore, *supra* note 13, at 72:

> Clearly enough the unresolved ambiguity in the relationship between § 75 and § 90 in the *Restatement (First)* has now been resolved in favor of the promissory estoppel principle of § 90 which has, in effect, swallowed up the bargain principle of § 75.

[563] The Author's imagery here is possibly an unconscious derivative of Gilmore's observation in his text quoted in the preceding footnote.

there is an obvious quid pro quo, whether express or implied. The classic fact pattern would be an express offer by one party to another, of sufficiently definite character, proposing a mutual exchange transaction. Promissory estoppel has no place here.

The same may be said of an implied-in-fact contract, where the quid pro quo is obvious to all, even though not stated expressly in words. The classic and seminal example is the 1609 case of *Warbrook v. Griffin*, where a man had stabled his horse with an inn.[564] Though the price of the inn's service had not been agreed explicitly, the fact that the inn's services were offered on a proposed commercial basis was clear as day, and the man was found to have constructively assented to the exchange transaction – thus including payment by himself – when he accepted the benefit proffered to him.[565] The promise is implied, not express. Promissory estoppel is here unnecessary, unwanted, and in fact completely unhelpful, as no explicit, verbally stated "promise" of any character whatsoever was made.

We turn now to what this book refers to as "promissory estoppel cases," which come in several variants.

14.1 *Definite Promise, Plus Benefit to Promisor*

First are those situations that satisfy the following criteria.

One party has in fact made a promise of sufficiently clear and unambiguous character, and spelling out the "terms" of a promise with sufficient specificity, that it would satisfy the traditional contract requirement of definiteness. We know what has been said.

At the same time, the promise does not state or propose a mutual exchange. It is simply a promise, nothing more.

Nonetheless, it is reasonably evident that the promise might in fact induce the promisee to take or forbear from some specific action. Detrimental reliance is thus entirely foreseeable, even if by no means certain.

Moreover, and vitally, the specific action or forbearance by the promisee would be of evident benefit to the promisor. From this fact alone, one might well infer that

[564] 2 Brownl. 254, 123 Eng. Rep. 927 (C.P. 1609).

[565] *Id.* ("[F]or it is an *implied promise* . . . of the part of the guest, that he will pay all duties and charges, which he caused in the house. . . .") (emphasis added). Case discussed in PLUCKNETT, *supra* note 57, at 648 (citation omitted):

> If an *assumpsit* could be implied, might not a contract be implied? This step was quickly taken, and in 1610 [sic] an innkeeper recovered the value of goods and services rendered to a guest who had not agreed upon a price. Soon a large variety of implied contracts, and eventually of quasi-contracts, were remedied by *indebitatus assumpsit*.

Likewise discussed in BAKER, *supra* note 92, at 367 (citations omitted):

> If a person ordered goods or services without first fixing the sum to be paid for them, he could be sued upon an *assumpsit* to pay what the goods were worth (*quantum valebant*) or what the performer of the services deserved (*quantum meruit*). Of course there may in some cases have been an express promise to pay whatever was deserved; but this seems inherently unlikely. When we see a *quantum meruit* count it is a fair guess that the undertaking was to be implied from the circumstances. This was openly stated to be so in 1609. . . .

the promisor made the promise for the purpose of inducing that specific detrimental reliance by the promisee.[566]

Finally, and likewise of critical importance, promisee will only benefit from fulfillment of promisor's promise if the promisee has in point of actual fact taken that specific action or forbearance (or change in legal relation)[567] in detrimental reliance. That is, promisor has promised to do something, and promisee takes action or forbearance in reliance, which the promisee views as beneficial to self, but in so doing, by virtue of that action or forbearance, has brought benefit to the promisor. Formulated more succinctly, promisee's benefit only occurs if promisee brings benefit to the promisor. We thus have a conditional "only if, then" structure of the type that lies at the heart of every bargain.[568]

566 Professor Jean Powers' thinking appears to have been along rather similar lines in her article arguing for a traditional contract law analysis of certain promissory estoppel cases. As here, in contemplating whether to apply a unilateral contract analysis to such a fact pattern, she wrote:

> I suggest that in the cases that should be decided as contract cases, the reliance is not only anticipated, but invited. It is that element that justifies the reliance in a way that distinguishes the enforceable promise from the purely gratuitous promise.

Powers, *supra* note 269, at 856.

567 The Restatement (Second) states that there are three distinct types of performance which, if bargained for, may constitute consideration: (i) an act; (ii) a forbearance; or (iii) "the creation, modification, or destruction of a legal relation." RESTATEMENT (SECOND), *supra* note 2, § 71(3). For simplicity of exposition – and in light of the fact that such a change in legal relation might very often be viewed as a species of act or forbearance – when discussing consideration, this book often simply refers to an act or forbearance, and if and when referring to the "creation, modification, or destruction of a legal relation," simply refers to a change in legal relation.

568 The reason this is such an important element of the analysis here is that a court will need to distinguish between (i) a pure unconditional gift promise, (ii) a conditional gift promise, and (iii) an implied mutual exchange. The former two categories are of course not enforceable in contract. The third category of course is.

To illustrate the fact pattern: (i), in the *Ricketts* case, the court was at great pains to paint grandfather's promise, by means of promissory note, to gift $2,000 to his granddaughter so "that you have not got to work any more," as a pure, unconditional gift. *See* Ricketts v. Scothorn, 77 N.W. 365, 366 (Neb. 1898). *See also* extended discussion of the case *supra* Chapter 11.2.1.4.1. The court stressed repeatedly that there was no quid pro quo, nothing the granddaughter had to do, in exchange for grandfather's promise. *See* Ricketts v. Scothorn, *supra*, at 366. She was not required to quit work in order to receive the gift. The grandfather's promise was unconditional. The grandfather was going to make the gift irrespective of what the granddaughter might do or not do. He was going to give her the money no matter what. Now, it is obvious that the grandfather might wish that his granddaughter might choose not to work any more, and that his purpose with the gift was to increase the likelihood that she might so decide. But because he was going to make the gift no matter what, the granddaughter would receive the benefit of his promise without having to rely detrimentally, and without having to confer any particular hoped-for emotional and psychic benefit back to the grandfather. She could just receive the money and keep working. If we take the court's factual characterization as valid, this sort of situation – a pure, unconditional gift promise – looks like so many other intrafamily gift promises, and would be unenforceable in contract. The promissory note in *Ricketts* was only enforced on the basis of what appears to have been a bad faith misreading – or at very minimum an utter misapplication – of extant doctrine and precedent on point. *See* discussion *supra* Chapter 11.2.1.4.1.

Fact pattern (ii), the conditional gift promise, is considerably more complex and the proper interpretation thereof far more parlous. A case in point is the famous Kirksey v. Kirksey, "Dear sister Antillico," case. Kirksey v. Kirksey, 8 Ala. 131 (1845). The court was divided in how best to view the

This is a "promissory estoppel case" in the sense that there was no explicitly stated quid pro quo. Yet, it would not be difficult, within the precinct of traditional contract law, for a court to find a constructive mutual exchange transaction to be present. The promisor has made a promise not in express, but in constructive, exchange for action or forbearance by the promisee.

This line of analysis still obtains even where promisee's specific action or forbearance is not certain to occur. In such a case, the promisor has made a promise in constructive exchange for an increased likelihood of that action or forbearance by promisee occurring. This can, ex ante, be an entirely rational course of conduct by a promisor seeking to maximize promisor's own expected net utility.

Thus, one would have a constructive, that is, implied, mutual exchange transaction, where promisor does not seek any counterpromise by the promisee, but solely promisee's action or forbearance. This can be considered an implied unilateral contract.

An excellent example of how this line of analysis could be applied to defang an entire line of "promissory estoppel cases" that have emerged over the years is in the

situation, with the judge who wrote the opinion of the court actually disagreeing with his majority colleagues in the decision. *Id.* at 133. Briefly put, the facts were that a landowner wrote to the widow of his deceased brother, saying that he was concerned for her welfare and the welfare of her children – "I feel like I want you and the children to do well" – and that if she moved down to his farm, "I will let you have a place to raise your family. . . ." *Id.* at 132.

The majority view was that this constituted a fact pattern (ii) conditional gift promise, not a fact pattern (iii) implied mutual exchange. *Id.* at 133. Yes, the sister-in-law did have to move in order to access the continuing gift, the benefit of promisor's promise; this geographic move constituting the "condition" that must be satisfied to receive the continuing gift. But the majority presumably viewed the intrafamily setting as one best interpreted as true gift promise, truly gratuitous, rather than as an exchange transaction giving rise to legal obligations.

The dissenting judge, by contrast, said that "[t]he inclination of my mind, is, that the loss and inconvenience, which the plaintiff [sister-in-law] sustained in breaking up and moving to the defendant's, a distance of sixty miles, is a sufficient consideration to support the promise, to furnish her with a house, and land to cultivate. . . ." *Id.* The dissenting judge's view is of course also eminently defensible, if one follows the line of analysis: that the landowner would derive emotional and familial benefit – thus an increase in his utility –if his nieces and/or nephews, and their mother, were to do well; that he desired this to occur; that he made his promise of a place and land to raise her family for the purpose of inducing his sister-in-law to move down to him with the children; and that the sister-in-law could only receive the benefit of the landowner's promise by doing the very thing that would bring benefit to him, namely, moving with the children down to his farm. Under this line of thinking, one could easily find an implied unilateral contract – if, and only if, Party B does what Party A wishes (which is of benefit to Party A), then Party B receives a benefit from Party A. The conditional "only if, then" structure of an implied quid pro quo, an implied bargain, an implied contract, is present. The dissenting judge thus viewed the case not as presenting a fact pattern (ii) conditional gift, but rather a fact pattern (iii) contract.

What makes the case tricky is the intrafamily context, where we ordinarily think not in terms of contract and binding legal obligations, but instead in terms of love and affection and care for each other. Viewed through that lens, the imposition of legal obligations feels artificial and unwarranted. But it is certainly possible from a technical point of view, if one decides to follow the dissenting judge's view.

And once we leave the intrafamily context, and cross over into commercial or other societal relationships, then it becomes child's play to find an implied unilateral contract on the factual predicates recited in the main text, without any resort whatsoever to novel, unprecedented, and thus artificial doctrines such as promissory estoppel.

context of subcontractor bids. The seminal case here is *Drennan v. Star Paving*, decided by Chief Justice Traynor of the California Supreme Court in the late 1950s.[569] Traynor chose to decide the case on the basis of Section 90 promissory estoppel.[570] He need not have done so. He could as easily have remained firmly anchored in traditional contract law with an implied unilateral contract analysis.

The case concerned the typical fact pattern where a project sponsor has put out a call for general contractor bids for the project as a whole.[571] The general contractor, before submitting such a general bid to the sponsor, turns to its stable of potential subcontractors for various portions of the project – such as plumbing, electrical, and so forth – and calls for subcontractor bids on those various components of the overall project. The "subs" submit their bids to the "general," who does not accept those bids, but relies on them in constructing and pricing the general's own general bid to the sponsor for the project as a whole.[572]

If the sponsor chooses a specific general's general bid, the general is now locked in and economically exposed to deliver at the quoted price.[573] The general now turns back to those subs upon whose bids and subcontract pricing the general had relied in constructing its own general bid. If a given sub now backs out, or changes its quoted pricing, the general would face an economic loss, due to the fact that its own general bid was presumably priced competitively low based on certain assumed subcontract prices.[574] The general would therefore be inclined to sue a sub that tries to back out, but would ordinarily have no basis for doing so by virtue of the simple fact that the general had not itself ever accepted the sub's bid in the first place.[575] If the general is not bound to the sub, how is it that the sub could be bound to the general, in traditional contract law? There would be no mutuality of obligation, and thus no contract. Or so it would at first glance appear.

Traynor decided the case in favor of the general using Section 90 promissory estoppel.[576] Sub made an offer, upon which the general's reliance was reasonably foreseeable, and the general did rely by using the sub's pricing as the basis in part for the general's own overall project pricing.[577]

[569] Drennan v. Star Paving Co., 333 P.2d 757 (Cal. 1958).

[570] *Id.* at 759–60.

[571] *See id.* at 758.

[572] *See id.* at 758–59.

[573] The general had to deliver a bidder's bond equal to 10 percent of the quoted general contract price. *Id.* at 758.

[574] *See id.* at 758–59.

[575] *Id.* at 759.

[576] *Id.* at 759–60.

[577] Traynor's recitation of the essential facts, and his predicate for applying a promissory estoppel analysis, was as follows:

> There is no evidence that the defendant [sub] offered to make its bid irrevocable in exchange for plaintiff's [general's] use of its figures in computing his bid. Nor is there evidence that would warrant interpreting the plaintiff's [general's] use of defendant's [sub's] bid as the acceptance thereof, binding plaintiff [general], on condition he

As a brief aside at this juncture, before we proceed further, there is a perhaps subtle technical point worthy of mention. Why, if sub made an "offer," are we talking about "promises"? This is because, as noted in the Restatement (Second), "[i]n the normal case of an offer of an exchange of promises, or in the case of an offer of a promise for an act, *the offer itself is a promise*, revocable until accepted."[578] It is a special kind of promise. It is not a point-blank unconditional promise that promisor will act or forbear in some specific manner, irrespective of what the promise does. Instead, an offer is a conditional promise, along the substantive lines of, "if you do X for me, I shall do Y for you." That is, it is a quid pro quo. And it is a promise that shall lapse if not timely accepted. Yet, a promise it is, nonetheless.[579] So now to return to the case under discussion …

Drennan could, however, in contradistinction to Traynor's approach, be viewed through the following traditional contract law lens. Sub made an offer, upon which the general's reliance was reasonably foreseeable, for the specific purpose of inducing the general to use the sub's bid and pricing as part of the basis for the general's own overall project pricing. If the general did so use the sub's bid, and the general were to win the overall sponsor award of the project, then the general would have an economic incentive to use that particular sub upon whose sub bid the general had relied in constructing the general bid. To do otherwise would invite an economic loss for the general. So the sub made a promise, in the form of an offer, for the

> received the main contract, to award the subcontract to defendant [sub]. In sum, there was neither an option supported by consideration nor a bilateral contract binding on both parties.
>
> Plaintiff [general] contends, however, that he relied to his detriment on defendant's [sub's] offer.… Thus the question is squarely presented: Did plaintiff's [general's] reliance make defendant's [sub's] offer irrevocable?

Id. at 759. And further:

> Defendant [sub] had reason to expect that if its bid proved the lowest it would be used by plaintiff [general]. It [sub] induced "action … of a definite and substantial character on the part of the promisee [general]."

Id.

578 Restatement (Second), *supra* note 2, § 24 cmt. a (emphasis added).

579 *Drennan* was decided in 1958, at a point in time when the First Restatement and Section 90 existed, but the Restatement (Second) had not yet been drafted. In the Restatement (Second), the result in *Drennan* was enshrined in a new Section 87(2), which specifically addresses offers and reads:

> An offer which the offeror should reasonably expect to induce action or forbearance of a substantial character on the part of the offeree before acceptance and which does induce such action or forbearance is binding as an option contract to the extent necessary to avoid injustice.

Restatement (Second), *supra* note 2, § 87(2).

The reporter for the Restatement (Second), Professor Farnsworth, subsequently made clear that Section 87(2) "endorses the result in the *Drennan* case.…" Farnsworth, *Ingredients in the Redaction of the Restatement (Second) of Contracts*, *supra* note 241, at 7.

purpose of inducing specific action by the general which – although it would not guarantee the general's subsequent choice of this particular sub for the project – would increase the likelihood that the general would choose this sub for the project.[580] Thus, the sub made a promise, deliberately intending to induce detrimental reliance, which reliance would, ex ante, increase the sub's expected net utility.

A court could find that in such circumstances an implied option contract had been created. Not a contract yet between general and sub for the subcontract itself. But an option contract pursuant to which the general, by using the sub's bid in constructing its own, at the instigation and desire and implicit request of sub, had taken action that increased sub's ex ante expected net utility, thus furnishing consideration for a constructive, implied promise by the sub not to withdraw or change the terms of its sub bid after having submitted it to the general.[581] The general could thus rely on sub bids with peace of mind, knowing that if its general

[580] This fact pattern also provides the "only if, then" conditionality requisite for finding the presence of a mutual exchange. If the general does not use the sub's bid in constructing its own general bid, then the general experiences no increase in utility from sub's bid. If, however, the general does use sub's low or otherwise attractive bid in constructing the general's general bid, this permits the general to make a lower or more attractive bid for the overall project, increasing the general's likelihood of being awarded the project by the sponsor, thus increasing the general's ex ante anticipated utility. And this reliance by the general on sub's bid, which brings higher anticipated utility to the general, is also precisely what makes it more likely that the general will ultimately use the sub for the project, thus increasing sub's ex ante anticipated utility. Therefore, promisee's benefit only occurs if promisee brings benefit to the promisor, and we have a conditional "only if, then" structure of the type necessary to a mutual exchange transaction.

[581] For similar discussion, see also Alden, *Reversing the Reliance Revolution*, *supra* note 2, at 1662–63.

Traynor was fully aware of the concept that an offer for a unilateral contract can be viewed as creating an option contract binding on offeror not to revoke the offer, once the offeree has commenced performance on the principal underlying contract offered. But Traynor appears to have considered that since the general had not commenced using the sub's services, no consideration for such an option had been given. He appears not to have considered the argument advanced here by the Author, that the general's use of sub's bid in constructing the general's bid, thus increasing the likelihood of sub ultimately being awarded the subcontract by the general – which use by the general in its own bid construction was deliberately sought by the sub – is sufficient in and of itself to furnish consideration for an implied option against the sub not to revoke its offer.

In his view, the facts in his *Drennan* case were similar to "the analogous problem of an offer for a unilateral contract," within the meaning of Section 45, comment b, of the First Restatement (which now appears in essential substance as Section 45(1) of the Restatement (Second)). Drennan v. Star Paving Co., 333 P.2d 757, 759 (Cal. 1958). He then quoted that Section 45, comment b, of the First Restatement, in relevant part, laying particular emphasis in his own thinking on the embedded reference to Section 90's principle of promissory estoppel appearing at the end of this passage:

> The main includes as a subsidiary promise, necessarily implied, that if part of the requested performance is given, the offeror will not revoke his offer.... Part performance ... may thus furnish consideration for the subsidiary promises. Moreover,

bid were accepted by the sponsor, the general could then return to the subs without risk of the subs backing out or changing terms to the general's loss.

This may all seem a bit elaborate at first blush. But once one case lays out the logic in this manner, the precedent is set, and can easily be cited and relied upon by other courts so inclined. Neither *Drennan* nor other subcontractor bid cases since then need have been decided on promissory estoppel grounds to protect the generals. The same judicial result could as easily be reached on the basis of traditional contract law *terra firma*.

14.2 *Vague "Promise," Plus Benefit to Promisor*

The next category of "promissory estoppel case" is a particularly challenging one.

This is where the "promisor" has not really made a "promise" at all – or at least, such characterization might be subject to genuine, good faith challenge by reasonable minds. The "promise" could really be any statement of forward-looking intent or anticipation, or frankly something even squishier than that.[582]

But the critical aspect is that, whatever was said, a "promisee" hearing the statement might reasonably be expected detrimentally to rely thereon – or at least, such detrimental reliance might arguably have been reasonably foreseeable, even though, again, reasonable minds might differ as to this characterization. And in those courts that also impose a requirement that the reliance not merely be reasonably foreseeable, but substantively reasonable in and of itself,[583] that such interpretive gloss to Section 90 has also been satisfied.

And finally, the specific type of detrimental reliance by the "promisee" would be of manifest benefit to the "promisor."

What to do?

The essential issue here, the core issue, is whether the "promisor" has in fact truly made a statement that can legitimately be considered a "promise." Everything turns on this inquiry.

It is the Author's contention that in this regard, the classic requirement of traditional contract law that a statement must be sufficiently "definite" to constitute an enforceable promise is well considered, well founded, and necessary for the proper and responsible administration of law. It should be respected and applied in this category of "promissory estoppel cases." Courts should step up to their judicial

> merely acting in justifiable reliance on an offer may in some cases serve as a sufficient reason for making a promise binding (see § 90).

First Restatement, *supra* note 2, § 45 cmt. b.

Again, as argued here by the Author, no application of Section's 90 promissory estoppel is required whatsoever in order to find an implied option against the offering sub. The same result can be achieved in this situation through traditional contract law as through promissory estoppel.

582 *See* Chapter 7.1.1, *supra*.

583 *See* Chapter 7.1.2.2, *supra*.

responsibility to conduct the requisite analysis and render a decision predicated thereon.

There are many circumstances in which a decent, honest person, acting in good faith, might not wish to make a binding commitment to another. This does not mean that they necessary wish brachially to reject another's inquiry or desire – and might very well be inclined to do, or at least to consider doing, what the other might hope for – but still not wish to be legally bound to do so. In such situations, normal people, at least in Anglo-American culture, are generally inclined to say vague, friendly, positive sounding things, without pinning themselves down to hard, irrevocable commitments. And this is widely culturally understood.

It would be perverse for the legal system to impose liability upon normal conversants for this kind of communication, one to another.

On the other hand, there also exist myriad instances in which one party, particularly in the business context, may in fact wish to "sucker" someone else into doing something the speaker wishes. The speaker uses vague but highly positive statements about the future, and butters up the listener with compliments and visions of bright and happy things to come. This is all done with the ulterior motive of encouraging optimistic, trusting, hopeful reactions in the other, while carefully avoiding, skirting, and dancing around any hard statements of commitment on the part of the speaker. This kind of communication is endemic, for instance, in marketing and sales activity. But by no means limited thereto.

An excellent example of this type of situation is provided by *Blinn v. Beatrice.*[584] In that case, an employee closing in on retirement age wished to ensure his income level for some years to come.[585] He had received an offer from a competing employer in another state.[586] Before accepting that competing offer, he went in to his own supervisor and said he would quit his current employment and accept that competing offer unless his current employer guaranteed him employment through retirement age.[587] The supervisor replied, "Bob, we've got at least five more years of work to do."[588]

The employee chose to rely on this statement as sufficiently solid – a point to which this discussion shall return shortly – stayed in his current employment, was fired less than a year later, and brought suit.[589]

The court found the "five more years of work to do" statement by the supervisor not to be sufficiently certain as to the terms of a commitment to provide a basis for determining the existence of a breach and for giving an appropriate remedy – that is,

[584] Blinn v. Beatrice Cmty. Hosp. & Health Ctr., Inc., 708 N.W.2d 235 (Neb. 2006).
[585] *Id.* at 240.
[586] *Id.*
[587] *Id.*
[588] *Id.*
[589] *Id.* at 240–41.

was not sufficiently "definite."[590] Thus, there was no promise enforceable in contract.[591] However, the court said, there was a genuine issue of material fact as to whether the statement by the supervisor, where the employee had threatened to quit unless given assurance of continuing employment, was of a type where detrimental reliance thereon was reasonably foreseeable.[592] "Definiteness" of the terms of commitment, required in contract, is not required in promissory estoppel under Nebraska law, stated the court.[593]

Did the court handle the decision the right way?

At least as presented by the court, the fact pattern reeks of manipulative communication by the supervisor. It would seem beyond reasonable question, at least as presented by the court, that the supervisor was seeking to induce the employee to continue his current employment and pass up the competing offer. And the supervisor did so while carefully choosing his own words so as not to actually say, "Yes, we will guarantee you employment for the next five years," or ". . . through your retirement."

On these facts, it would not have been difficult for the court to find sufficient definiteness in the supervisor's statement to find in favor of the employee. This is because the statement was not made casually, perhaps while sipping pints at a company social event, or off the cuff during an ordinary day's work, but in specific response to a pointed, direct question and threat by the employee. The employee had stated, either you guarantee me the employment I seek or I will quit here and now.[594] The "five more years of work" statement was the supervisor's specific response to that point-blank ultimatum.[595]

590 *Id.* at 246:

> [T]he assurances offered to him were not sufficiently definite in form to constitute an offer of a unilateral contract. The statement that "we've got at least five more years of work to do" is not a clear offer of definite employment and does not manifest an intent to create a unilateral contract.

591 *Id.*

592 *Id.* at 247. On this point, the court reversed and remanded in part.

593 *Id.* (citations omitted):

> Under Nebraska law, the doctrine of promissory estoppel does not require that the promise giving rise to the cause of action must meet the requirements of an offer that would ripen into a contract if accepted by the promisee. . . . Simply stated, there is no requirement of "definiteness" in an action based upon promissory estoppel.

594 *Id.* at 240 (emphasis added):

> Blinn then went to the Beatrice administrator, Larry Emerson, seeking assurances about the permanency of Blinn's position with Beatrice, and drafted *a resignation letter he intended to submit to Beatrice unless he received full assurances that Beatrice wanted him to stay*. Blinn said:
>
> Well, I went in and asked him if I could visit, and I shut the door in his office *and handed him this letter, and he read it*, and he told me that he did not want me to leave. He assured me that I was doing a good job, and most importantly, he said, "Bob, we've got at least five more years of work to do."

595 *Id.*

This is, in fact, structurally quite similar to the earlier *Embry v. Hargadine* case, in which a similar ultimatum was made by an employee, a similar vague response given – vague, but manifestly intended and worded in a manner designed to allay any concerns on the part of the employee – and the court found the employer in that case to have accepted the employee's offer of a term employment contract.[596] While there are certain distinctions between the two cases, the substance and logical implications are in both instances very closely related.

The same approach as in *Embry* could have been taken by the court in *Blinn*. To any reasonable third party, the employer's response could have been seen as a specific response to a specific question – as assent to a proposition from the employee – and thus sufficiently definite to provide a basis for enforcement in contract against the employer. This comports with the Author's own view and evaluation of the facts as presented by the court.

Alternatively, however, as reasonable minds can differ on arguable points, the court in *Blinn* could have concluded that the employer did not intend to be legally bound, and wanted to convey to the employee a need for employee's services and thus likelihood of continued employment, but not a guarantee thereof.

In support of this alternative view is the simple and irreducible fact that the employee chose to rely on a somewhat elusive response from the employer that did

[596] Embry v. Hargadine, McKittrick Dry Goods Co., 105 S.W. 777 (Mo.App. 1907). In *Embry*, a term employee whose prior employment contract had just recently come to a close sought a fresh one year term employment contract. The employee went in to the president of the company

> and said to him, that as appellant's [employee's] written employment had lapsed eight days before, and as there were only a few days between then and the 1st of January in which to seek employment with other firms, if respondent [the company] wished to retain his services longer he must have a contract for another year, or he would quit respondent's service right then and there. That he had been put off twice before and wanted an understanding or contract at once so that he could go ahead without worry. . . . McKittrick [the company president] then said: "Go ahead, you're all right. Get your men out, and don't let that worry you."

Id. at 777.

The court concluded that this response, to that request, under those circumstances, constituted assent:

> We think no reasonable man would construe that answer to Embry's [employee's] demand that he be employed for another year, otherwise than as an assent to the demand, and that Embry had the right to rely on it as an assent.

Id. at 779. "The answer was unambiguous, and we rule that . . . it constituted in law a valid contract of re-employment." *Id.* at 780.

Thus, the court implicitly found that the response, coupled with the specific terms of reemployment sought and communicated by the employee, was sufficiently "definite" to form a contract.

not squarely, head-on, answer the employee's ultimatum.[597] This happens all the time in real-life interactions. Anglo-American culture, in particular, shies away from direct, head-to-head, verbal conflict. The employee might have known or sensed that if he had pushed the issue, if he had forced a straight up answer from the supervisor, the response might then have come back in the negative. And the employee would then have had to carry through on his threat to quit, and incur all the hassle, disruption, and loss of social connections generally incident to moving from one geographic location to another. So, to avoid that unpleasant result, the employee chose to satisfy himself, for the moment, with the supervisor's elliptical response.

And herein lies the problem.

Ever since contract law has existed in the Western world, the law has recognized the profound social problems that would arise if it becomes unduly easy to engage the machinery of the state to claw defendants' assets from them upon the mere allegation by a plaintiff of some alleged oral agreement.

In Roman times, this was addressed by permitting enforcement only of (i) formal contracts of high evidential character (*stipulatio*), (ii) certain named, well-established categories of certain common transactions (such as sale–purchase, lease, partnership), and (iii) lastly, as a catch-all category, any other contractual agreement (pacts) provided they were founded upon a mutual exchange transaction.[598] Similarly, in the earlier phases of English law, enforcement was limited to (i) formal contracts of high evidential character (reflected in a written "deed") and (ii) as to informal contracts, principally the writ of "debt upon contract," under which a plaintiff could only bring suit after having rendered their own performance.[599]

Later, once the universal use of the tort writ of assumpsit in all contract actions had been permitted by *Slade's Case* in 1602 in order to obviate the hitherto preclusive affirmative defense of "wager of law,"[600] it was observed at the time that plaintiffs could far too easily allege the existence of oral contractual agreements. As stated by Chief Justice Hale at the time, two people could hardly have a conversation, without one of them being able to allege that some type of oral contract had been entered into.[601] The response to this problem was legislative,

[597] Again, the court considered the supervisor's response to have been "unambiguous," and the Author personally shares this view and ultimate weighing of the language and circumstances, but others might reasonably see the matter differently.

[598] *See supra* Chapter 1.

[599] *See supra* Chapter 3.1.

[600] *See supra* Chapter 3.2.5.

[601] *See* Buckeridge v. Sherly, Treby's reports, MT MS. 651 (1671) (Hale, C.J.), *reprinted in* English Sources, *supra* note 45, at 444:

> [A]ctions on the case are become one of the great grievances of the nation; for two men cannot talk together but one fellow or other who stands in a corner swears a promise and cause of action. These catching promises must not be encouraged. It were very well if a

namely, the Statute of Frauds of 1677.[602] By imposing a writing requirement for the enforcement of many of the more important species of contract of the day (substantial sale of goods, sale of land, etc.), the Statute of Frauds reestablished a minimum hurdle for plaintiffs to clear in proving up the existence of an alleged contract.

Promissory estoppel, of course, exacerbates this problem, given the noncomprehensive categorical coverage of the Statute of Frauds, which generally does not address vast numbers of services contracts.[603] Williston's new doctrine eliminates the requirement of mutual agreement, and of mutual consideration, and, indeed, in a number of courts, even the minimum contractual threshold of definiteness for enforcement. The long-recognized, age-old problem of unduly easy allegation by plaintiffs has been aggravated.

There are compelling reasons in all areas of the law to draw reasonably discernible lines as the predicate for enforcement. Indeed, it is the very essence of the rule of law, the very definition of what a "law" is, that a rule be stated in a form reasonably understandable to all, of a nature where an individual can conform their conduct accordingly, and applied in a nondiscriminatory manner across different parties. Where the lines become blurry, or worse, completely effaced, what we are left with is no longer law whatsoever, but rather judicial fiat.

Cases such as *Blinn*, which have declared inapplicable the requirement of definiteness as a threshold for enforcement in promissory estoppel, nearly obliterate the distinction between bargaining negotiations understood by the parties as preliminary to legal obligation, and those ordinary, day-to-day statements of intent or anticipation that constitute such a large part of normal discourse among normal people. It is a breeding ground for disputes and litigation.

In particular, *Blinn* and its doctrinal brethren generate moral hazard. They encourage someone like the employee not to pursue clear communications where each party knows with reasonable certainty whether they are legally binding themselves or not. Rather, the employee now has every incentive not to push the issue with the supervisor, knowing that a negative response might ensue. The employee has incentive to "play the line," as it were. The employee in *Blinn* could easily have requested that the supervisor clarify, and state definitively whether employment was guaranteed for the period sought by employee. The employee chose not to do so. Despite the initial presentation of the case that gives the impression of an innocent victim, the employee was not in fact fully innocent. He was part of the problem. It takes two to tango. The supervisor made a statement presumably intended to give

law were made whereby some ceremony, as striking hands etc., were required to every promise that should bind.

602 The Statute of Frauds, 29 Car. II, ch. 3, *in* 5 STATUTES OF THE REALM 840 (1677), *reprinted in* ENGLISH SOURCES, *supra* note 45, at 445.

These developments, namely, the metastasis of easy allegations as to oral contracts, and the legislative response thereto, are discussed in detail in BAKER, *supra* note 92, at 349–50.

603 For a generic listing of contractual categories covered by statutes of frauds enacted by the various US states, see RESTATEMENT (SECOND), *supra* note 2, § 110.

the employee a warm and happy feeling and induce him to stay without legal obligation by the employer. And the employee chose not to seek clarity and force the issue to a head. The lack of pellucid communication and understanding was a two-party affair, not solely one-sided.

What the courts should enforce are rules that encourage private actors to be precise in their communications, for the purpose of establishing clarity as to legal obligations and freedoms therefrom. The requirement of definiteness in contract is precisely such a salutary rule of law.

The Author therefore submits that the court in *Blinn* should have stepped up to tackle head-on the issue of definiteness as to the supervisor's statement and render its decision upon that basis. Again, reasonable minds might differ as to whether the supervisor should be seen as having made a sufficiently definite commitment, or successfully skirted commitment by declining to state an actual guarantee of employment. The issue is not what the result in the case is. The issue is the basis on which it was decided. After declaring the supervisor's statement too indefinite for contract, the court remanded for a determination of reasonable foreseeability under the promissory estoppel claim. The court should instead have decided the case on the basis of contract alone, turning on the issue of definiteness as to the supervisor's statement.

This approach can and should, it is here maintained, be applied by courts across the board when confronted with a vague or ambiguous statement. They should resist the temptation to bail out at 35,000 feet and pull the conceptual ripcord of promissory estoppel. Rather, they should pilot the craft to safe landing on the firm doctrinal ground of traditional contract law.

14.3 *Definite Promise, No Quid Pro Quo*

The next category of "promissory estoppel case" to be addressed are those situations where the promisor has indeed made a clear, explicit promise, reasonably definite in terms, but is asking for nothing in return, and where there is no reason to believe that the promisor is attempting to induce detrimental reliance by the promisee of benefit to the promisor.

If the situation at hand is a gift promise, as described multiple times *supra*, the traditional contract law rule is that such promises are not enforceable, as there is no consideration for them.

If the promisor wishes to lock the gift in, and make it legally binding, all the promisor has to do is actually deliver the gift. If the gratuitous commitment is of a nature only intended to occur in the future, the promisor could – albeit at legal expense and hassle – set up a trust or provide for disposition in promisor's will.

Precisely because it is so very easy for family members to allege the existence of gratuitous intrafamily gifts and gift promises, and there can be so much contention among various competing family member claims, this area of the law features numerous protective requirements. The delivery requirement for currently effective gifts is one such. The evidentiary requirements for formal wills are another. These rules have been established over time for good and compelling reason, and it may very well be best to simply leave them alone, not to innovate whatsoever in this space.

If, however, one were to reach the conclusion that the current legal structure for intrafamily gift promises does not adequately address the *Ricketts* fact pattern – where one family member wishes to enter into a legally binding obligation to make a gift in the future, though without reflecting obligation in a will or trust – two alternative approaches lie readily to hand.

The first would be to alter the law of property with respect to deemed delivery of a gift, as already suggested by the Author as a possibility in connection with the *Ricketts* case, *supra*. The suggested new deemed delivery rule would obtain if a family member has made a clear, definite gift promise, has consistently behaved since that time in a manner consonant with the declared gift promise, has never revoked the gift promise either explicitly or implicitly, and has never formalized the gift promise in a trust or a will. In such case, upon the promisor's passing, delivery would be deemed to occur at such time, prior to probate. This suggested rule would honor the promisor's evident and still effective intention at the time of passing.

A second possible approach would be to reinvigorate formal contract in this connection. A rule could be established that a promisor wishing to make a gift promise could render the gratuitous promise legally binding, without consideration, by utilizing some level of formality to do so. This would ensure that both the admonitory and evidentiary functions of formality have been fulfilled. At the most relaxed end of the spectrum, a rule could be established under which a mere writing would be deemed sufficient. Somewhat more rigorous would be to require that the writing be notarized, perhaps with additional witnesses to the signature, and perhaps filed with the court or other administrative agency.

But in either case, the proposed solution to any perceived lacuna in the current structure of the law could and should be carefully targeted to a clearly identified problem crying out for attention. There is no call whatsoever for the massive blunderbuss of Section 90's promissory estoppel to be fired at the issue.

14.4 *Vague "Promise," No Quid Pro Quo*

It should go without saying that where the "promisor" has not made any definite commitment, but rather some vague statement of future intent or anticipation, and it is not evident that the statement would lead to detrimental reliance by the promisee of benefit to the "promisor," liability should not be imposed.

The "promisor" in such a situation has done nothing wrong, has not entered into a bargain, has not made any firm commitment. Moreover, the "promisee" has chosen to rely on a statement that perhaps they should not have relied on.

By choosing to change position in detrimental reliance, without having paid or promised to pay anything to the "promisor" by way of recompense, the "promisee" has assumed the risk that the "promisor" might change their mind, or simply not conduct themselves in the way that "promisee" had anticipated. We are all responsible for our actions, "promisee" as well as "promisor." The "promisee" did not have to change position in detrimental reliance. They chose to do so. They own that decision. They are responsible for it, and for the consequences thereof.

Yet, promissory estoppel would permit liability to be imposed on the "promisor" in such a situation, particularly if the court applies Section 90 as written and does not add the interpretive gloss that "promisee's" reliance must itself have been substantively reasonable. Clearly, such a liability result should be rejected. There should be no liability in promissory estoppel, and none in contract.

14.5 *Promise Learned of by Third Party*

The foregoing considerations apply a fortiori to the astounding ambition of the Restatement (Second) to elevate third parties – *to whom no promise was even directed* – into the class of potentially aggrieved victims as promissory estoppel plaintiffs. This unwarranted and unprecedented attempt to expand the scope of liability merely adds the potential for overbreadth inherent in third-party beneficiary claims to the already manifest potential for overbreadth inherent in promissory estoppel. It is an exponentially more dangerous concept, and should be rejected as such.

15 RECOMMENDATION FOR THIRD RESTATEMENT TO REVERSE PROMISSORY ESTOPPEL

There is only one effective way to reverse the artificial doctrine of promissory estoppel back out of American contract law, to return to the way things were. That is to recur to the origin of the doctrine itself, namely, the ALI's Restatement.

The First Restatement was drafted in the 1920s, and published in 1932. The Restatement (Second) was drafted in the 1960s and 1970s, appearing in 1981. It is time for a Third Restatement, one designed to pull up by the roots promissory estoppel and a host of related provisions scattered throughout the Restatement.

The following recommendations would largely effectuate such objective.

15.1 *Section 90: Promissory Estoppel*

The doctrine of promissory estoppel is set forth in Section 90, "Promise Reasonably Inducing Action or Forbearance." The principal recommendation of this book is that Section 90 be deleted in its entirety.[604]

[604] To the extent one wished to retain the caselaw exception to the consideration requirement for promises to make charitable contributions, that exception could be set forth in a new

In the wake of such deletion, the analytic framework proposed in Chapter 3 of this book can and should be applied going forward to decide so-called promissory estoppel cases.

The result would be to return American contract law to the well-designed, smoothly functioning legal machine it was prior to the wrench of promissory estoppel having been thrown into the works.

15.2 *Section 87(2): Promissory Estoppel Applied to Offers*

Closely allied with Section 90 is application of the same principle to offers that have not yet been accepted by the offeree. This appears in the current Section 87(2) (a subpart of Section 87, "Option Contract"), which reads as follows:

> An offer which the offeror should reasonably expect to induce action or forbearance of a substantial character on the part of the offeree before acceptance and which does induce such action or forbearance is binding as an option contract to the extent necessary to avoid injustice.[605]

In other words, an offeree need not accept an offer, and thus make a counter-commitment to the offeror, to lock the offeror in place. All the offeree has to do is assume that the offeror cannot revoke the offer, commence detrimental action in reliance thereon, and while maintaining the offeree's liberty simply to walk away at any time, without any obligation to the offeror. It is a free one-way option against the offeror.

It is worth noting, of course, that this is precisely what Traynor did in the *Drennan* subcontractor bid case, discussed *supra*. He gave the general a free option against the sub. Now in *Drennan*, the result may well have felt just, because the sub desired that the general rely on sub's bid in constructing the general's own bid, as this would increase the likelihood of the subcontract ultimately being given by the general to the sub. However, as argued earlier, Traynor need not have used promissory estoppel whatsoever to reach his desired result, which he could have attained through an implied unilateral option contract analysis.

freestanding section of its own. If so, however, serious inquiry should be made as to whether such exception is justified in circumstances where the charitable institution literally has not even detrimentally relied on the promise, as current Section 90(2) would have it: "A charitable subscription or a marriage settlement is binding under Section (1) without proof that the promise induced action or forbearance." *Id.* § 90(2).

The Author's own recommendation is that removing even the detrimental reliance element from the enforcement of promises for charitable donations is ill-advised. In the Author's view, unless and until a donor has in fact delivered a gift to the donee, or made irrevocable legal provision for it, such as through an irrevocable trust, it is still the donor's money or land. The donor should, by any moral standard in a free society, have the right to decide the disposition of the donor's own assets, and should thus be at their liberty to change their mind until the point they have actually made a grant of the property in question.

[605] *Id.* § 87(2).

As also noted by Judge Learned Hand in *Baird v. Gimbel*[606] – an earlier subcontractor bid case that is not precisely on all fours with Drennan but nonetheless bears significant structural similarity to that later case – there is no per se compelling reason why generals must necessarily enjoy free options against subs. The general in *Baird* "might in advance have secured a [sub]contract conditional upon the success of its [general] bid. . . ." That is, the *Baird* general could have entered into an immediately effective subcontract with the sub it had in mind for the project, in which subcontract the general's duties to proceed were subject to a condition precedent that the general have won the overall general contract bidding process with the project sponsor.

By contrast to the carefully constructed approach suggested by Learned Hand in *Baird*, where the parties make their contractual obligations clear through precise drafting and structuring of their agreements, the *Drennan* promissory estoppel approach is a cheap, quick, dirty and, above all, sloppy approach to regulating the rights and responsibilities of parties to the subcontracting process. The parties are not encouraged by the legal framework to clarify and make explicit their legal arrangements, rather quite the converse.

More to the point, Section 87(2) is in no way limited on its face to *Drennan*-type fact patterns. It has the potential on its face to apply to any and all manner of offers across the entire contractual landscape.

One might be tempted to say that Section 87(2) should be removed and deleted for the same reasons as Section 90, and just leave it at that. But the situation with Section 87(2) is arguably even more aggravated than with Section 90 itself. This is because 87(2), by specifically targeting offers, is addressing head-on promises that by their very terms are not intended to become operative unless and until they have been accepted by the counterparty. The promise is tautologically conditional in nature – "if you do, or agree to do, X for me, then I will do Y for you." The offeree knows – *knows* – that they do not have a deal, and are thus not invited or permitted to rely on the offer unless they have first accepted and entered upon a counter-obligation to the promisor. Unless we are dealing with a *Drennan*-type fact pattern, where it can credibly be argued that the offeror intended and desired that the offeree engage in detrimental reliance on the offer without yet having accepted the offer and made any countercommitment whatsoever to the offeror, then Section 87(2) runs counter to the entire premise of what the offeror intended to communicate in making an offer.[607]

[606] James Baird Co. v. Gimbel Brothers, Inc., 64 F.2d 344 (2d Cir. 1933).

[607] This very point was made by Learned Hand in *Baird*, where he wrote that

> an offer for an exchange is not meant to become a promise until a consideration has been received, either a counterpromise or whatever else is stipulated. To extend it would be to hold the offeror regardless of the stipulated condition of his offer.

Id. at 346.

Suffice it to say, this book recommends that Section 87(2) be removed and deleted in the same manner as Section 90.

15.3 *Section 139: Promissory Estoppel Circumventing the Statute of Frauds*

Another principal innovation in the Restatement (Second) was the creation of Section 139, which purports to use promissory estoppel to sweep aside the Statute of Frauds:

> A promise which the promisor should reasonably expect to induce action or forbearance on the part of the promisee or a third person and which does induce the action or forbearance is enforceable notwithstanding the Statute of Frauds if injustice can be avoided only by enforcement of the promise.[608]

As described by Farnsworth:

> This section has already had an important impact. When a sharp rise in the grain market in 1973 and 1974 caused sellers to repudiate their oral agreements after buyers had already made arrangements to resell, courts searching for a ground to reject the sellers' Statute of Frauds defense placed heavy emphasis on section 139.[609]

General concerns with promissory estoppel are, in this instance, exacerbated by the fact that Section 139 runs directly counter to statutory law. Section 139 is nothing more than a suggestion by the academics and others who compose the ALI to disregard precisely and directly the entire policy objective of the Statute of Frauds, which is to provide a defense to enforcement of mere allegations of certain oral agreements of significant character. To employ Section 139 would "be in direct conflict with the purpose and policy of the Statute,"[610] and "render the [Statute of Frauds] entirely nugatory."[611]

Unlike the Restatement, the Statute of Frauds is democratically legitimated, having been enacted at the state level throughout the United States. Section 139 thus represents not the exercise of equitable powers by a court around the fringes of a legal rule, to prevent injustice. It is the purportedly proper use of equitable powers simply to deny the relevant legislature's intent and judgment altogether.

One might note here, by the by, that Learned Hand in the quoted passage, in contradistinction to the Restatement (Second), holds the view that an offer does not become a promise until accepted. The Restatement (Second) view is that an offer is indeed a promise, but one that is conditional in nature. In the Author's view, the difference in description is largely six of one, half a dozen of the other, in terms of ultimate legal consequence, with the Restatement view having somewhat greater intuitive and logical appeal. The Restatement view has therefore formed the basis for discussion in the principal text here.

608 Restatement (Second), *supra* note 2, § 139(1).

609 Farnsworth, *Ingredients in the Redaction of the Restatement (Second)*, *supra* note 241, at 7.

610 Ayres et al., Studies in Contract Law, *supra* note 228, at 460.

611 Ozier v. Haines, 103 N.E.2d 485, 487 (Ill. 1952).

As such, it is here recommended that Section 139 likewise be removed from the Restatement. If and to the extent that academics wish to pursue a relaxation of the strictures of the Statute of Frauds, they should propose and advocate for the adoption of amendments thereto by state legislatures. The ultimate decision would thus be subject to the will of the people, via their elected representatives.

15.4 *Ancillary Sections to Be Revised*

The foregoing three major recommendations would effectively bring the Restatement's advocacy of promissory estoppel to an end. There are, however, quite a few other provisions littered throughout the Restatement that Williston manifestly built into the nest of contract law for the purpose of welcoming the cuckoo's egg of promissory estoppel. Having addressed the principal pillars of promissory estoppel thus far, it is therefore further recommended that these ancillary provisions likewise be "cleaned up," as it were, to return them to their proper classical contours. The exercise puts one in mind of Napoleon's dictum, "*frappez la masse, et tout le reste vient par surcroît.*"[612] Having struck the center, the recommendations now turn to "the rest."

15.4.1 Section 1: Definition of "Contract"

Prominent among these other provisions is the very definition of "contract" itself, set forth in Section 1 of the Restatement (Second):

> A contract is a promise or a set of promises for the breach of which the law gives a remedy, or the performance of which the law in some way recognizes as a duty.[613]

This definition is, of course, absurdly overbroad. In essence, it says that a contract comprises any species of enforceable promise. What it manifestly omits is any indication of which promises shall be enforced, upon what bases, upon what preconditions. This is obviously by design, not accident.

Very specifically, this definition omits any mention of mutual agreement, or mutual consideration. Quite clearly it was so written to permit the misclassification of promissory estoppel as a category of "contract."

Historically, commonly cited definitions of "contract" declare mutual assent and mutual consideration to be the two criteria that literally define the concept. For example, the standard definition of the term stated in the seminal Slade's Case of 1602 sounds as follows:

[612] Quoted and translated as "strike the center, and the rest will follow," by Mark Helprin, *The Heart of the Matter*, CLAREMONT REVIEW OF BOOKS (Fall 2022), https://claremontreviewofbooks.com/the-heart-of-the-matter/.

[613] RESTATEMENT (SECOND), *supra* note 2, § 1. The definition was already crafted thusly in the First Restatement as well, by Williston himself. FIRST RESTATEMENT, *supra* note 2, § 1.

> a mutual agreement between the parties for something to be performed by the defendant in consideration of some benefit which must depart from the plaintiff, or of some labour or prejudice which must be sustained by the plaintiff.[614]

In 1765, Blackstone defined contract as "an agreement, a mutual bargain. . . ."[615] Similarly, William Wetmore Story in his major treatise on contract law in 1844 specified that a "contract is a deliberate engagement between competent parties, upon a legal consideration to do, or to abstain from doing, some act."[616] He further wrote of the "*reciprocity of consideration*, and *mutuality of agreement*, which are necessary to constitute a parol agreement. . . ."[617]

Also noteworthy in Williston's newfangled definition is that it excludes the well-known and well-established concept of an "executed" contract, that is, one which is immediately performed by both sides, as distinct from a contract which is unilaterally or bilaterally "executory," namely, based on promise yet to be performed in the future.[618]

It is evident that the effect of this omission is to downplay mutual exchange as the true foundation of contract. Instead, "contract" is now to focus exclusively on promise, rather than exchange. This shift in the essential philosophical underpinnings of the concept helps open the path to enforcement of promise standing alone, irrespective of whether mutual exchange is present. Promissory estoppel beckons.

15.4.2 Section 79(c): Mutuality of Obligation

One of the somewhat subtle subversive moves made by Williston was to declare the requirement of "mutuality of obligation" nonsensical and incorrect.

"Mutuality of obligation" is, of course, nothing other than another way of stating the mutual consideration requirement for the formation of contract. It is, therefore, tautologically correct, at least in its essential core.

Williston's attack on mutuality of obligation was conducted by undermining the essential legitimacy and applicability of the concept with a series of technically

[614] *Slade's Case*, *supra* note 181, at 429 (remarks of Tanfield "before all the justices of England, assembled at Serjeants' Inn," Michaelmas term 1598). Tanfield spoke of this as "assumpsit," which as discussed *supra* became in effect the universal writ of choice for contractual actions as a result of the decision in Slade's Case.

[615] 2 Blackstone, *supra* note 3, at 443.

[616] 1 Story, *supra* note 205, at 1.

[617] *Id.* (emphasis added). A "parol agreement" is one which is neither an obligation of record nor under seal. *Id.*

[618] "Executed" contract is defined and discussed in inter alia 2 Blackstone, *supra* note 3, at 443; 1 Story, *supra* note 205, at 8.

The drafters of the Uniform Commercial Code, initially appearing in 1952, declined to follow Williston's attempt to shift the foundation of contract law in this respect, clearly including within the definition of the term "contract" a "present sale" of goods. *See* U.C.C. § 2-106(1) (Am. Law Inst. & Unif. Law Comm'n 2022).

correct statements around its fringes, and with reference, of course, to promissory estoppel, his true objective. Section 79(c) reads as follows:

> If the requirement of consideration is met, there is no additional requirement of . . . "mutuality of obligation."[619]

A comment to the section spells out his justification for this statement:

> The word "mutuality," though often used in connection with the law of Contracts, has no definite meaning. "Mutual assent" as one element of a bargain is the subject of Topic 2. . . . Clause (c) of this Section negates any supposed requirement of "mutuality of obligation." Such a requirement has sometimes been asserted in the form, "Both parties must be bound or neither is bound." That statement is obviously erroneous as applied to an exchange of promise for performance; it is equally inapplicable to contracts governed by §§ 82–94 and to contracts enforceable by virtue of their formal characteristics under § 6. Even in the ordinary case of the exchange of promise for promise, § 78 makes it clear that voidable and unenforceable promises may be consideration. The only requirement of "mutuality of obligation even in cases of mutual promises is that stated in §§ 76–77.[620]

This is rather like declaring the generalized statement, "the sky is blue," to be "obviously erroneous" because sometimes the weather is overcast, sometimes it is night, and so on. But it is far more egregious than that. The instances in which the sky is not, in fact, blue can occupy a significant portion, if not all, of any given day. Particularly in London, England, or in Seattle, Washington, as many of us know from personal experience. Nonetheless, every sensible individual understands full well the essential point being made by an affirmation of the sky's generally blue color. The exceptions to the general principle cited by Williston are indeed merely minor, ancillary side points to the general verity of the statement that mutuality of obligation is required for the enforceability of contract.

To begin with, an "exchange of promise for performance" will most typically be present when the offeree accepts through commencement of performance.[621] In such a case, the law reads in an implied covenant, thus a promise, by the offeree now to complete performance in full.[622] Thus, there is indeed mutuality of obligation in such situations. It is the comparatively rare case of an offer for a unilateral contract, such as a brokerage contract, or a reward offer, that the offeree remains unbound while they commence and attempt to complete performance.[623]

The reference to formal contract is correct, but effectively irrelevant in the American context, where formal contract has as a practical matter retreated to vestigial status.

[619] Restatement (Second), *supra* note 2, § 79(c).
[620] *Id.* § 79 cmt. f.
[621] *See id.* § 62(1).
[622] *Id.* § 62(2).
[623] *See id.* § 45 cmt. e.

The reference to voidable or unenforceable promises constituting consideration covers such comparative rarities as voidable promises made by a minor lacking legal capacity, or contractual obligations subject to affirmative defense due to the statute of limitations or bankruptcy.

It is therefore true that the vast majority of all contracts do in fact require mutuality of obligation to be enforceable.

Thus, the true objective behind Williston's denigration of the concept of "mutuality of obligation," his casting of this phrase as some sort of intellectual error, some species of fundamental misunderstanding of the subject, is to undermine one's instinctive sense that mutuality is required for contract. Although he has hedged his statement with the prefatory words, "if the requirement of consideration is met" – which of course means that mutuality if present and thus effectively guts the rest of the statement negating the mutuality requirement – this is a clear delegitimation attack. It is manifestly intended to provide intellectual and political cover for the novum of promissory estoppel, as seen in his reference to those "contracts" "governed by §§ 82–94."

The more responsible way of handling the matter would be to remove this reference in Section 79(c) to mutuality of obligation and address it perhaps as a mere comment to Section 17, which addresses the requirement of "bargain" for the existence of contract.[624] "Bargain" means mutual assent to a mutual exchange.[625] That suggested new comment on mutuality could simply state that – with the exception of those handful of unusual circumstances listed by Williston – "mutuality of obligation" is indeed required in all bilaterally executory informal contracts. These constitute, of course, the vast majority of all contracts at their point of inception.

15.4.3 References to Sections 90 and 87(2) Throughout

Throughout the entire Restatement, there appear references to Sections 90 and 87 (2) as exceptions to the ordinary rules of contract otherwise applicable. It is as if a portal, a wormhole, to an imaginary alternate world exists, one in which neither mutual consideration nor mutual assent are required. It is the imposition of liability for unfulfilled "promise," untethered from its historical moorings. Consequent to the removal of Sections 90 and 87(2), these many references to those elided sections, and the exceptions they currently claim to the normal rules of contract, should likewise be removed. For brevity, a number of these are illustratively listed here by footnote.[626]

[624] *See id.* § 17(1).

[625] *Id.* § 3.

[626] *See, e.g., id.* § 17(2); § 17 cmt. e; § 25 cmt. c; § 34 cmt. d; § 45 cmt. f; § 50 cmt. b; § 62 cmt. d; § 69 cmt. c; § 71 cmt. b, c; § 72 cmts. b, c; § 74 cmt. d; § 79 cmts. b, d, f; ch. 4, topic 2, intro. note; § 82 cmt. a; § 84 cmt. c; § 87 cmt. e; § 88(c); § 88 cmt. d; § 89(c); 89 cmt. d.

Conclusion

What this book has attempted to do is trace the genesis, method of execution, marketing, and effect, of what amounts to a massive academic fraud.

No fraud would have been present had Sections 90, 87(2), and 139 all been clearly identified as mere suggestions by the American Law Institute (ALI), rather than "the law as it is." And no fraud would have been present had the historical development of contract law doctrine and more recent American cases been honestly and fairly presented. But such is not the record.

What the record reveals instead is that the newfound doctrine of "promissory estoppel" was point-blank invented, that its artificial nature was obfuscated through its presentation as an organic element of "the law as it is," and that it was slid past the natural intellectual defenses of the legal profession, widely marketed on the basis of misleading claims of historical precedent.

The American public deserves better. Our Anglo-American ancestors, who built the magnificent and comprehensive structure of classical contract law, deserve better. And our descendants – who rely on our generation to pass along to them predictable principles characteristic of the rule of law, rather than a system riven with potential judicial fiat and subject to a high risk of doctrinal metastasis and consequent overbreadth over time – deserve better.

ANNEX A

Blackstone*

The "choppy water" referred to here by the Author relates to a certain terminological ambiguity when it comes to the word "consideration" in the context of whether a deed will be recognized and honored as having legal effect. Briefly put, Blackstone set forth and described in this context a rather unfortunate linguistic distinction – presumably not his in origin – between a "valuable consideration" and a "good consideration." "[A] valuable consideration is such as money, marriage, or the like, which the law esteems an equivalent given for the grant; and is therefore founded in motives of justice"; whereas "[a] good consideration is such as that of blood, or of natural love and affection, when a man grants an estate to a near relation; being founded on motives of generosity, prudence, and natural duty. . . ."[627]

In his discussion, the former, a "valuable consideration," is the consideration with which we are familiar, that is, a component of the reciprocal exchange that renders a contract enforceable. A "good consideration," by contrast, in the sense used by Blackstone, does not necessarily and in fact would generally not be expected to constitute a mutual exchange, but rather a gratuitous transfer by deed to a family member. It would, in fact, be better referred to simply as one's "motive" for granting property to another. Blackstone's use of the common word "consideration" in these two antipodal contexts presents, of course, a rather extraordinary risk of conceptual conflation.

The potential for misunderstanding, however, is perhaps sufficiently resolved by the fact that Blackstone's discussion of so-called good consideration generally relates to gifts and grants, both of which he defines to involve fully executed, thus consummated, transfers of possession and property interest by one to another: "Grants or gifts, of chattels *personal*, are the act of transferring the right and the possession of

* From Chapter 4.3 ("Blackstone"), note 201.

627 2 Sir William Blackstone, Commentaries on the Laws of England 297 (London, W. Strahan, T. Cadell in the Strand, & D. Prince, Oxford, 9th rev. ed. 1783) (Garland Pub. photo reprint 1978) (1765–69).

them; whereby one man renounces, and another man immediately acquires, all title and interest therein. . . ."[628]

By contrast, when he turns to the enforcement of executory promise, of a contract, Blackstone then speaks of "sufficient" and "valuable" consideration, and makes his strong statements quoted here in the main text regarding reciprocity of exchange as the key criterion and requirement of such enforcement.[629]

The reason Blackstone engaged with the concept of "good" consideration whatsoever appears to be solely a concern that a purported transfer of property, not arising from a mutual exchange transaction, and not motivationally grounded by familial love and affection, raises red flags. "Deeds made upon good consideration only, are considered as merely voluntary. . . ."[630] "Merely voluntary," of course, means that one is not legally compelled to undertake the act, in contradistinction to the legally compulsory requirement that one deliver or perform the consideration one has agreed to furnish pursuant to a mutually agreed mutual exchange. A "conveyance, when merely voluntary," Blackstone continued, "is somewhat suspicious; and is usually construed to be fraudulent, if creditors or others become sufferers thereby."[631] For this reason, "every grant or gift of chattels, as well as lands, with an intent to defraud creditors or other, shall be void as against such persons to whom such fraud would be prejudicial; but, as against the grantor himself, shall stand good and effectual. . . ."[632]

Critically, Blackstone's discussion of the concept of "good" consideration in the foregoing cited text does not relate to the enforcement of executory promise. Rather, it relates to whether there exist grounds for invalidating an already fully executed purported gift or grant:

> A true and proper gift or grant is always accompanied with delivery of possession, and takes effect immediately. . . . [I]t is not in the donor's power to retract it, though he did it without any consideration or recompense [Author's note: this is fully consistent with current law concerning the legal validity and effectiveness of an executed, delivered gift, as distinct from a promise to make a gift in the future, which is unenforceable]; unless it be prejudicial to creditors; or the donor were under any legal incapacity, as infancy, coverture, duress, or the like; or if he were drawn in, circumvented, or imposed upon, by false pretences, ebriety, or surprize.[633]

Thus, the initially confusing reference to "good" consideration resolves into simply a factual trigger for heightened legal scrutiny when it is absent from the circumstances of an already consummated transfer of property.[634]

628 *Id.* at 441 (emphasis in the original).
629 *See id.* at 442–45, and Chapter 4.3.
630 *Id.* at 297 (emphasis added).
631 *Id.* at 441.
632 *Id.*
633 *Id.*
634 For additional, consonant discussion of the matter, see Alden, *Reversing the Reliance Revolution in Contract*, 93 Wash. L. Rev. 1609, 1622-25 (2018).

That this analysis of Blackstone's explication of a terminological distinction between "valuable" versus "good" consideration was widely understood in the same manner as set forth here, see, for example, W. W. Story's 1844 treatise on contract law:

> *The law requires not only a consideration but that it be valuable. A valuable consideration is distinguished from a good consideration. A good consideration* is an equitable consideration, founded upon mere love, or affection, or gratitude, and *will not support an action on a contract*; but a valuable consideration is a legal consideration. . . .[635]

Likewise, Joseph Chitty's 1851 treatise on contract law discussed Blackstone's distinction in terms substantively quite similar to those set forth here, noting specifically:

> We may premise, that considerations, as they relate to *deeds*, are, in general, divided into *good* and *valuable* considerations. . . .
>
> We must, however, observe, that the term *good* consideration, as thus used in the case of deeds, does not apply to *simple* contracts [i.e. contracts not under seal], to support which, mere relationship, or natural love and affection, is not a sufficient consideration.[636]

Two other respects in which Blackstone's explication of contract law might initially raise a question are his treatment of (i) bailment, that is, a circumstance in which an owner of property has temporarily entrusted custody thereof to another and (ii) borrowing.

As to bailment, Blackstone refers to this general category as a "contract," and indeed the many specific examples thereof that he furnishes nearly all involve clearly mutual exchange situations, such as goods delivered to a common carrier for delivery, a horse handed over by a guest to an innkeeper and his stablehands, a pawnbroker taking possession of items as security for the repayment of a loan, and the like.[637] In each such instance, the duty assumed by the bailee to return the property in good condition is compensated in some manner, and mutual consideration is therefore present. At the end of his enumeration of bailment types, however, Blackstone refers to one friend temporarily entrusting property to another friend, a presumably gratuitous situation.[638] The bailee friend is of course obligated to return the bailor's property upon demand. But as to liability for damage to or loss of the property while in possession of the friend bailee, Blackstone makes clear that

[635] 1 William Wetmore Story, A Treatise on the Law of Contracts Not under Seal 72 (Charles C. Little & James Brown 1844) (emphasis added).

[636] Joseph Chitty, Jr., A Practical Treatise on the Law of Contracts Not under Seal; and Upon the Usual Defences to Actions Thereon 27–28 (Springfield, George & Charles Merriam 8th Am. ed., from 4th London ed., 1851) (emphasis in original).

[637] *See* 2 Blackstone, *supra* note 627, at 446, 451–53.

[638] *Id.* at 452.

> now the law seems to be settled, that such a general bailment will not charge the bailee with any loss, unless it happens by gross neglect, which is an evidence of fraud: but, if he undertakes specially to keep the goods safely and securely, he is bound to take the same care of them, as a prudent man would take of his own.[639]

That is, liability in the gratuitous bailment situation only arises if there has been negligence or gross negligence, in other words, tort rather than contract. Although Blackstone has overbroadly referred to the entire category of bailment as "contract," his treatment of gratuitous bailment makes clear that liability in this specialized circumstance is not predicated upon contract at all, but rather upon tort.

Thus, Blackstone's overbroad characterization of all bailment of contract is not correct as a technical matter, presumably the result of incautious drafting of his text, but his further explication of the matter does not in any way suggest that a naked, uncompensated promise, without more (i.e., without tortious negligence), could lead to liability. His statement therefore in no way lends any support to the purported principle of promissory estoppel, which asserts potential liability for failure to fulfill uncompensated promise even in the total absence of any tortious negligence.

That modern law regarding liability in the gratuitous bailment setting remains entirely consistent with Blackstone's treatment centuries ago is likewise well known.[640]

As to gratuitous borrowing, Blackstone again incautiously refers to this as "contract," though it is of course not contract at all.[641] Just as with gratuitous bailment, however, his further explanation illustrates that no support for the purported doctrine of promissory estoppel can here be sought. What Blackstone describes as borrowing is in fact nothing other than the gratuitous grant of a temporally limited possessory interest in certain property, by the owner to a borrower.[642] In other words, it is the gift of possession for a limited period of time, at the end of which the borrower must return the property to the owner/lender. Nowhere in the discussion is there any whisper of attempting to enforce some sort of executory promise. Thus, although Blackstone as a matter of drafting improperly tossed gratuitous borrowing into the "contracts" pot, such borrowing, properly seen, has nothing to do with contract whatsoever. A borrower's express acknowledgment of a duty to return the borrowed property upon expiry of the temporally limited right to possession is nothing more than acknowledgment of a limitation upon one's property right. Return of the borrowed property would be obligatory irrespective of whether the borrower had acknowledged that borrower's temporary possessory interest would at some point terminate. It is simply a matter of property law, not contract, where the gratuitous borrower's rights are fixed and legally determinable irrespective of the

639 *Id.*
640 *See* Alden, *Rethinking Promissory Estoppel*, 16 Nev. L.J. 659, 688–92 (2016).
641 *See* 2 Blackstone, *supra* note 627, at 453.
642 *Id.*

presence or absence of any statement at all by the borrower. "Promise" by the gratuitous borrower is irrelevant to the analysis. And thus gratuitous borrowing is irrelevant to so-called promissory estoppel.

Thus, we emerge from the brief interlude of conceptually choppy water onto the calm seas of clarity and crystalline exposition seen in Blackstone's forceful doctrinal statements of the law of executory contract.[643]

[643] *See* Chapter 4.3.

ANNEX B

Langdell*

One of the truly regrettable developments in the academic explication of contract law principles and doctrine was an undue, exclusive emphasis placed by Professor C. C. Langdell of Harvard Law School in the late 1800s on detriment to the promisee – rather than benefit to the promisor – as the definitional touchstone of the term "consideration."

This misplaced emphasis has served for now close to a century and a half as a red herring that distracts students' attention from the true ethical and practical grounds for the creation and enforcement of contract law as explained in the principal text of this book – namely, promoting the entry into and full performance of Pareto improving transactions that increase the net utility of both parties to an exchange. That is, it ignores the true basis for entering into exchange transactions – the excess of the benefit enjoyed by receiving consideration from the counterparty over the detriment incurred in providing consideration to the counterparty – in favor of an exclusive focus on the detriment incurred in providing consideration. It is a seriously misleading half explanation, rather than a true, complete and fully explanatory presentation of the issue.

In the Author's experience, Langdell's exclusive emphasis on detriment to the promisee thus routinely leads to doctrinal confusion for students during their first year contracts course. Far more seriously and consequentially, it has had the broader deleterious effect of acting as a philosophical pied piper of Hameln, seducing American lawyers away from understanding the foundation of contract law as originating in exchange transactions, off to thinking of contract law as a species of remedy for tortious conduct. That is, Langdell's emphasis – presumably entirely unwittingly and unintentionally – began to lay the conceptual cornerstones for Williston's later doctrinal apostasy with the invention of promissory estoppel.

* From Chapter 12.2 ("Pareto Analysis of Traditional Contract Law"), note 536.

Specifically, in his major treatise on contract law, Langdell made the following rather striking categorical statement:

> [I]t is frequently laid down as a rule, that a consideration must consist of some benefit to the promisor or some detriment to the promisee, as if either one of these would do; and in applying this rule, it is a common practice to inquire first if there is a benefit to the promisor, as if an affirmative answer to that question would render all further inquiry superfluous, and as if that were the quality which every consideration ought to possess to place it entirely above suspicion. In *Scotson v. Pegg*, Martin, B., said expressly, "that any act done whereby the contracting party receives a benefit is a good consideration for a promise by him." In truth, however, *benefit to the promisor is irrelevant to the question whether a given thing can be made the consideration of a promise*, though it may be very material to the question whether it has been made so in fact. There may be a clear benefit to the promisor, and yet no consideration, *e.g.* where the benefit does not come from the promisee. On the other hand, detriment to the promisee is a universal test of the sufficiency of consideration; *i.e.* every consideration must possess this quality, and, possessing this quality, *it is immaterial whether it is a benefit to the promisor or not.*[644]

What could have motivated Langdell to make such a strong doctrinal assertion? The answer can be arrived at through carefully parsing his statement and reading further into related portions of his text.

To begin with, Langdell is absolutely correct in asserting that a necessary element of the inquiry into consideration is that it has come from the promisee. He is correct in criticizing the passage he cited which claimed "that any act done whereby the contracting party receives a benefit is a good consideration for a promise by him." For example, a recitation in a written document reflecting a donative promise to a university, to the effect that the donor promises to make the gift "in consideration of my interest in furthering education of the public," does not constitute consideration sufficient to render the gift promise enforceable. There is no specific undertaking by the university, nothing that it has committed to provide or do from its side, in exchange for donor's promise. Yes, the donation will further public education and this result will be to the moral satisfaction and psychic gratification, and thus benefit, of donor. But there is no bargain, no quid pro quo, nothing promised in return, by the university, by the promisee. No consideration is present. Consideration requires a bargain, a mutual exchange.

In related discussion, Langdell articulated a sharp distinction between motive and consideration. Here arises the issue. Langdell wrote:

> In debt there is practically no distinction between consideration and motive, but in assumpsit the *consideration need not in fact constitute* the whole, or even *any part, of the motive* for making the promise. Thus, in the common case *where the*

[644] Christopher Columbus Langdell, A Summary of the Law of Contracts 81–82 (Boston, Little, Brown, & Co. 2d ed. 1880) (emphasis added) (citations omitted).

> *consideration is received by a third person* and *inures wholly to his benefit, it would be an abuse of terms to say that the consideration is the promisor's motive* for making the promise, *his true motive being a desire* either *to confer a benefit upon the person who receives the consideration*, or to obtain from the latter some advantage for himself. But even when the consideration is received directly by the promisor, the latter may be induced to make the promise by something wholly different. In other words, it may be clear that the promise would never have been made if the consideration had been the only inducement to make it. Thus, in *Thomas v. Thomas* the consideration for the defendant's promise was the plaintiff's promise, but a desire to comply with the will of the defendant's testator was clearly the defendant's inducement to make the promise. So a promise may be made for a nominal consideration, that is, the consideration may be given and received for the mere purpose of making the promise binding; and in all such cases, there must of course be some motive for the promise besides the consideration.
>
> *It must not be supposed*, however, *that motive, as distinguished from consideration, can constitute any element of a contract, or that it is a thing of which the law can strictly take any notice*. On the contrary, as every consideration is in theory equal to the promise in value, so it is in theory the promisor's sole inducement to make the promise. As *the law* cannot see any inequality in value between the consideration and the promise, so it *cannot see any motive for the promise except the consideration.*[645]

What has occurred here in Langdell's conceptual framework is a complete divorce between consideration and motive, with motive being then summarily banished from further notice, sent to the analytic doghouse, so to speak. But in reality, the two concepts cannot really be divorced and separated from each other.

This is because any act, forbearance, or change in legal status, by the promisee – that is, the detriment to promisee – only constitutes consideration for promisor's promise if it was bargained for. Only if the promisor insisted on promisee engaging in that act, forbearance, or change as the necessary precondition to promisor's obligation to perform. Or in the case of implied rather than express contract, the promisor clearly intended to induce promisee so to act, forbear, or change. To cut to the chase, promisee's detriment is only consideration if promisor *wanted it* to occur. Promisor thus desired the result of promisee's act, forbearance, or change. Desiring that result is promisor's motive.

To view it from the other end first, it is only that motive which actuated promisor's promise, with either the express or implied intent of causing promisee to act, forbear, or change legal status, in a specific manner. Only the presence of that motive means that we are dealing with a bargain, with an actual quid pro quo, with mutual consideration.

And one only desires something to occur if one will experience an increase in one's own utility, one's own sense of gratification or well-being, either physical,

[645] *Id.* at 77–79 (emphasis added) (citation and footnote omitted).

emotional, or otherwise intangible, as a result of that occurrence. That increase in one's own utility is the benefit to promisor, and is what always and invariably actuates the promise, in the hope of inducing promisee's act, forbearance, or change in legal status.

In Langdell's initial example of debt, the connection between the motive and the consideration is so obvious and manifest it requires no further thought. Promisor wants the money, that is the motive, and promisee's transfer of that money to promisor is the consideration for promisor's promise to pay it back, presumably with interest.

Other factual situations may pose a tad more analytic complexity. For example, the benefit to be received by promisor might not be money, or anything tangible such as goods or real property. It might instead be a service received, which brings with it either physical or mental well-being, an increase in promisor's utility. Paying money to attend a concert, for instance, is absolutely a contract predicated upon mutual consideration, even though no money or tangible property is conferred by the promisee musicians. They produce music, which is (hopefully) pleasurable to listen to, thus increasing the payor's well-being, payor's utility.

Similarly, the immediate, first-order consideration and thus benefit might run to a third person, as Langdell points out. But the promisor will only have bargained for this to occur if the benefit to that third person is of some indirect, second-order benefit to the promisor. The quintessential example is of course a parent promising to pay a doctor for medical services to be provided by the doctor to the parent's child. The immediate consideration of medical services runs to the child, but the promisor, who receives nothing directly, clearly benefits in myriad and profound ways from that benefit to their child.

To state it baldly, no one but a pathological sadist would bargain for detriment to the promisee for its own sake. A psychologically normal individual only bargains for something to occur because in some manner, either tangible or intangible, either direct or indirect, either immediate or second order, the promisor will benefit, will experience an increase in utility. Benefit to the promisor is always, tautologically, present in every bargain, and thus in every contract. The flip side of the transactional coin from promisee's detriment and decrease in utility is promisor's benefit and increase in utility. And the promisor doesn't care about promisee's detriment and decrease in utility. That's not what motivates promisor. The promisor desires, and is focused on, the benefit to promisor. That is why people enter into voluntary exchange transactions. To benefit themselves in some manner, even if intangible or indirect.

The rubber really hits the road when it comes to deciding whether an implied contract should be viewed as being present in a given situation, or not. In an express contract, the act, forbearance, or change in legal status by promisee is explicitly sought by promisor. Where, however, the promisor has made a promise, or a statement of intent or anticipation that qualifies as a promissory estoppel "promise," upon which "promisee" detrimentally relies – but where there is no actual agreement, no express articulation of any mutual exchange transactions, any quid pro quo – the crucial inquiry becomes whether the promisor in fact sought to induce that reliance. And here we apply Occam's razor: if the promisor stood to benefit in some reasonably cognizable manner from promisee's detrimental reliance, then a court may infer that the promisor intended to induce that reliance. Inferentially, promisor's motive for making the promise was to experience an increase in utility from promisee's reliance, and inducing that reliance was therefore promisor's purpose. If so, and if the promisee can only benefit from promisor's promise by relying in the manner sought by promisor that benefits promisor (i.e., there is a conditional "only if, then" logic structure present), then it is child's play to find the presence of an implied unilateral contract under traditional contract law, and promissory estoppel is thus wholly unnecessary.[646]

Conversely, if the promisor did not stand to benefit in some cognizable manner from promisee's detrimental reliance, then presumably promisor had no motive to see such reliance occur and thus no purpose to induce that reliance. No implied unilateral contract would be present. But promissory estoppel might step in. Precisely the danger of this novel, artificial doctrine is that it permits punishment of the promisor even where the promisor did not seek to induce promisee's detrimental reliance. It is a strict liability tort for unfulfilled "promise."

Promissory estoppel is therefore in this entire context either unnecessary, or dangerous and ill-advised, from both a practical and a moral perspective.

Returning to Langdell's statement, we thus see the danger in ignoring the intimate, indeed necessary and tautological connection, between motive, purpose, intent, bargain, quid pro quo, and thus consideration. This is particularly important when it comes to analyzing potential implied unilateral contract situations.

What so easily and frequently gets lost in the shuffle is that many students of the field remain unaware, or fail to think through clearly, that promisee's detriment constitutes consideration *if and only if* the detrimental change in position which occasions that detriment has been sought by promisor. Countless times the Author has seen students take Langdell's words (or more precisely, later repetitions thereof in various books, treatises, commercial outlines, and bar prep materials) to indicate that the presence of detriment to the promisee ipso facto means that consideration is present. Not so.

The more conceptually robust, salutary, preferable, and frankly normal way to commence analysis of nearly any contractual fact pattern is to do precisely what Langdell objects to, namely, start with the question of what benefit to self the promisor seeks.

If there is a benefit to self that the promisor seeks, even if intangible and/or indirect, then obtaining or experiencing that benefit is promisor's motive. Promisor

[646] *See* extended discussion of this point in Chapter 14.1.

makes the promise in order to receive that benefit. In order for a mutual exchange to be present, it is indeed necessary, as Langdell correctly observed, that the detriment moves from the promisee and not from some other third party or general circumstance. A quid pro deal, a deal, mutual consideration, is only present if the promisor is offering something to promisee in exchange for *promisee's* act, forbearance, or change in legal status.

Thus, stated in terms of formal logic, that the promisee have incurred a detriment is a necessary, but not sufficient, requirement for the presence of contract. Promisee's detrimental change in position must also have been bargained for, or implicitly sought, by the promisor. Now we have a contract.

So, in summation, the reason Langdell's formulations in the quoted passages, to the effect that benefits and motives are wholly irrelevant to the analysis, are unfortunate is that they so often seduce students of the subject into a misunderstanding of the true meaning and requirements for the presence of consideration. It leads them to ignore benefit to the promisor, thus promisor's motive, and what promisor's purpose and intention was, in making the "promise." And this becomes problematic when potential "promissory estoppel" fact patterns are confronted.

Contract law is all about benefits. That is why parties enter into exchanges. That is why we have contract law. To achieve benefits that exceed the cost of obtaining such. For both parties. That is, to increase the net utility of both parties. In microeconomic terminology, to achieve Pareto improvements.

In every contract, benefit and detriment are two sides of the same coin. They are inextricably and necessarily connected to each other. We want the benefit, and seek it, and are willing to incur the cost of detriment to pay the price therefor. Benefit is not irrelevant. It is at the heart of the inquiry. Nobody bargains for detriments to others. We bargain for net benefits to ourselves.

Index

www.ingramcontent.com/pod-product-compliance
Lightning Source LLC
LaVergne TN
LVHW091530200926
848483LV00002B/358
* 9 7 8 1 0 0 9 3 6 7 6 1 5 *